Understanding China's Growth

Understanding China's Growth

Forces that Drive China's Economic Future

Chi Lo

First published in 2007 by
PALGRAVE MACMILLAN
Houndmills, Basingstoke, Hampshire RG21 6XS and
175 Fifth Avenue, New York, N.Y. 10010
Companies and representatives throughout the world.

PALGRAVE MACMILLAN is the global academic imprint of the Palgrave
Macmillan division of St. Martin's Press, LLC and of Palgrave Macmillan Ltd.
Macmillan® is a registered trademark in the United States, United Kingdom
and other countries. Palgrave is a registered trademark in the European
Union and other countries.

ISBN-13: 978–0–230–51557–4
ISBN-10: 0–230–51557–6

This book is printed on paper suitable for recycling and made from fully
managed and sustained forest sources. Logging, pulping and manufacturing
processes are expected to conform to the environmental regulations of the
country of origin.

A catalogue record for this book is available from the British Library.

A catalog record for this book is available from the Library of Congress.

10 9 8 7 6 5 4 3 2 1
16 15 14 13 12 11 10 09 08 07

Printed and bound in Great Britain by
Antony Rowe Ltd, Chippenham and Eastbourne

For my sons **Bun Bun** *and* **Chung Chung**

Raising them is both a joy and a challenge. What amazes me is the inspiration they have given me without which this book would not have come true.

Contents

List of Figures

List of Tables

Foreword

China's rapid economic development over the past, nearly 30 years is rightly regarded as one of the economic wonders of the modern world. At the same time, the very speed of its development process, coupled with an extraordinarily high ratio of fixed asset investment to GDP and continued concerns about high levels of non-performing loans in the banking sector, poor asset allocation and corporate governance have led many to question the sustainability of this process. Given the rising role of China in both the global economy and global financial system, any substantial missteps could have implications far beyond the Chinese economy itself. Moreover, the very success of the process has created new problems, including social strains and high pressure on resources such as commodities and the environment.

China's economic development process has interest not simply in its own right, but also as one of the latest variations of what is widely referred to as the 'Asian model' of economic development. Beginning with Japan in the 1950s, the model has varied by country, but broadly includes the following major aspects: rapid growth fuelled by high levels of capital investment, including foreign direct investment and importation of advanced technology; a strong orientation towards fostering export-oriented industries and encouraging competition in global markets, which typically has led to the development of current account surpluses; protection of domestic markets against foreign competition; aggressive intervention by the government to direct the course of economic development, especially via the banking system; and a high level of domestic savings which made high rates of guided investment possible. On the negative side, the Asian model has paid short shrift to Western notions of capital return and shareholder interest. Against this template, China stands out mainly in terms of its size, being the most populous country on earth, and the fact that the process was orchestrated by a nominally communist government.

The Asian model has been demonstrably successful in terms of rapidly lifting Asian economies to high levels of per capita income and other measures of development. However, regarding the overall assessment, the jury is still out. This is primarily because the Japanese economy, which pioneered the Asia growth model, has floundered in the past

17 years, going from bubble to bubble bursting to painful recovery. Even though the post-bubble adjustments have largely been completed, i.e. the elimination of the three 'excesses' – capital, labour and debt – the Japanese economy still appears to be hobbled in some respects. Although trend growth is generally estimated to be in the range of 1.5 per cent–2 per cent, the share of private capital investment in nominal GDP is over 16 per cent, compared with just over 10 per cent in the US, implying relatively low capital efficiency. This is also reflected in relatively low returns on capital, although they have improved over the past decade. Finally, in the process of stabilizing the balance sheets of private sector companies, the government itself accumulated enormous amounts of debt, and it remains to be seen whether this debt burden will be worked off without major side-effects. Although China remains some decades behind Japan in terms of its stage of development, the experience of Japan provides important lessons about the strengths and weakness of the Asian growth model that Chinese policymakers will have to take into account.

China resembles other more economically advanced Asian nations in another respect, i.e. the prospect of a rapid ageing of its population as a result of the combined effects of a sharp decline in fertility together with rapidly increasing life expectancies. The expected rise in the dependency ratio and the ageing of society poses major challenges for the savings rate, which heretofore provided the fuel for high levels of investment spending, prospective fiscal burdens related to future obligations connected with pensions and health care, and the trend growth rate.

These challenges suggest that Chinese economic management and the economic system itself will have to adapt in response to a more challenging environment than it faced previously. Reform of the system is the crucial ingredient for successful adaptation. Chi Lo's analysis in this book provides a unique and valuable guide to understanding what forces have driven the Chinese economy to date, and how these are likely to change in coming years as a result of the prospective reform process. This includes reforms of state-owned enterprises, the financial system, the legal system, the currency system and the national pensions system. He also examines other factors related to economic stability, including the ageing of society and potential socio-political stresses. Chi Lo's analysis provides substantive reasons for being optimistic that the reform process will keep the Chinese economy on a sustainable growth path, and that other features of the

Chinese economy will not prove to be insuperable hurdles. Perhaps the biggest challenge policymakers will face is to gradually cede much of their own role to market forces. Otherwise, the potential gains from capital allocation and productivity growth will not be fully realized.

Peter Morgan
Chief Economist
Asia-Pacific, HSBC

Preface

China has come a long way in lifting itself out of poverty since late paramount leader Deng Xiao-ping started economic reforms in 1978. Structural changes have transformed the Middle Kingdom into an economic powerhouse in recent years. After over 20 years of economic reform, China's development has come to a crossroads. The easy part of reforming the primitive economy has been done. Cross-currents affecting future structural changes are getting stronger and political and economic forces that shape future reforms are getting more complicated.

Generally, China observers have agreed that the country faces significant challenges from a fragile banking system, rising unemployment, a large public debt/deficit overhang, an inefficient state sector and serious corruption. All these cause difficulties to future economic reforms and disrupt social harmony. However, they see quite different paths into which China would develop, as there is always evidence for supporting the most contradictory arguments. The imperfection of the Chinese data does not help in clarifying the issues.

It is thus not surprising that there is a sharp divergence in views on China's economic future. There are those who see China becoming the next America and those who see it becoming the next Latin America. The optimistic case has been well documented, while the pessimistic view has served to give a counterbalance to the China debate. However, both views are often exaggerated and distorted because both camps have often overlooked, or misread, the underlying drivers for assessing China's economic future.

Hype has often influenced the views of many sanguine China observers, who have based their assessment on straight extrapolation of some short-term favourable trends into the future without rigorous examination. Meanwhile, many pessimists have often focused exclusively on China's economic woes and structural flaws in the system. They put China under microscopic scrutiny in a static environment; they assume no economic dynamism so that from this view China's past and current problems would continue to accumulate until they crushed the system.

The truth is that rapid changes are taking place in China, making some current information swiftly outdated. Unfortunately, many China watchers tend to dwell on yesterday's glory and problems and lack the foresight for spotting the underlying, but often hidden, economic dynamism that drive China's economic future. These hidden trends are only reflected by subtle changes at the margin of the system, and thus have not yet been filtered into mainstream thinking.

For example, a Beijing high court decision in June 2006 to overturn a ruling by China's patent-review board (PRB) in favour of US pharmaceutical giant Pfizer[1] is a case showing that significant, but often overlooked, changes are taking place in China's huge bureaucratic system. China's PRB sided with a group of local generic-drug makers in July 2004 to challenge Pfizer's patent on sildenafil citrate, the essence for making Viagra, the impotence-curing drug.

Beijing's ruling in favour of a foreign company's intellectual property rights is unusual. Less than one in ten foreign companies appealing a ruling in China have succeeded, according to industry observers. While the Beijing high court's decision could build political capital for China at a time when economic liberalization is creating significant piracy problems, the ruling could also open up more legal battles from other foreign firms against Chinese suppliers. These suits may, in turn, hurt many Chinese infant industries in the high-tech, high value-added areas.

Granted, implementation of the patent would still be tough. That is because there is a lack of policy coordination between the central and local authorities and a lack of local compliance on implementation due to incentive incompatibility problems. Pfizer and other foreign firms in China will have to continue to fight against counterfeit products even after the Beijing ruling. But this is an old problem, and China critics should not be dwelling on it.

Beijing's overturning of the PRB's ruling is a new, and strong, signal of its willingness to improve protection for intellectual property rights. The changing dynamics is seen in the fact that the ruling had followed other moves to change China's intellectual property protection habit. In early 2006, China ruled, in favour of Miscrosoft corporation that all major computer makers must ship their products together with legitimate operating-system software installed. Before that, computers were often sold as shell units so that buyers could install pirated software. In December 2005, a Shanghai court ruled against a local company that had copied into Chinese the name and logo of US coffee chain Starbucks without its agreement.

There are other significant changes, such as Beijing's experiment to scrap the population control system and privatize lending rights based

---

[1] *The Wall Street Journal – Asia* (2006).

on market forces, taking place at the margin of the system. It is amazing how misinformed and distorted the views of many China critics are, especially those from America. Their views often focus on generic problems that exist in most emerging economies. But those problems have been generalized and imposed on China as if they were unique to it. Many of these biased views have little substance or research backup and, unfortunately, they are often promulgated in the professional arena[2].

Cutting through hype and distortions, by provoking innovative thoughts and drawing on unpublished research and data, this book seeks to inspire further technical research on better understanding China's growth dynamics, update the trends that have affected the Chinese economy, anatomize the driving forces that will shape its economic future, and provide the intellectual ingredients for a healthy debate on China's impact on the world economy.

The book combines rigorous research thoughts, data, facts and economic logic with real-world examples and anecdotes to elaborate the arguments. While some of the issues discussed here may be controversial, the discussions are not US-centric (as are many China books in the market). Views and arguments here are backed by research and evidence so that they should serve as bases for intellectual debates.

However, it is important to note that China is a very complicated country with an intriguing development pattern. Despite its effort to probe into the hidden issues and look outside conventional wisdom, this book is not meant to be an exhaustive treatment of China's future development. A complete analysis is beyond the scope of this book. There are many other issues that are best left to other specialists than macro-economists.

The issues discussed in this book are long-term events of great public and political interest. Together with the high information quality and density, the book should have a long shelf-life in the years to come. In addition to its intellectual research content, the book is also written from a market perspective, representing the thinking and application of analytical tools by market practitioners.

Academia and students of Asian studies, financial market practitioners, corporate executives and government advisors seeking to understand China and Asia's economic and financial development should find this book particularly useful for brainstorming, further research and developing business and policy strategies.

CHI LO

---

[2] A notable example of these distorted views is found in Chang (2001; 2006).

List of Abbreviations

AMCs	Asset management companies
Big Four	Bank of China (BoC), China Construction Bank (CCB), Agricultural Bank of China (ABC), Industrial and Commercial Bank of China (ICBC)
BoJ	Bank of Japan
CBRC	China Banking Regulatory Commission
CCDI	Central Commission on Disciplinary Investigation
CPI	Consumer price index
CSRC	China Securities Regulatory Commission
FDI	Foreign direct investment
FIEs	Foreign-invested enterprises
GATT	General Agreement on Tariffs and Trade
IMF	International Monetary Fund
IPD	Implicit pension debt
KEB	Korean Exchange Bank
M&As	Mergers and acquisitions
MBOs	Management buy-outs
MoF	Ministry of Finance
NBS	National Bureau of Statistics
NPLs	Non-performing loans
OTC	Over the counter
PAYG	Pay as you go (pension system)
PBoC	People's Bank of China
PPC	Production possibility curve
PPI	Producer price index
PRD	Pearl River Delta
QDII	Qualified Domestic Institutional Investors
QFII	Qualified Foreign Institutional Investors
RMB	Renminbi (or Chinese yuan)
RTC	Resolution Trust Corporation
SASAC	State-owned Assets Supervision and Administration Commission
SDRC	State Development and Reform Commission
SEZs	Special economic zones
SOEs	State-owned enterprises

TPF	Total factor productivity
TVEs	Township and villages enterprises
UN	United Nations
UNPD	United Nations Population Division
WIPO	World Intellectual Property Organization
WTO	World Trade Organization
ZIRP	Zero interest rate policy (in Japan)

Introduction

Most people who talk about China's economic ascent to the world stage are referring to its rise from the three decades of instability between 1946 and 1976. This period was characterized by civil wars (1946–50) and the Maoist era which encompassed the Cultural Revolution (1966–69), though many would include the years up to 1976 when the Gang of Four were arrested. However, this characterization misses the historical perspective. The omission is indicative of a common problem of many observers focusing on partial information in reading China's economic development.

China was in fact once the world's most advanced economy between the first and late thirteenth centuries. It then went into a prolonged, seven centuries, economic decline well into the twentieth century due mainly to its neglect of scientific development and foreign trade. Strictly speaking, China's recent economic ascent is an economic comeback. But China's development trends are not as straightforward as they were in the old days. Global geopolitical and socio-economic forces are more complicated today. The Chinese economy and development process, in a hybrid system that combines market forces with planning mechanisms, are also more intriguing these days.

Opinions about China's economic future are divided sharply. But they have one thing in common. Generally, observers and analysts tend to dwell on China's past problems and glory, and look for clues to the future in past trends. As a result, they have overlooked, and often ignored, the crucial changes that are taking place at the margin of the system. But these subtle changes are key to determining China's future.

This habit of dwelling in the past and overlooking subtle changes applies to all of us, and it has to do with the way we think. The trouble, especially when it comes to analysing China, is that our thoughts are often bounded by conventions. In other words, our thinking pattern is boxed in systematic grids. Figure I.1, which plots a nine-point grid,

1

illustrates this interesting issue. Now try to join all the nine points with four straight lines without lifting the pen off the paper or folding it. Puzzled? We shall return to this a little later. Let us first look at China to put the economics into this grid-lock perspective.

The fall from global economic pre-eminence

China was a rich country with a per capita GDP of US$450,[1] according to Professor Angus Maddison,[2] under the Han Dynasty in the first century. Ordinary Chinese were living well above the subsistence level. The royal family was even able to lead a luxurious life afforded by rich tax revenues from the domestic economy and contributions from neighbouring foreign states.

Per capita GDP in Western Europe was about the same as China at that time. But the fall of the Roman Empire depressed Continental Europe's economic growth, while China managed to grow steadily throughout the first century. From about 960 onwards for three centuries, China's economic and population growth continued to rise.

China's superior growth relative to that of Western Europe during this period owed much to its merit-base system set-up. By linking merits to rewards, such a system created incentive compatibility between the ruling elite and the people. It was far more efficient in driving economic growth than Western Europe's feudal institutional framework, which often lacked economic incentives. Indeed, China's agricultural productivity gains soared during this period, spurring overall economic growth.

However, the table turned by the late thirteenth century when the Sung Dynasty crumbled into the hands of the Mongolians (the Yuan Dynasty 1291–1368). China's per capita GDP stalled between the late thirteenth and early nineteenth centuries. Meanwhile, Western Europe discovered the economic formula of growth rejuvenation via trade expansion within the Mediterranean Basin, capital accumulation and technological advancement. This also sowed the seed of capitalism in

Figure I.1   Grid puzzle

Europe. By 1820, China's US$600 per capita GDP was about half that of Western Europe's.

China's fall from its economic pre-eminence stemmed mainly from its inward-looking policy, which also led to a complacent attitude towards technological development and neglect of foreign trade. For example, in the early fifteenth century, China had built a vast maritime empire with one of the most technologically advanced navies at the time. The Ming (1368–1644) navy had more than 3,800 ships, many of which were several times larger than their Portuguese counterparts. The Ming Admiral Zheng He made seven major expeditions to the 'western seas' (*si yang*) between 1405 and 1433, with the aim of expanding the Chinese maritime empire across the oceans.

However, a weak fiscal position and domestic economic chaos constrained the Chinese government's outward perspectives. Instead, it turned inward by building waterways and roads with the hope of boosting the economy and fixing the fiscal deficit via domestic spending. By 1470, the Chinese navy had shrunk with most of the shipyards closed. China also turned its back on technology development at that time.

In the mid-twentieth century, China's GDP per head had dropped by over 25 per cent from its level a century ago. In contrast, Western Europe's per capita income was over three times higher, while North America and Australia's were on average eight times higher. Arguably, China's inward policy created a complacent attitude that set it back at a time when the western world started pushing for technological and foreign trade expansion. The result was disastrous. China's income per head was less than 10 per cent of the western nations' by 1950.

China's relative economic decline was notably rapid between the early nineteenth and mid twentieth centuries, as the fall of the Manchu (*Qing*) Dynasty (1644–1912) caused institutional disintegration and internal volatility (including civil wars, social unrests and religious uprisings). Foreign trade during the *Qing* Dynasty was completely detrimental to China because it was driven by the imperialism of the western powers forcing open China's door for unfair trade, especially for opium.

Any gains from trade during this period were only accrued to foreign residents and firms in China. Despite expanded foreign trade, there was absolutely no technological transfer from the western powers to China. There was also no development of educational institutions to raise local skill and technology levels. Despite large investment and economic development, especially in major cities such as Shanghai and Tianjin, there were no productivity and efficient gains in most of the Chinese economy between the 1800s and mid 1900s. Per capita GDP fell by an average 0.6 per cent a year between 1913 and 1950.

The pessimists

China's economic fortune started to turn the corner after 1950. Growth started to rise exponentially after 1978, when late paramount leader Deng Xiao-ping launched economic reforms that remade China's economic foundation. Nevertheless, cynics and pessimists argue that the future of China's economic comeback is bleak. They see a doomed system, with the state as an oppressive drag on the future. Most state-owned enterprises (SOEs) are hopelessly inefficient and unprofitable. They suffer from excessive government intervention and distorted economic incentives, which make them incapable of competing with the private firms. As the economy continues to open up, market forces will crush the SOEs, dragging the economy along with them.

Aggravating this oppressive factor is a crumbling banking sector. Pessimists see no reform incentive for the financial sector and incentive incompatibility plaguing the whole reform process. After all, the state still owns the bulk of the banking sector, with administrative and policy objectives overriding commercial motives. That is why banking reform has moved at a snail pace and capital market reform has gone nowhere.

Add to this pile of problems an ageing population, a broken pension system, and rising income inequality and socio-economic tension, and many critics just cannot help but see China heading down the path of becoming another Latin America. Some observers even compare China with the former Soviet Union, as both are states under communist regimes. Despite rapid growth rates and being seen as an economic development model between the 1960s and mid 1980s, the USSR did not escape the fate of economic and political disintegration.

Cynics have also drummed up a 'waste theory' for China, seeing massive and unsustainable waste eventually eroding the Middle Kingdom down to the ground. The 'theory' starts with the tenets that human beings must eat, clothe, shelter and defend themselves against macro- and micro-predators like wild beasts and diseases. But once these basic needs are met, any extra energy left over can be wasted on unnecessary pursuits.

In economics context, productivity gains (which allow more output to be made with less inputs), which China has achieved significantly in recent years, is meaningless unless the saved inputs are used in other better ways. Similarly, the extra outputs must be put to good use. Otherwise, there is no point in having them. Some argue that China's mixed system of planned and market mechanisms was perfect for creating an extremely wasteful system, with productivity gains in the market segment generating extra output for the planners to waste. This is unsustainable and the system will crumble sooner or later.

In a macro-economic context, the command part of the Chinese system has a high tendency to generate excessive savings, which are reflected in China's large current account surplus. The 'waste theory' argues that these must be wasted by the communists on the back of the productivity gains achieved. Hence, the command economy misallocates credit to investment in value-destroying production, making goods that no one wants to buy. This system of resource wastage is needed to ensure everyone gets a job and thus has income to save from.

Whereas the state produces the waste in a command system, the consumer is responsible for the waste in the market economy. Watching a movie, playing football, going to the gym are different ways of 'wasting' energy after the basic needs are met, according to the 'waste theory'. In China, these 'wasteful' activities are rising on the back of increasing affluence.

In an international context, there is another major wasting that China engages in. And that is lending to the rich economies, notably America, to allow them to produce their physical wastage at home. If the current excessive spending of debt-building trends continue in the US, odds are high that China's credits to America are not going to be repaid in full. That would make it an outright waste of Chinese financial resources.

There are also those who claim that China is damned as a consuming nation. Its strong growth and energy use are blamed for pushing up global oil and commodity prices, for climate change and for the resurgence of nuclear energy, just to name a few. As the world's largest importer of unprocessed wood and tropical timber, China is seen as one of the key destroyers of the global environment. As a producer and an exporter, it is hammered for providing cheap goods that put people in importing countries out of work. In the US, for example, unions have been pursuing legal channels to curb Chinese imports on the grounds they destroy US jobs and lower labour standards.

The optimists

On the other hand, others cite evidence of profit recovery in the SOEs, which is still the backbone of the economy, and see continued improvement in the state sector. They reckon that state firms are too important to be left completely to market forces and private ownership in the short term. There have been structural changes in the corporate sector, albeit at a slow pace. The state, in the optimists' view, should in fact strengthen the competitive position of the SOEs to enable further reform and sustain growth for China. Indeed, the losses of the SOEs are yesterday's problem because, in aggregate, they have become profitable on a flow basis.

Meanwhile, despite the large stock of non-performing loans (NPLs), Chinese banks are on the mend. There has been material progress in bank restructuring. The authorities are selling local bank stakes to foreign and retail investors to invoke market discipline for pushing banking reform. Capital market reform is seen as the next step.

Unlike many other emerging economies, China does not have any more state-owned 'black holes' that siphon off massive fiscal resources. Productivity gains are on the rise, as capital deepening[3] develops and resources allocation improves gradually. High public and social welfare burdens are certainly critical issues, but they are mostly a historical legacy and Beijing is putting in place measures for tackling them. Hence, optimists see China becoming the next America in the not too distant future.

However, the focus on these positive forces has created some overly bullish views based mostly on hype. Many have casually projected that sustained high growth would allow China to become the world's leading economic superpower. Others have called China's growth a miracle that would consistently outperform global growth so that the rest of the world would not be able to catch up even in the long term.

These overly optimistic views are distorted. Fundamentally, there are doubts about the quality of the Chinese economic data, which have generated heated debates among the academics.[4] Many China books' discussions are distorted. The investment community is especially concerned about data problems in GDP growth, industrial output, investment, inflation, retail sales and even exports.[5] The data problem is largely due to China's personal and relationship-driven power structure. Government officials derive their power and build their political bases solely by gaining favours and trust from their superiors. This creates a strong incentive for officials to please their superiors by fudging their economic reports to ensure that they are politically correct.

Arguably, there is no miracle in China's growth. In terms of growth rates, China's experience is no different from Japan and the Asian tiger economies[6] during their high-growth years.[7] The Japanese economy grew by an annual average of 8.5 per cent between 1955 and 1975, and so did Singapore, South Korea and Taiwan in their high-growth years between 1965 and 1995. Hong Kong, Malaysia and Thailand were close behind, with annual growth rates averaging over 7 per cent during that period.

In terms of growth model, China is just like Asia – not really a miracle.[8] China's high growth rate is mainly attributable to massive savings, which support high rates of capital accumulation, augmented by total factor productivity growth. For sure, its domestic saving rates are much higher than Asia's (Figure I.2). There is really no reason to be hyper about China's growth. But a high savings rate is not going to enable China to 'take over the world', as some have feared.

Just look at Japan. After many decades of economic development, it still has a gross domestic savings rate of 26 per cent of GDP and an investment-to-GDP ratio of over 20 per cent. But its average growth rate since the early 1990s has dropped to a mere fraction of the peak growth rates in its golden years. The same is seen in the Asian tiger economies. These Asian economies have not taken over the world economy, despite their high saving rates.

Understanding China's economic future

These divergent, and often exaggerated, views reflect the difficulty of reading China because there is always evidence to support the most controversial arguments. Further, both critics and supporters of China often overlook some hidden trends that are developing in the Chinese system, thus leading to partial or biased understanding of China's development. However, due to the complexity of the Chinese system and its development process, comprehensive coverage is provided only on the key issues here. Any attempt to evaluate these complicated forces exhuastively is beyond the scope of this book.

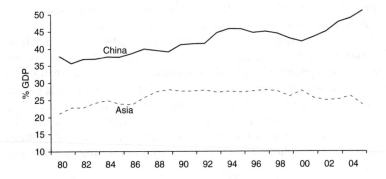

Figure I.2   Chinese vs Asian savings*
* GDP – private and public consumption, nominal terms
Source: CEIC

It is true that China's hybrid system of state ownership and growing market influence is creating problems that are manifested in the misallocation of resources and a shaky financial system. Meanwhile, low and fixed interest rates and severe state intervention in resources allocation have led to over-investment and highly volatile economic performance.[9]

However, significant changes are taking place at the margin, with the authorities taking deep-rooted measures to restructure the economy. Reform progress will raise the odds for China to become a more stable and efficient system over time. In particular, Beijing has shown resolve in taking the crucial decisions to make necessary, and often tough, changes. They include liberalizing the economy by opening it up to competition, expanding foreign trade and enabling creative destruction to replace the loss-making SOEs by sunrise industries and private sector firms. The authorities have also avoided the grave mistake of creating cross-sector state holding firms, and have started to retreat from mass subsidizing of the state sector.

The government is improving the regulatory and institutional frameworks in which the market mechanism works, and continues to open up domestic industries to foreign and local competition. Meanwhile, market-opening requirements from the World Trade Organization (WTO) will continue to act as an external discipline for guiding and pushing China's domestic economic reforms.

The central government has become more organized in its privatization efforts, as seen in the creation of the State-owned Asset Supervision and Administration Committee (SASAC) in 2003. There is also now an exit strategy for Beijing from the banking system, by selling stakes to foreign strategic investors and listing of the Chinese banks overseas. Withdrawal of political intervention from the banking sector is of utmost importance for improving resources allocation and growth outlook.

Beijing is also experimenting with scrapping the *hu-kou* (or household registration) system and allowing private investors to set up lending companies to price credit according to market forces. These are unprecedented and bold moves to restructure the old system by allowing market forces to work better. Together with financial liberalization, including the Qualified Domestic Institutional Investors (QDII) scheme and the creation of the SASAC, these are initial steps to break the communist policy icons of public asset ownership, population control and financial repression.

Many of these changes are still in their initial stages. That is why they are not noticeable and not factored into mainstream analysis yet. But these are the signposts for where China will be heading down the growth path. Crucially, these changes fly in the face of those who have dwelt on China's past problems and continued to claim that China's leaders are failing to make changes and rendering the system to an eventual collapse. In these myopic views, China's instability has risen with its increase in prosperity. Die-hard pessimists cite the rising numbers of violent protests in recent years (Figure I.3) as an indication that the Chinese system is unable to handle discontent.

China's structural changes have certainly created losers in the process, but it is wrong to see this by-product as a sign for a systemic collapse. The rise in the reported cases of unrest is partly a result of better media coverage, which should be seen as a positive development. Granted, social unrest is worrisome, but the demonstrations remain largely unorganized and impulsive. They are localized grievances rather than large-scale discontent, for example, about broader political reforms. There does not seem to be any national network or coordinating mechanism of dissent.

The social issues are not an imminent threat to China's stability, but they should not be taken lightly. Socio-economic tension is indeed the trickiest issue confronting the Chinese authorities. While Beijing is trying to be sensitive and respond vigorously to the first sign of organized protests, it is undeniable that the bureaucrats still do not have any long-term remedies for the problem yet. If mishandled, the social problems could be the Achilles heel of China's economic future.

In the structural context, China's economic reform has come to a crossroads, and a new policy approach is needed to sustain long-term growth. For all its virtues and success, the old approach of gradualism and reform experiments is becoming inappropriate, as the distortions resulting from it are intensifying and threatening systemic instability

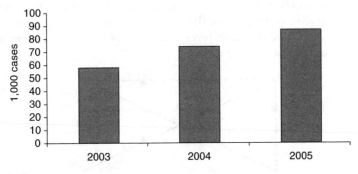

Figure I.3 Total number of protests

Source: Media reports

down the road. Beijing's leaders must find new ways of managing an economy that is subject to ever-increasing market forces.

All this brings us back to the thinking problem discussed earlier. Conventional analytical toolkits often do not work in China due to its strong idiosyncratic characteristics and the opaque system set-up. It is natural to be comfortable with dwelling on our old habits and the conventional wisdom. But when it comes to understanding China, thinking creatively is crucial, just like solving the grid puzzle (Figure I.4).

The plan of the book

Chapter 1 opens up the discussion on China's economic future by digging into the heart of its economic problems and probing into its incentive compatibility issues. In particular, the discussion addresses the conflict between a strong reform incentive from the central leadership and stubborn resistance to change at the local government levels. It assesses how far structural reforms will go and what the next steps will be.

Chapters 2 and 3 look at the banking and state sectors under the reform umbrella. Chapter 2 reassesses the fragility of the banking sector, its inherent incentive problems, reform progress and obstacles, and future outlook. It argues that the 'WTO threat' to Chinese banks is illusive. Despite being illegal and a symbol of financial distortion, informal lending in China in fact makes positive economic contributions where the formal banking market fails. Beijing should learn from the underground capital market experience for financial reform.

Chapter 3 examines the role of the state in the economy, and argues that the state and its Marxist legacy would continue to dominate in the medium term. Even the private sector still behaves pretty much like state firms. But there have been crucial changes at the margin that signal further creative destruction of the state sector. The discussions also seek to chart the future course of privatization, corporate sector reform and the fate of the state-owned firms.

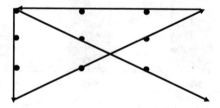

Figure I.4   Solution to the grid puzzle

Chapter 4 revisits the ageing population issues, including the pension 'time bomb', China's labour shortage and the labour-intensive growth model. It argues that a lot of these problems have been misunderstood and exaggerated, and that there is another side to the story. Nevertheless, if China is to deliver sustainable growth in the face of adverse demographics, the government must change economic incentives in the system to react to the greying problem.

Chapter 5 anatomizes the myth and truth of China's socio-economic problems. It argues that unemployment is not really a factor causing social unrest, and Beijing has fiscal ability to resolve the social problems. Social problems in China are not structural, not yet at least. But China's hybrid economic system is a hotbed of corruption, which will only fade when the country embraces market forces more fully. If mishandled, income inequality and corruption could be the Achilles heel of China's future growth.

Chapter 6 discusses the paradigm shift and sustainability of China's growth model. Though the Chinese authorities have handled the growth transition quite well so far, the system needs more market discipline to move forward. Arguably, Beijing's gradualist reform approach has become increasingly untenable and caused an increasing amount of distortions after years of experiment. China needs to move reform into 'uncharted waters' and proceed in bigger strides and a more coordinated fashion to sustain long-term growth.

Chapter 7 assesses China's policy visions for future growth. Beijing has been adapting to the increasingly complex economy and facilitating its next transformation to higher value-added and more capital-intensive production with various policy vision and inspiration. But some of these need to be reassessed carefully. Its future currency policy is especially crucial. It will be a grave mistake to shift the RMB regime in the short term, as such a move could sink the Chinese and the global economy and leave legacy problems for the long term.

Chapter 8 concludes that China needs a new, bolder and more integrated policy approach to keep the country on a sustainable growth path. The current approach, which combines control, flexibility, adaptability and pragmatism, is creating distortions and threatening systemic instability down the road. The leadership must break the old mentality, think innovatively, and move to increase market discipline and economic freedom. Given its track record, it stands a reasonably good chance of being the first socialist state to transform itself successfully into a market system and make great contributions to the global economy in the future.

All economic data, data estimates and figures used in this book are created from the databank provided by CEIC Data Company Limited, unless stated otherwise. Established in Hong Kong in 1992 and acquired by ISI Emerging Markets in 2005, CEIC provides economic, corporate and industry sector time-series data on Asian and other major economies. It has strategic presence in Asia and sources the data from national governments, government agencies and prime releasing entities.

1
China's Reform Puzzle

Structural reform lies in the heart of the debate on China's economic future. The Middle Kingdom's rapid economic growth since economic reform started in 1978 has created admiration, fears and envy about its development. Many people even think that a rising Chinese economic power might eclipse the US within a decade or so, if its current growth rate persists. Whether one takes a benign or cynical view on China, the most crucial factor that decides its future growth is economic reform. Here, mixed signals have confused many observers. Some see a total lack of reform incentive, and argue for an eventual collapse of the Chinese system under the increasing weight of economic imbalances. Others, while sanguine, are puzzled by China's snail-pace reform despite a strong push from the central authorities.

There are indeed significant changes taking place in the system. But many of these changes have often been overlooked because they are subtle changes at the margin of the system and hence are not yet obvious in mainstream thinking. One of the problems in analysing China is to judge its reform by quantity. It is more crucial to assess the progress of reform, or the lack of it, by the momentum that it generates. Evidence suggests that its forward momentum is strong. Beijing is experimenting with dismantling the classical communist policy icons, such as public asset ownership, population control and financial repression.

The need for reform[1]

Economic reform serves to raise output efficiency so that the available resources can be better and fully utilized to sustain and raise long-term growth potential. This can be seen in a simple Production Possibility Curve (PPC) framework (Figure 1.1). The PPC shows the tradeoffs an economy faces when it chooses its output combination of any two goods. We use consumption and capital goods in our generalized example here. In other words, each point on the PPC represents some maximum output combination of any two goods, given all the resources available.

The PPC is concave in shape due to rising opportunity costs. In our framework, as more and more output is shifted towards the capital good, the production shift cuts deeper into the stock of resources used for the consumption good. In all likelihood there will not be resources to move that are as good at making the capital good and as poor at making the consumption good as the previous output shift. Hence, to get the same increase in the output of the capital good, more units of the consumption good must be forgone. This result is symmetric. Shifts going the other way towards more consumption good raise the opportunity cost of capital good with each shift.

Economic inefficiency suggests that China's economy is operating inside the PPC, for example point U in Figure 1.1, with massive unemployed and/or underemployed resources. Implemented properly, economic reform can purge the structural flaws in the economy and move employment towards the PPC by better allocating resources and raising output efficiency. For example, any output bundle within triangle UBC in Figure 1.1 is superior to bundle U. In the longer term, economic reform enables technological progress, thus expanding resources supplies and rejuvenating productivity growth. This will, in turn, push the PPC outwards, allowing the economy to enjoy larger output bundles.

Indeed, structural changes have shown their impact on the Chinese economy by reducing the amount of economic inefficiencies. Various studies[2] have found that China's total factor productivity (TPF)[3] grew by

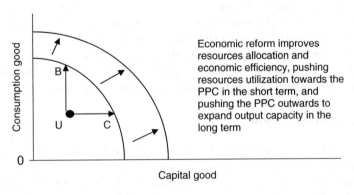

Figure 1.1   Production possibility curve

an annualized average of 3.5 per cent a year since reforms began in 1978. Further, China's TPF contributed an average of 1.5 percentage points to annual real GDP growth between 1978 and 2000. This growth contribution was comparable to that of the Asian average.

This steady growth of productivity suggests that there is a lot more to the Chinese growth story than just a wasteful model of forcing excessive amount of capital into unproductive activities. Growth in various parts of the Chinese economy has been led by efficient private sector firms, with increasing numbers of the corrupted state-owned enterprises (SOEs) dropping out of the picture. In a nutshell, the role of the market has risen sharply since the 1980s despite continued, but diminishing, state influences on investment and output decisions.

Reform incentive, now you see it ...

While theoretically the need for reform is clear, the question remains whether China's mandarins have the will to do it. This is because, the sceptics argue, shaking up the system would risk eroding the Communist Party's power base and hence its survival. Take financial reform. Though China has made some good progress in reforming its banking sector (see next chapter), many analysts remain doubtful about its reform incentive and the judgement of foreign investors buying into the Chinese banks.

Critics argue that foreign investors were just minority shareholders, with influence being capped by the Chinese government, which is still controlling the banking system. Does China have a heart in its financial reform, and if so why? Is Beijing selling off state assets too cheaply to attract foreigner investors in Chinese banks? Are foreigners overly optimistic about Chinese banks? These are some key questions puzzling pessimists and optimists alike.

Between 1998 and 2005, China spent US$260 billion on cleaning up its banking system. The amount was about twice as much as Korea spent on restructuring its banks after the 1997–98 Asian crisis. The effort included capital injection in the Big Four state banks[4] and transference of some US$170 billion worth of bad loans to the four asset management companies. Over the years, Chinese banks have also improved their technical ability by raising accounting and regulatory standards and improving management and incentive schemes.[5]

Recognizing these improvements and Beijing's opening of the Chinese banking sector for foreign investment, foreigners poured over US$18 billion into China's banking sector between late 2004 and 2005: a jump of 36 times from the accumulated investment in that sector in

2003. However, foreign investors remain minority shareholders in Chinese banks. Sceptics argue that their influence would likely be limited to the degree of graciousness. They cite Korea as an example.

Though Commerzebank had become a 30 per cent shareholder in the government-controlled Korea Exchange Bank (KEB) after the Asian crisis, it had failed to kick the KEB's old habits, which eventually got it into trouble again. The same thing happened when the country's major credit-card issuer, LG Card, failed after a consortium of international investors had acquired over 20 per cent of its equities. Foreign investors held board seats in both the KEB and LG Card, but they failed to bring about effective changes in the way these firms were run. The point that can be deduced from all this is that for foreign investors to be effective in pushing through the restructuring the controlling shareholder must be willing to accept changes.

Another example is Hyundai Motor chairman Chung Mong-koo, who was indicted in May 2006 for fund embezzlement (Won 100 billion, or US$820 million, in company money to create a slush fund used for bribery activities) and breach of trust for allegedly incurring Won 300 billion in damages to Hyundai. The indictment of Mr Chung, one of Korea's most respected industrialists, brought to boil tensions that had simmered for years between the country's secretive corporations and regulators seeking to raise standards of corporate governance. The problems at Hyundai, LG Card and KEB highlight Korea's painful effort to grow beyond an Asian development model that many see as having outlived its usefulness. They also show that the Koreans were still not biting the bullet.

If Korea, being once dubbed the IMF's model reform pupil after the Asian crisis, could not get its reform house in order, what difference would China make? Why would Beijing want a fundamental clean-up in the banking system, which would loosen its control of the financial system, give the market a bigger role in the economy and thus threaten the power base of the Communist Party?

From a strategic perspective, there is indeed a sound reason for Beijing to be serious about banking reform. Contrary to conventional wisdom, this reason is not the need to prepare the local banks for expected competition from global banks. China was required to open up its banking sector to full foreign participation under World Trade Organization (WTO) requirements from December 2006 onwards.

The power of the WTO factor to push banking reform has often been exaggerated. Even China is required by WTO rules to fully open up its banking sector; invisible barriers to entry, such as red tape, a difficult distribution network, shifting regulations and cumbersome and expensive licensing requirements, still exist (see Chapter 2, 'The WTO threat to Chinese banks' section for more). WTO rules will not be effective to force a true opening of China's banking market if it does not want to open up.

Japan is an example. It has been incorporated in the world trade system and brought under international trade laws and requirements since September 1955, when it became a member of the GATT (General Agreement on Tariffs and Trade, which was later replaced by the WTO in 1995). But the Japanese market, from retail to banking to cars, was never opened up to foreign participation until the early 1990s, when the auto trade agreement with the US cracked it. The close knit Japanese system and bureaucracy allowed it effectively to fend off foreign competition in defiance of international trade rules. Things only started to change when the Japanese were truly willing to open up.

China's distribution network is a formidable entry barrier. It will take decades and billions of dollars in investment for any foreign bank to replicate the network franchise of the large Chinese banks. Without such a web of branches, foreign banks will not be able to make any meaningful headway to compete with the local banks, especially in retail banking, which is the jewel of the business under financial liberalization. This boils down to how much the Chinese are willing to give to the foreigners.

With its massive economy, opaque markets and rustic (though developing) regulatory and institutional frameworks, China can easily replicate Japan's previous effort to fend off foreign competition within the WTO. So for China to be willing to change, there must be some significant and visible benefits accrued to the country, and at the same time those changes will not threaten the power of the Communist Party.

A robust reform incentive indeed stems from China's self-interest in building a strong economic system to sustain long-term growth, which is key to securing the Communist Party's leadership. Since China is moving towards a fully convertible currency and building an open capital market, its weak and inefficient banking system is not consistent with economic stability and not conducive to sustainable economic growth. Without a sound banking system, volatile capital (especially portfolio) flows will inflict excessive and damaging shocks in the economy and wreak havoc on the local markets if and when the capital account is opened up. Thus, contrary to the bearish view, there is indeed compatibility between reform and political incentives. This incentive is, arguably, the strongest in reforming the banking sector.

A strong banking system is as essential to a healthy economy as a heart to a healthy human body. Despite years of strong growth and reforms and the emergence of some efficient economic units, China's overall economy remains inefficient and wasteful. This can be seen in the diminishing marginal returns[6] on capital over the years (Figure 1.2). On international comparison, it takes more capital for China to produce a unit of GDP than it does in other developed economies (Figure 1.3). This diminishing returns problem shows not only over-capitalization of the Chinese economy (due to excessive savings), but also misallocation of capital. Without an efficient banking system to allocate capital better, China virtually stands no chance of graduating from its developing economy status.

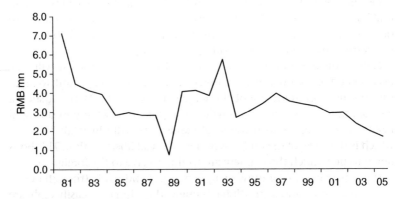

Figure 1.2   China's declining marginal returns on investment*
* Change in GDP divided by change in fixed-asset investment (4-year ma)
Source: CEIC

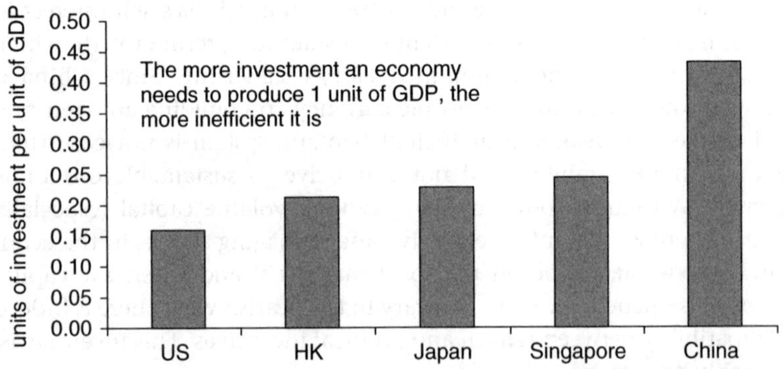

Figure 1.3   China's excessive investment
Source: CEIC

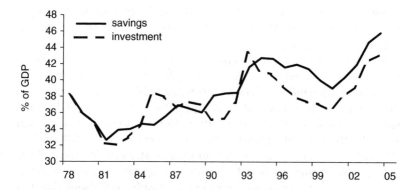

Figure 1.4 China's national savings and investment*
* Savings = GDP − consumption − govt spending; inv't = fixed inv't + inventories
Source: CEIC

China's economic inefficiencies have not yet dragged down its economic growth because growth has been driven by excessive savings boosting investments (Figure 1.4) from a low base. However, this model of throwing in ever more resources to generate a given amount of output will reach its limit eventually, as diseconomies of scale[7] will cause output to contract (or, equivalently, cost to rise disproportionately to increasing output) on an ever-increasing amount of inputs if the current inefficiencies persist.

As the savings are channelled into investments by banks, the inefficiencies and wastefulness have turned many of projects into bad debts. To sustain growth over the long term, China has to clean up its banks, kick their habit of underwriting bad loans and develop a true commercial culture. Beijing will have to withdraw from the sector ultimately to allow all this to happen. A sound banking system will allow more efficient allocation of resources so that the economy can grow on the basis of improved factor productivity but not on input accumulation alone.

From a macro-perspective, there is also strong compatibility between reform, growth and policy incentives. China's low production cost is not a panacea for the issues confronting its future growth. Indeed, low wages could even be a trap for dragging down future growth. While low cost helps Chinese manufacturers to compete, it also locks the economy in low-end production and deprives it of the ability to climb the value chain.

Many of China's low-cost manufacturers have been trying to protect margins or enhance returns in a tough environment by buying up established global brands (Table 1.1). Most of these moves are desperate attempts. Notably, the moves by Chinese manufacturers, such as Shanghai

Automotive Industry, television maker TCL and computer maker Lenovo, to acquire foreign well-known brands in recent years reflected the trouble with the low-wage trap.[8]

The trouble is not limited to manufacturers. It has spread to retailers, such as Beijing-based Gome Electrical Appliances Holding. Gome's offer of US\$4.9 billion bid for China's third-ranked China Paradise Electronics Retail in July 2006 was another example of the low- to mid-end business struggling for survival via consolidation. Fierce local competition, made worse by the entry of aggressive foreign retailers (such as US-based Best Buy) into the Chinese market, has cut the industry's profit margin down to the bone. Some of these high-profile, desperate, expansion moves have already run into trouble. Evidence as of early 2007 shows that TCL is piling up huge losses on the RCA and Thomson TV brands it bought in August 2004. Lenovo's purchase of IBM's PC business for US\$1.25 billion in December 2004 has seen its global market share shrink. There are many examples of smaller Chinese companies getting into trouble after buying into foreign competitors.

In general, razor-thin margins and cut-throat competition in the white goods and low-tech manufacturing and retail markets have pushed

Table 1.1   Top ten deals of Chinese acquisitions of foreign assets (as of September 2006)

Date	Chinese buyer	foreign target	US\$ bn (excl. debt)
August 2005	China National Petroleum	PetroKazakhstan	4.18
January 2006	China National Offshore Oil	Akpo Offshore Field	2.69
January 2006	China Petroleum &Chemical	Udmurtneft OAO	2.46
September 2005	Andes Petroleum	Ecuadorian oil assets	1.42
December 2004	Lenovo Group	IBM PC business	1.25
June 2006	China Petroleum & Chemical	Angolan oil assets	0.92
May 2006	China Petroleum & Chemical	Omimex de Columbia	0.80
June 2001	Beijing Orient Electronics	Hyundai Display Tech	0.65
January 2002	China National Offshore Oil	Repsol energy assets	0.59
August 2004	TCL	Thomson	0.52

Source: Media reports

Chinese firms to fight for survival by acquisitions and diversification. But being stuck in low-value production lines, these expansion moves have only trapped them in more low-margin, cut-throat businesses instead of one or two. Structural reforms to boost China's value-added are the only way out of this trap and to strengthen the leadership's governing legitimacy.

Critics argue that Beijing was selling Chinese bank stakes cheaply to amass funds for plugging the black hole in the banking system. This view is wrong. China has more than enough money to repair the banking mess. Total bad loans are estimated by the government at 7.2 per cent of GDP (US$160 bn) at the end of 2005. Private analysts estimated that the ratio might be as high as 30 per cent of GDP, or US$670 bn. But China has US$1.7 trillion (and growing) in household saving deposits in the banking system and US$1 trn (and growing) in foreign reserves. All of these can be mobilized to contain any systemic crisis. In a nutshell, China's banking system is unlikely to collapse (see Chapter 2, 'A system that won't collapse' section).

Then why did Beijing sell off some of the local banks under private placement to some foreign investors at prices as low as half the amount the stock market was pricing them? Such a question misses the big picture because the effective costs of buying the Chinese banks were much higher for foreign strategic investors than the books showed. These foreign investors had to commit significant time and resources in due diligence, transferring technology and taking a risky role in restructuring and managing the acquired bank. Further, Beijing wants commitment from foreign strategic investors. To prevent them from simply taking a ride, the Chinese government has required them to hold onto their stakes in the Chinese banks for at least three years.

The opportunity cost of all this was far higher than the cash that other investors paid for buying the banks in the stock market. Further, the due diligence and primary research work by the strategic investors during their buy-out process was an externality[9] to the public. Thus, investors buying the Chinese banks from the stock market should have to pay for these unintended benefits in the form of higher stock prices.

Some also think that China's bank sale to foreign investors is all about getting money to recapitalize the Chinese banks. This is simply not true. The Big Four state banks already have massive capital injection from Beijing, and the system is not short of funds for repairing the mess. The purpose of attracting foreign strategic investors is really inducing external market discipline in the Chinese system and transferring better technology, governance and management to help speed up reform momentum.

Chinese leaders have a good understanding of what it would take to sustain economic growth, though they still need to refine their reform vision.[10] Such understanding underpins their resolve to push through banking reform. Arguably, China is in an enviable position of having enough resources to reform its banks without foreign financial help.

By and large, policy lending has become history. Despite its limitations, the China Banking Regulatory Commission has tightened regulations and forced banks to pare bad debts (see Chapter 2, 'Reality check on the banks' section). The People's Bank of China (PBoC) has started liberalizing interest rates and building up a local capital market since late 2005. Other steps are also being taken to slowly improve the banking culture, such as experimenting with legalizing private lending rights (see below).

Attracting foreign investors and listing of the Big Four are signposts for Beijing's reform progress. Granted, Chinese banking reform still has a long way to go and the road ahead will be tough and bumpy because the easy part of reform has been done. There is a good chance, however, that the leadership is pursuing strategies that will make China the next America rather than the next Latin America.

... now you don't

If there is a strong incentive to reform, then why has reform moved so slowly? There is also stubborn reform resistance from various levels of the government. Aren't these signs of unwillingness to change? Indeed, there are technical and structural barriers hindering China's reform pace, despite a genuine strategic motive in Beijing.

The structural drag is rooted in the Marxist legacy, which has prevented the reform mindset from filtering down to the lower levels from the top leaders. This lack of trickle-down effect has created incentive incompatibility problems at the local levels that, ironically, clashes with the incentive compatibility (between reform and political survival) at the central level. The Maoist system set-up has also retarded the pace of change. Overall, the replacement of the old Marxist thinking by liberalized technocrats, many of whom are foreign-trained, can take place only gradually.

Hence, one should not try to judge China's reform by quantity. It is more important to assess the structural changes by the momentum at the margin. On a positive note, Beijing has been testing the grounds for withdrawing control, ranging from asset ownership to population growth and movement. It has also progressively, albeit slowly, instilled market forces into the system.

From a policy perspective, Beijing has a sharply focused objective to the exclusion of almost all other policy issues. This objective is to sustain economic growth, subject to the constraint of keeping economic stability. Stability is a constraint because it keeps the leadership from taking risks by accelerating reforms. The top policy priority has been job creation to contain potential social unrest that structural changes might bring.

This priority is especially crucial for the financial system. Beijing will not go too fast on reform, despite calls to do so from both within and outside China. It fears that fast changes would risk a massive exodus of deposits from the banks and trigger a systemic collapse. The exodus might come from external and domestic channels. On the external side, there is a concern about large capital outflow if the capital account were opened up too quickly. The worsening of China's over-invoicing problem may be a sign of capital leaving the country if the floodgates were opened.

In over-invoicing, a Chinese firm will inflate the import bill by charging the import price of some commodity at a much higher rate than the actual cost. This allows the passing of capital overseas, as the foreign (exporting) entity credits the amount of the excess payment into its Chinese counterpart's bank account outside China.

One, though imperfect, estimate for over-invoicing is the difference between China's import values and the export values of its corresponding trading partners. In principle, after allowing for the small foreign exchange rate differences used in the different official reporting systems, they should be the same. But the data show that China's inflated imports bills seem to have been getting larger in recent years (Figure 1.5), suggesting a rising incentive of capital outflow.

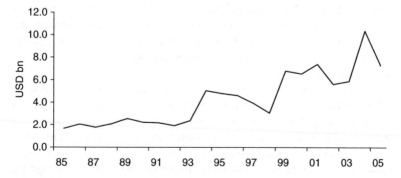

Figure 1.5 Estimated over-invoicing of Chinese imports
Source: CEIC

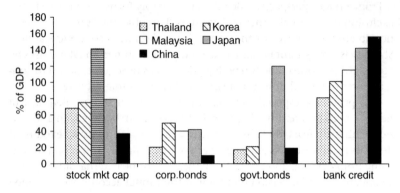

Figure 1.6   Size of the capital market
Source: CEIC

On the domestic side, the authorities have been reluctant to nurture a domestic capital market, despite its importance for financial reform. The Chinese economy relies predominantly on bank credit for capital allocation, with the capital market remaining underdeveloped even compared with its Asian neighbours (Figure 1.6). On one hand, this reflects financial repression, which enables the government to have firm control of the banking system and, hence, capital allocation, at its discretion. On the other hand, this is also largely due to the authorities' concern about deposits flowing to alternative investment vehicles in the capital market, thus hurting the banks, retarding their restructuring process and potentially triggering systemic instability.

To keep the system stable while the banks are struggling to shed bad loans, the PBoC has been helping to rebuild bank balance sheets by ensuring fat margins from their lending business. Hence, deposit rates have been kept low and lending rates have been kept high to ensure a persistent spread of three to four percentage points for the banks since 1999 (Figure 1.7).

If capital market development were to speed up before the banks are reformed to stand on their own feet, the damage on the banks would be big. For example, a one-year Chinese Treasury note yields 2 per cent at the time of writing, while a one-year bank loan costs 6.12 per cent. A firm that could borrow in the bond market at a two-point spread over government bond yield would still be paying only 4 per cent; that is over two percentage points fewer than it would have to pay by borrowing from the banks. So if firms were allowed to issue bonds, they would rush to do so.

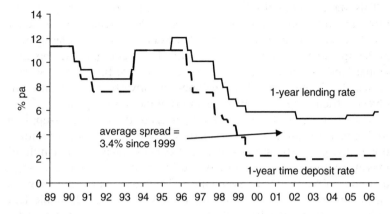

Figure 1.7 Chinese bank margins
Source: CEIC

The point is that the banks would lose their best clients to the bond market. They would also lose deposits, as savers flee the low-paying (2.25 per cent at the time of writing) bank deposits and head for higher-yielding (4 per cent) corporate papers in the capital market. Until the local banks can manage credit risk better and diversify revenues from lending, it makes sense from the policy perspective to keep capital market reform slow.

The fundamental drag on the reform pace comes from the old communist mindset. Despite the constitutional amendment in March 2004 to elevate the status of private property to the same legal status as state-owned property, Karl Marx's legacy still dominates. The government still discriminates against private firms, albeit in a more subtle way than before.

The amended constitution clearly treats state property as 'sacred and inviolable', but it never says the same for private property. The amendment also states that only 'lawful' private property is protected, but all (lawful or not by implication) state property is protected by the constitution. While no constitution would protect unlawful property, the emphasis on 'protecting lawful private property' only suggests a stubborn mindset of suspicion of private sector businesses.

The mentality has not changed much. Two years after the constitution amendment, in March 2006, at the National People's Congress the Communist Party failed to pass the draft civil code that was designed to protect private property rights. The problem, according to opponents of the code, was that the draft law failed to declare socialist property as inviolable!

This Marxist mentality has created serious incentive incompatibility problems in the local bureaucracies and hindered reform implementation from land to financial reforms. For example, on the surface, China broke up its collective farms in the early 1980s and gave farmers individual land-use rights. It was hoped that by granting them the land rights, the farmers would make long-term investment and raise and diversify their output and income. But that did not happen.

While farmers got individual land parcels in the farm break-up, they were given no assurance for property ownership. The old communist rule of the game still stood – local cadres could readjust the landholdings at any time, shuffling farmers to different parcels to reflect changes in household and village population. The reason for reshuffling the farmlands was often an excuse for bribery. Such a readjustable land rights system, on the back of rampant corruption, had deterred the farmers from making long-term investments, thus defeating the original purpose of the land reform programme.

The top leadership in Beijing knew and adopted a solution to the land rights security problem. It passed the Rural Land Contracting Law in March 2003, which scrapped the readjustable practice and gave farmers 30-year transferable property rights. But the law has not been implemented effectively because Beijing's initiatives have not trickled down to the local levels. The local cadres have resisted the change so as to protect their rent-seeking opportunities.

Indeed, it is generally known among the investment community, and even in the Chinese policy circle, that whenever there are policy directives from above, there are always counter-moves from below to offset these directives ('shang you zheng ce, xia you dui ce', as the Chinese say). In the land reform perspective, many officials still see collective ownership of rural land as one of the few remaining badges of the Communist Party. They fear the explosion of divisive political debate if this bit of constitutional dogma is changed. They also worry that allowing peasants to trade their land freely would restore the landlord class, which the communist had fought hard to eliminate. Farmers might rush to sell their land and move to ill-prepared cities, creating shanty towns and pushing up crime rates. Thus, despite years of central initiatives, the resistance to genuine land reform still remains.

On the financial side, it took over five years for the proposal of Qualified Domestic Institutional Investors (QDII), which allows Chinese institutional funds to invest overseas, to be approved and implemented in April 2006. Meanwhile, despite the sorry mess of the domestic securities industry, the clean-up effort has been minimal. This is mainly because of regulatory forbearance by the China Securities Regulatory Commission (CSRC).

Though some brokerage licences have been revoked, the too-big-to-fail policy still rules. Even industry consolidation is scanty. All this again reflects the old mindset, as the CSRC is unwilling to rock the system and offend the regional governments, who are the owners of most securities firms.

Incentive incompatibility has also persisted between the asset management companies (AMCs) and the firms and banks they target to restructure. The programme has not worked properly because the AMCs and the state-owned enterprise (SOE) managers have different motives. Modelled after the US Resolution Trust Corp. (RTC), the Chinese government set up the AMCs in 1999 to solve the banking mess using debt-equity swaps. Under the programme, the banks should be able to clear their books of large amounts of bad debts, the SOE borrowers should be able to remove oppressive loan obligations to lenders and the AMCs should be able to implement structural changes, such as governance, operational and financial reforms, in the SOEs by becoming their shareholders.

In principle, these debt-equity swaps should enable the banks to break the log-jam of bad debt that has been hurting their performance and ability to lend, and break the state banks' habit of pouring household savings into the bad SOEs. They should also allow the AMCs, through their ownership rights, to restructure some of the bad SOEs back to health either for continued operations or for sale later. The AMCs will eventually sell their equity stake back to private, including foreign, investors to recoup their purchase cost and to bring market discipline to the underlying companies.

However, the AMC programme has failed to function properly due partly to inadequate legal and institutional frameworks and operational problems, and partly to incentive incompatibility problems among the banks and the SOEs. While the debt-equity swaps are meant to be a market selection process to identify the bad SOEs for restructuring, many state firm managers still see them as just another way to save the crumbling SOEs.

Meanwhile, the banks have no incentive to recover the bad loans because they also see the AMCs as public bailout agencies to absorb their losses. This situation has improved recently, but the bailout mindset still overwhelms the pulse of market discipline. Overall, both the bank and SOE managers still see the state firms as public entities and thus sacred, and the purpose of reform is to preserve the state's assets.

It is clear that the communist mindset of public ownership and government control that prevails in the general level of the system goes against Beijing's top leaders' reform initiatives. The Maoist system set-up has prolonged this incentive incompatibility problem at the local level.

The banking system was initially set up to manage the official supply and distribution of credit in the economy. There was never a commercial culture based on risk and reward. Local party committees controlled appointments and the future of bank staff, who thus pledged their loyalty to the Party but not to shareholders and the market. Banks were basically the spending arms for local governments; credit officers were trained as bureaucrats not commercial bankers.

Reform momentum

This problem has persisted through to today, and change from this mindset has been painfully slow. However, the reform momentum is strong at the margin, suggesting a strong will from the central leadership to speed up reform in the medium term. Reform resistance should fade as the reactionary forces retreat and the old attitudes change over time.

To address the inefficiency problem, Beijing's top leadership is looking to cut the 167 central government-owned enterprises through mergers and sales to foreign or local investors either directly or through stock listing. The current plan is to keep about 80 strategic industries under the government's wings. This initiative builds on Beijing's already shrinking portfolio of SOEs (Figure 1.8). The move to shrink the state sector has already shown improved profitability results (Figure 1.9).

Meanwhile, reform initiatives in the financial sector are strong. The authorities have shown resolve to move ahead by purging the structural faults in the system and building a better institutional framework upon which an eventual change in mindset can be based. Following its initial financial liberalization moves in 2003, which saw the creation of forward contracts and allowance of short selling in the bond market, the

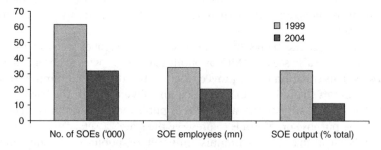

Figure 1.8 The shrinking state sector
Source: CEIC

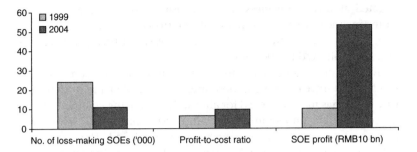

Figure 1.9 Improved SOE profits
Source: CEIC

Ministry of Finance (MoF) started a wave of financial reforms in 2005 and 2006. Chinese commercial banks have been freed to set their lending rates, according to market forces, above the PBoC's base rate, though the lending rate floor and control on deposit rates have yet to be scrapped.

The PBoC aims at withdrawing interest rate control gradually. It intends to set only the one-year deposit base rate in the near future and relinquish control of all the rest. As of 2007, the PBoC was still setting base rates for each term of deposit, from three months to five years. Deposit rates are usually the slowest to be liberalized, particularly on the upside. This is because banks may have incentives to maximize deposits using irrationally high rates, despite the costs involved, if they are assured of a bailout.

There is another crucial, but unheralded, step in interest rate liberalization. It is the introduction of 'fixing'[11] for short-term money market rates. The National Inter-bank Trading Centre has been issuing fixings for overnight and seven-day repurchase (or repo) contracts since March 2006 when the fixing was introduced. This is an important financial reform step as the fixings can be used as rates for pricing foreign exchange and interest rate swap, which are important instruments for hedging and financial market development once allowed.

When the Chinese authorities want to implement some important changes, they usually start with experiments in some small cities before rolling them out as national policies. This was what the MoF did in a move to test the liberalization of interest rates. In early 2003, it approved an unprecedented experiment with banking overhaul in the eastern city of Wenzhou by allowing market forces to set interest rates for bank deposits and loans. It also lifted the ban on the city's private-sector investment in local commercial banks, and set up a small-loan system targeted at private business. These measures go a long way towards correcting the distortion of interest rate controls and capital misallocation that deprive the private sector of credit. A wave of financial liberalization then followed in 2005 and 2006.

The long-delayed capital market reform has also seen some signs of acceleration since late 2005 as booming financing demand from the private sector has made the need for alternative financing channels urgent. Listed firms are undergoing ownership restructuring and investment products for domestic investors are being broadened. The reform will help provide effective financing instruments and facilitate good governance through information dissemination and monitoring. All this, in turn, will help to induce technological changes, improving allocation efficiency and productivity.[12]

Beijing is also embarking on a programme to reduce the discrepancy between the values of the tradable and non-tradable shares. As recently as 2005, two-thirds of the Chinese listed companies were still state-owned or state-controlled, and 60 per cent of these shares were still not tradable in the secondary market. The small 'float' of the Chinese listed companies creates an illiquid market and a price discrepancy between tradable and non-tradable shares. The lock-up of shares in government hands has also distorted incentives for holding shares, with non-tradable shareholders often taking myopic views and actions at the cost of tradable shareholders, who tend to focus on bottom lines.

In late 2005, the Ministry of Commerce and the CSRC started to restructure the ownership of the list companies by swapping shares between tradable and non-tradable shareholders with a cash incentive scheme and by encouraging foreign strategic investors to buy into Chinese firms. More institutional investors, such as security funds, insurance companies, social securities funds and qualified foreign institutional investors (QFII) are allowed to invest in the domestic A-share market, the bond market and mutual funds. All this is part of capital market reform and meant to help reduce both the price discrepancy between the two types of shares and to reduce the incentive distortion.

Even the long-neglected fixed-income market development has received a boost in the recent reform initiatives. For a start, the MoF has taken measures to encourage the issuance of short-term (one year or less) commercial papers in the interbank market since mid 2005. Despite the mini-economic bubble between 2002 and early 2004, which led to a temporary burst of short-term paper issuance, the interbank money market has grown steadily since its inception in the late 1990s (Figure 1.10). Going forward, the MoF is endeavouring to ensure steady

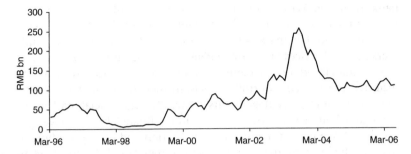

Figure 1.10 Interbank money market turnover*
*3-month moving average
Source: CIEC

growth of the market with proper supervision and to minimize policy volatility in the market. The government is also improving the development of the domestic bond by merging trading in the interbank market (in which only treasury and government agency bonds trade) and the stock exchanges (in which both treasury and corporate bonds trade), and by introducing more products such as asset-backed securities.

Many steps have also been taken to modernize the foreign exchange market. Following the reform in 2005 that expanded the forward market, introduced currency swaps and derivative products, the PBoC followed up in early 2006 with the formation of market makers in currency trading. It started over-the-counter (OTC) trading in the interbank foreign exchange market. Despite the delay and political hassle behind its approval, the QDII scheme is another significant move on financial liberalization. Qualified banks, insurance funds, securities companies and mutual funds are allowed to invest overseas upon approval under the scheme. The QDII programme, when fully implemented, will go a long way to liberalize investment and foreign exchange controls and facilitate capital allocation efficiency in China. All these are steps towards eventual capital account convertibility, which should expose the domestic system to international discipline.

The list of reform initiatives is growing, as new measures are being implemented over time. The point is that Beijing is moving forward in dealing with the structural problems in the economy. It is not sitting on its hands, as many China critics have claimed, to allow the woes to accumulate and risk a systemic collapse later. While capital market reform may raise short-term economic volatility as it purges the bad financial institutions, it should also help contain credit risk in the banking sector. When fully liberalized, market interest rates should reflect underlying economic fundamentals, as artificially low interest rates are replaced by market-driven rates. The informal lending (or curb) market, which prices credit by market forces, may offer some clues for how China's interest rates might move after they are liberalized from the distorted government-controlled levels. In 2006, the curb market's lending rates were 15 percentage points higher than the official market.

In a nutshell, new reform initiatives in the financial sector have been visible. They include interest rate liberalization and technical improvement in the local interbank and foreign currency markets. But there are other less visible and perhaps more crucial initiatives that point to a sea change in future reforms.

In particular, Beijing is experimenting to end the half-century-old *hu-kou* (or household registration) system.[13] By tying individuals to their birthplace via registration which determines their state benefit entitlements and rights of abode and work in their birth provinces, the system has retarded labour mobility, urbanization and income growth. Indeed, the *hu kou* system has dragged on urbanization, despite rapid industrialization. In 2003 (the latest data available at the time of writing), 58 per cent of the labour force was employed in the non-farm sector – a proxy for industrialization. But only a third of the labour force was registered under the urban *hu kou* system – a proxy for urbanization.

Consumer demand growth tends to be slow when urbanization lags because the 'illegal' migrants outside their home provinces tend to be poor and have fragmented demand for goods and services. For example, among the 100 million rural migrant labourers, the majority of them are single individuals rather than those with families. Their major consumption tends to remain in their home towns. This includes buying or renting homes for their families, schooling for their children and consumption of medical and other services. Since the home towns of these migrants are mostly poor, overall consumption growth under the *hu kou* system tends to be weak.

Starting in 2006, Jinan, the capital of Shangdong province, has officially scrapped the *hu-kou* system and replaced it with a system that registers individuals based on where they live rather than where they were born. Jinan was the first prefecture-level city that removed the *hu kou* system for all residents within its jurisdiction. If implemented fully, the removal of the *hu kou* system will allow free flow of people between provinces, improve labour mobility, reduce labour market distortion and improve allocation efficiency. This will have a significant positive impact on consumption growth in the long term.

Further, Beijing has started allowing domestic investors to run lending companies in the Pingyao county of Shanxi province. The move could be a harbinger for a breakthrough in China's financial reform by legalizing private lending rights. Following simple regulations and prudential guidelines, individuals and firms can form lending companies to make loans based on market-driven interest rates. The emergence of private lending institutions will likely facilitate the development of small and medium-sized enterprises, which are deprived of funding opportunities under the banking system.

In a nutshell, privatizing lending rights goes a long way to relax the private sector's budget constraint, making intertemporal choice for spending more readily available to private firms and individuals. This reform experiment in Pingyao could also be the first step towards legalizing China's informal lending market (see Chapter 2, 'Implications from the curb market' section), which has emerged to fill the financing gap left open by the official banking market.

Even the QDII scheme imparts a will to loosen financial control. When fully implemented, the scheme will be a major step towards capital account convertibility. At the current experimental stage, it is only applicable to institutional investors. But this is the first time that domestic Chinese households and firms have been granted the opportunity to invest abroad. This is also the first time that domestic residents have been granted official approval for converting renminibi (RMB) funds for foreign portfolio investment purposes. These are the aspects that give the QDII scheme historical importance.

Though these are experiments currently running at the margin of the system, they are likely forerunners of similar national policies later. More crucially, they are bold moves to restructure the old system by allowing market forces to work better. Through this reform momentum, Beijing is showing leadership in scrapping the communist policy apparatus, such as asset ownership, population control and financial repression.

The next steps

China's economic future depends on its reform process and its ability to sustain the reform momentum. Banking reforms so far have focused on restructuring the state banks. Deregulation of the financial sector has yet to come into full force. The incentive problems between the banks, the AMCs and the SOEs will remain as long as the government owns the majority of these banking and corporate assets. Institutional and legal frameworks are still insufficient to sustain deeper reforms; for example, bankruptcy is still not a viable solution for most banks because, in the Chinese mindset, 'too-big-to-fail' still rules. Hence, the bankruptcy law has been underdeveloped and institutional set-up for asset disposal after bankruptcy is poor.

Significant legal and institutional reforms are thus needed to push reform further. And the situation is starting to change. For example, China's highest law-making body, the Standing Committee of the Chinese National People's Congress, finally approved the new Enterprise Bankruptcy Law in August 2006 (effective in June 2007) after 12 years of drafting and deliberation. The new law will replace the old one issued in 1986 that applied only to SOEs. Efforts to draft a new bankruptcy law began in 1994, but opponents had blocked it for years, in part because they were worried that it would lead to a rash of new bankruptcies at the troubled SOEs.

The new bankruptcy law is the start of a big step towards modernizing China's bankruptcy procedures by breaking the back of the old communist practice that ignores the rights of creditors. The old law required insolvent companies to pay off obligations to employees before they addressed creditors' claims. The new law, which covers both privately owned firms and SOEs, instead requires companies that go bankrupt to repay creditors first, with employee salaries and other obligations paid out of what remains.

The old law gave little guidance for dealing with insolvent companies in an increasingly market-driven economy. But the new law is a milestone for China's economic overhauls that will strengthen creditors' rights and bring China closer to international legal standards. But proper implementation of the new bankruptcy law remains a challenge, as is the case for any other reform initiatives handed down by the central authorities in Beijing.

On banking reform, continued progress can be expected but speed will remain slow. This is because, under the current system, risks of the banking sectors will be very much affected by a sharp fall in economic growth, a rapid fall of deposits if the banking sector is opened to fierce foreign competition or capital market development or there is a drop in the savings rate due to demographic change and unexpected shocks to the economy.

Thus, banking reforms will progress only slowly, with recapitalization, privatization and operational restructuring as the key forms of change in the medium term. The restructuring will take a few more years to complete. After that, financial deregulation and capital market liberalization will become the main reform focus. Beijing's move to allow the entry of non-deposit-taking lending institutions[14] into the credit market indicates that the informal credit sector will be legalized soon, at least partially.

To correct the incentive problems in the state banks, restrictions on foreign investors to hold Chinese bank shares will have to be relaxed. For joint stock commercial banks and city commercial banks, majority foreign ownership is possible in the near future. The recent development in the domestic capital market will speed up after the bank restructuring process is completed. Success in deregulation will go a long way to reduce systemic risk in the financial sector, which will also become China's largest service sector boosting economic growth for decades to come. Ultimately, withdrawal of government controls is what the banking system needs to change fundamentally for the better. But it is also a long-term process; shock treatment for the existing financial woes will not work.

Tax reform is crucial to fiscal stability and improvement of economic efficiency. Initiatives are being undertaken to simplify the tax system and make it a more level playing field between local and foreign companies in China. Under the current dual tax system, local firms pay a 33 per cent corporate income tax every year, while foreign firms and firms (including joint ventures) located in the high-tech and special economic zones enjoy a preferential tax rate of only 15 per cent. Further, foreign firms with an investment horizon of ten years or longer are eligible to a two-year income tax holiday after they first make a profit. Then, they will only have to pay tax on half of the income earned for the following three years.

During the early days of economic reform, when the market mechanism was largely absent, the risk of investing in China could be very high. The difference in the tax rates paid by local and foreign investors could be seen as the risk premium for foreign investors to justify their return on risky investments in China. However, structural changes since 1978 have created a market mechanism in the Chinese system so that the risk premium of investing in China (hence the tax rate differential) should be lowered going forward.

The Eleventh Five-Year Plan, approved by the National People's Congress in March 2006, calls for unifying corporate income taxes within five years. Under the new tax regime Beijing will cut the local tax rate and raise the foreign preferential rate to something near 25 per cent for everyone. Nevertheless, there will still be tax incentives for priority areas, such as energy-saving and environmentally friendly industries and scientific development.

Improving and simplifying tax administration will also reduce the problem of tax evasion and capital flight. Under the current tax regime, many local Chinese firms have been illegally sending capital outside China, most commonly to Hong Kong, and then taking it back under the guise of foreign investment to take advantage of the preferential tax treatment. This process is known as 'round tripping' and is estimated to have accounted for an average of 30 per cent of capital flight from China over the years.[15]

The tax reform aims at correcting the distortions created by the current dual tax system. A unified tax would no longer discriminate against enterprises based on who is investing and where investment is being made. The intended objective is to promote fair competition and resource-efficient and environmentally friendly growth in the future. While foreign investors may see tax rate unification as negative to them in the short term, they should benefit from the long-run impact of the reform if strong growth and improved market efficiency offset the increased tax burden after the reform.

If implemented properly, the unified corporate income tax rate would confirm the direction of market-based reform going forward. It would not affect foreign investors' comparative advantage in technology and high-value goods and services production. However, competition in some sectors, most likely in the labour-intensive and low-tech sectors, would increase sharply and margins in these industries would be squeezed. This would force some foreign, especially small-scale, enterprises to relocate their business outside China in the future.

A genuine great leap forward for China will be the implementation of true and proper land reform, the progress of which has so far been retarded by the communist mindset and incentive incompatibility problems. Under paramount leader Deng Xiao-ping, China's agricultural output soared, as for the first time under the communist regime farmers were allocated plots, though not given full ownership, of land to farm for private earnings. This marked the start of the economic transformation that has raised the world's eyebrows today. But Mr Deng kept in place two pillars of the Maoist rural order: collective land ownership and an apartheid *hu kou* system that barred rural residents from moving to the cities.

Beijing is now experimenting with scrapping the *hu kou* system, due to economic pressure from the manufacturing boom on the demand for cheap labour. But true rural land reform has yet to start, despite the breaking up of the collective farms in the early 1980s and the adoption of the Rural Land Contracting Law in 2003. Nonetheless, despite its defects, the partial rural reform did achieve a more equitable land distribution for the farmers, and this has been a powerful factor in reducing social tension and the potential for unrest (see Chapter 5, 'Unemployment is not the real problem' section).

Improving property rights will go a long way to improve income and investment growth because, as some studies argue,[16] the poor have more assets – shacks, stalls, plots – than one might think. But since they lack title to these assets, the poor cannot use, pass on, divide up or offer their assets as collateral for loans to expand their makeshift business and fully utilize their entrepreneurial energies. Thus, their assets remain embalmed as 'dead capital'. However, others argue[17] that granting land title *per se* was not enough to lift the poor from their desperate plight if their access to financing means, such as bank loans and credit cards, had not improved. The land titles must also be made transferable in the market-place. In addition to income growth and wealth accumulation, transfer-able land title (which allows the owner to cash in on the land-use, rights, thus enhancing wealth) is a necessary and sufficient condition to unlock the dead capital from the poor.

All these arguments are relevant to Chinese farmers and rural land reform. The Chinese government must carry out genuine rural land reform by giving farmers marketable ownership rights and developing a legal system to protect these rights. Only then would the farmers be able to mortgage their land and raise money for investment. Only then could the farmers sell their land to raise money to move to the cities, thus facilitating urbanization. In a nutshell, full landownership with transfer-able rights would give the farmers the incentive to invest and start life anew in the cities, which are key to boosting productivity and con-sumption growth.

It is inevitable that land reform will loosen the Communist Party's control in the long run. But this is the cost of economic progress and the Chinese authorities have shown a willingness to take a risk for the sake of it. Take housing reform as an example. Before it started in 1998, almost all urban housing was state-owned. However, in one of China's most dramatic and successful economic reforms, most urban housing is now privately owned. This has fostered the growth of a middle class that wants property ownership rights free from state interference. Property owners even elect their own landlord committees, independent of the Party, to lobby for and protect their rights. And a new breed of lawyers, not Party clones, has emerged to defend the rights of private property owners from state threats and politics. All these have been tolerated by the state.

In general, China's Community Party has shown its willingness to take big risks to its power grip where economic development requires this. This is clearly seen in the massive creative destruction where SOEs were closed or privatized to make way for the rise of the private sector, and tens of millions of state jobs were lost over the past two decades. The leadership seems to indicate that the time has come for them to complete the unfinished business of structural reform.

There is no need for the Party to fear economic reforms, as the upshot of new reform experiments in Ningxia has shown. Ningxia, a province in a remote part of northwest China, is predominantly rural, has a hard time in attracting foreign investment, few private enterprises, and serious soil erosion and water scarcity. It has also seen rising grievances in land-use rights, along with the collapse of affordable education and healthcare systems (which is also a nationwide problem).

Part of the leadership's solution has been to spend money. The central government has provided southern Ningxia with a large annual subsidy equal to fifteen times the tax revenues that the local government collects. Farmers are also given direct subsidies to grow grains and raise livestock. But structural measures are also being put in place to correct the problems inherited from the communist legacy, such as control on population movement and the lack of education opportunity. The Ningxia government has introduced free primary education in the province and has measures for helping residents travel to and work in the booming coastal cities by providing skills training and organizing work contracts.

Through measures for raising education opportunities and facilitating residents' moving to cities to make a better living, 'Ningxia-nomics', as the experiment is called, has boosted the local government's popularity sharply. By pursuing Ningxia-nomics, the leadership evidently wants to improve the distribution of economic prosperity so that those at the bottom of the pile have a chance of moving up and escaping poverty. Ningxia-nomics is just further evidence showing that reform and political incentives can indeed be compatible.

2
Financial Fragility Revisited

Despite more than twenty years of structural reforms, the stability of the Chinese banking system remains a key concern for China's economic outlook. Many China observers are ambivalent about the health of the Chinese banks. Die-hard pessimists have argued for an eventual collapse of the banking system, dragging the economy down with it. Some others see the opening up of the banking system to fierce foreign competition under World Trade Organization (WTO) requirements aggravating China's inherent financial woes, leading to an eventual banking implosion. There is also concern about the informal credit market, or the curb market as it is sometimes called, wreaking havoc on the formal banking system and reducing the effectiveness of monetary policy on demand management.

To the surprise of the pessimists, and despite their repeated predictions, no banking crisis has happened so far. It is unlikely that one such crisis would emerge, unless the authorities make serious policy mistakes. There is concrete evidence of progress for banking reform, though the completion of reform will likely take longer than most optimists think. There is no doubt that a lot still needs to be done to correct the inherent financial woes. But there are no signs of imminent financial instability threatening China's long-term economic outlook. Systemic risk has fallen sharply over the years, and WTO-induced competition is not likely to shock the Chinese system into chaos. Arguably, despite its being a symbol of financial distortion, the curb lending market also makes positive contributions to China's economy where the formal banking sector fails.

A system that won't collapse

Pessimists have been predicting a Chinese banking system collapse, which leads to their doom-laden view of the whole economic outlook.

Despite all the positive headline changes, such as a shrinking state sector on the back of a bourgeoning private sector, China's credit market is still dominated by the Big Four state banks – Agricultural Bank of China, Bank of China, China Construction Bank and Industrial and Commercial Bank of China. There are also three state-owned policy banks – Agricultural Development Bank, China Export and Import Bank and State Development Bank. Altogether, these state banks account for slightly over 60 per cent of the assets and deposits in the system. The rest is accounted for by other commercial banks, urban and rural credit cooperatives, postal savings banks and foreign-funded banks (see Figures 2.9 and 2.10: p. 54).

There are huge bad-debt problems with these state-owned banks. The improvement in China's accounting standard in the banking system only makes these woes more easily seen. Since 2001, the state banks have adopted a five-tier classification system broadly in line with international practice. They have also made some progress in improving internal accounting and reporting structures. The government's recent estimate of just over 10 per cent non-performing loans (NPL) ratio for the Big Four state banks is based on this reformed accounting system. Despite the greater transparency, most external experts still put China's NPL ratio at over 30 per cent of total assets.

The official number is still misleading, many sceptics argue, because the Chinese reporting system still suffers from serious problems. They arise from both the branch level and senior management. While the head office accounting procedures may be stringent, the quality and reliability of local audits still remain poor when the new accounting and reporting procedures are carried out at branch level. The fundamental problem is that many senior staff at the state banks are appointed civil servants. They face a conflict of interest where the pressure to report accurate data often weighs against the incentive to show good numbers to their superiors.

Further, the official 10 per cent or so bad-debt ratio for the Big Four is an understatement due to their exclusion from the NPL calculation of the RMB1.4 trillion (US$175 billion) bad loans transferred to the four asset management companies (AMCs) in 1999 and 2000. Arguably, excluding these bad assets is wrong because they remain NPLs on the AMCs' balance sheets before they are sold. Hence, they are still a burden on the financial system. Putting these bad loans back into the state banks' balance sheets would yield a 25 per cent NPL ratio, which makes China's NPL the biggest in Asia (Figure 2.1).

Based on this evidence, the pessimists cannot help but keep calling for a financial collapse in China. But that has never happened. There are

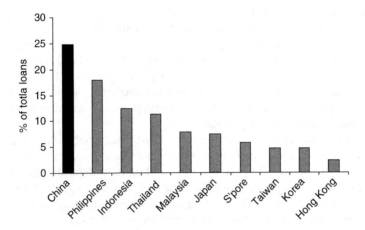

Figure 2.1 Asia's NPL ratios (2005)
Source: CEIC

several reasons for this. First, the conventional wisdom for a banking crisis does not apply to China. Second, China's half-baked market economy has turned out to be a blessing in disguise for keeping the system from falling apart. Third, the overall banking environment in China has improved, reducing the risk of a systemic meltdown. Fourth, Chinese banks have made some progress on improving their operations and system controls. Last, but not least, the central bank is phasing in, albeit slowly, market-determined interest rates, thus improving market discipline for controlling system risk.

The conventional wisdom is that a bank goes under when it is insolvent,[1] and the banking system collapses when most, if not all, of its banks are insolvent. But in China's context, the key is not whether Chinese banks are solvent but whether they have positive cash flow.[2] On a systemic basis, there is a confidence issue. A bank will not go bankrupt simply because it is insolvent, unless there is a loss of public confidence that prompts all depositors to withdraw their money. This will cause a run on the bank, draining its liquidity and eventually forcing it to fail. In China, the government's 'too-big-to-fail' policy essentially underwrites the stability of the banking system. The implicit government guarantee of the banking system has kept public confidence high so that the probability of bank run is low.

Technically, a bank becomes non-viable when it lacks money from its interest income to pay its depositors: that is when its cash flow turns negative. A bank's cash flow is determined by the spread that it charges, i.e. the difference between the lending and the deposit rates. As long as the interest charged on the performing assets covers the interest paid to the depositors, the bank has a positive cash flow and will not go bust. Thanks to official interest rate control policy that have kept China's lending rate consistently and significantly above the deposit rate since 1995 (Figure 2.2), Chinese banks are always liquid, or cash-flow positive, despite all the bad-debt problems.

In other words, the higher the ratio of the lending rate to the deposit rate, the more liquid the bank is. Consider a Chinese bank that lends at 6 per cent and pays 2 per cent on its funding from deposits and a Thai bank that earns 8 per cent from lending and pays 4 per cent to its depositors. The Chinese bank's lending rate is three times higher than its deposit rate, implying that it could sustain an NPL ratio of 66 per cent without getting into negative cash flow.

On the other hand, the Thai bank's lending spread is twice its funding cost, meaning that its net cash flow will turn negative as soon as its NPL ratio goes over 50 per cent. On this basis, the Chinese bank is less susceptible to NPL shocks than the Thai bank. Indeed, this is exactly the case in the entire Chinese banking system. On a regional basis, Chinese banks have the highest lending-to-deposit rate ratio (Figure 2.3), making it easier for them to bear the bad-debt burden.

The absence of a banking crisis so far in China can also be attributable to its half-transition from a planned economy to a market system. This mixed system has allowed the authorities to perform an economic balancing act

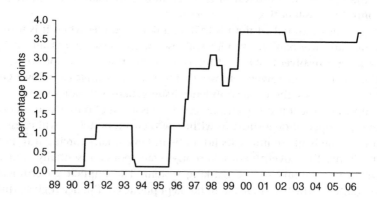

Figure 2.2   Chinese bank lending spread*

* 1-year base lending rate – 1 year time deposit rate
Source: CEIC

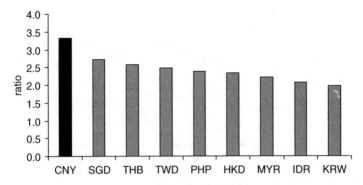

Figure 2.3 Asia's lending-deposit rate ratios
Source: CEIC

between growth and reform. The combination of a closed capital account and a small foreign debt has shielded China from the risk of withdrawal by the foreign creditors.[3] In other words, unlike those Asian-crisis economies, China's banking system is not held hostage by foreign creditors.

Meanwhile high savings, averaging 40 per cent of income over the past decade, and robust income growth have generated a huge amount of liquidity. With capital controls locking liquidity in the local system and without a developed capital market to offer alternative saving products, the bulk of household savings goes into the state bank deposits. China also limits the operating scale of non-state commercial banks and foreign banks through licensing requirements and restrictions on funding sources. The full opening of the Chinese banking system in December 2006 under WTO requirements may not change this much going forward (see pp. 56–9). All this has helped direct household savings to the state banks, keeping them liquid.

China's overall banking environment has improved. The progress, though slow, should continue to help contain the risk of a banking crisis. The bulk of the bad loans in the system are a legacy of the old woes. Since 1998, not only has the state sector downsized, but overall internal governance and transparency at Chinese banks have improved. The shrinkage of the state sector suggests that the role of state-directed lending has declined.

Indeed, the Big Four's working capital loans to the state-owned enterprises (SOEs) have dropped sharply in recent years. With the closure of many SOEs, there is simply a smaller need to lend to the state sector. There has also been faster loan growth at smaller non-state banks, which are less susceptible to policy-driven lending. Meanwhile, the state banks

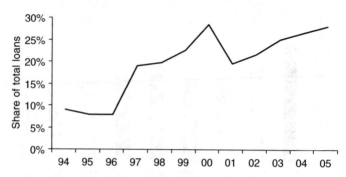

Figure 2.4   Private and non-state sector loans
Source: CEIC

have been developing new business, such as consumer lending, mortgage loans and investment-related finance, instead of continuing to throw good money after bad at the SOEs. Bank loans to private and non-state sector firms[4] have risen sharply in recent years (Figure 2.4).

This is not to say that state banks are not generating new bad loans. Indeed, they will continue to add NPLs as reform continues because many SOE loans will turn bad as the inefficient state firms are restructured or closed down. However, the pace of bad loan growth has slowed (see next section). The official revelation of a high bad loan ratio also suggests improvement in transparency, though the problem is not resolved completely.

Chinese banks are also making progress on reforming their operations, reducing the risk of failure. On the audit side, banks have adopted new accounting standards and the international five-tier system for classifying NPLs. They have broadly computerized and centralized credit databases, though audits are still done internally with local auditors. Banks have also gone through significant risk management training. Granted, in a controlled interest rate environment, there is little scope for serious implementation. But even this may be starting to change.

Since late 1999, all Chinese banks have been putting in efforts to improve credit-risk management, especially in the underwriting of new loans. Most of them have used credit checking processes that are familiar to western bankers. Not surprisingly, many SOEs – the banks' traditional borrowers – cannot meet the new lending criteria. Hence, lending to the SOEs has dropped while loans to government projects and to individuals buying houses and durable goods have risen. The banks have also been investing funds in government bonds to improve asset quality on their balance sheets. From a portfolio risk and cash flow angle, this is an improvement, though the change is still slow. Meanwhile, major Chinese banks have vastly raised their bad-debt provisions and cut NPLs by increasing write-offs.

The People's Bank of China (PBoC), China's central bank, is allowing more interest rate flexibility under market forces. In early 2003, it tested full interest rate liberalization and a complete banking overhaul in the eastern city of Wenzhou by allowing market forces to set interest rates for bank deposits and loans. The Ministry of Finance (MoF) also approved hedging activity in the Chinese bond market by allowing investors to use risk-hedging tools, such as forward contracts and short-selling,[5] in the domestic Treasury bond market. The purpose is to encourage Chinese banks, which are the main investors in government bonds, to hedge exposure to government debt.

This is a crucial start for liberalizing interest rates and the capital market. Without hedging instruments, Chinese banks have lacked the tools to protect themselves from price volatility in the Treasury market as interest rates fluctuate. It is thus obvious that by experimenting with market-driven interest rates and allowing interest-rate risk hedging, Beijing is committed to liberalizing interest rates, allowing them to be determined gradually by market forces.

The more relevant risk for China's banking system is a 'Japanese quagmire'. If financial reform loses steam, the cost of sustaining the banking system will rise. More crucially, this rising cost will mean lost opportunities and faltering growth. Tolerance of the financial woes, such as waiting for economic growth to bail out the system, would mean a prolonged period of moral hazard, interest rate controls, capital account inconvertibility and onerous rules that will stifle the development of a market-based system.

An impaired financial system with falling savings, due to an ageing population and a structural rise in consumption over time, could trim China's real growth rate in the future. Japan is an example of this. Its ageing population, falling savings, high pension and debt liabilities and insufficient reform have left the country with no growth, a spiralling fiscal burden and structural stress.

China can only calm investor concerns by moving decisively to fix the banking woes. The state banks are unable to repair their balance sheets on their own. Thus, the government has to step in to bring them back to health. Beijing has already started the recapitalization process when it created the AMCs in 1999 with a total of RMB400 billion (US$49 billion) paid-in capital from the MoF. However, that was only a small sum compared with the estimated RMB2.5 trillion that is needed to bring the state banks into reasonable condition for privatization. The amount of funds required has raised another grave concern about Beijing's fiscal ability to fix the mess without blowing up its budget deficit. Adding in China's pension liability, Beijing's total requirement for funds to fix the whole financial system may exceed 100 per cent of GDP.

To tackle this formidable challenge, China must expand the capital market as part of the reform package by promoting equity and bond instruments as alternative saving and funding instruments. This, in turn, argues for full interest rate liberalization so that market forces can set the price of capital and banks can develop risk-management capabilities. When these conditions are met, China can fully open up the capital account and allow full RMB convertibility.

An open capital account involves allowing local funds to invest abroad. The approval of the qualified domestic institutional investors (QDII) scheme in April 2006 was the first step towards capital account convertibility. Allowing local capital to invest abroad is as crucial as attracting quality capital inflow. The current foreign exchange controls have locked up a huge amount of domestic savings, forcing local capital to invest at home even when returns are poor. Much of this investment has taken the form of bank lending to the SOEs, though banks have started to diversify their business lines and client base recently.

China's broken banking system cannot fully utilize the funds available, leading to excess deposit accumulation. At the end of 1999, the surplus of deposits over loans in China's banks amounted to RMB1.5 trillion (US$182 billion). By mid 2006, it had grown seven-fold to over RMB10 trillion. The surplus will grow as long as the banks remain dysfunctional and there is a lack of investment choice for savers.

The problem is manifested in a persistent fall in the loan-to-deposit ratio (Figure 2.5), which in China's case amounts to financial suppression. It not only misallocates capital and deprives domestic savers of better returns, but also creates highly volatile economic cycles. This is because the government owns the lion's share of the financial system, directly controls the price of capital and provides implicit guarantee to the banks' funding. Under this set-up, bank managers and borrowers have an incentive to take excessive risk, in the belief that funds will always be cheap and the government will always cover the banks' losses.

Meanwhile, the huge amount of surplus savings has propelled an unsustainable investment boom in recent years. Eventually, run-away investment will drive up inflation, forcing the government to slam on the monetary brakes and end the party in tears. Beijing is aware of the problem.

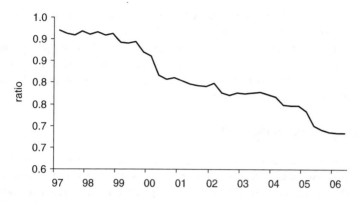

Figure 2.5   China's loan-to-deposit ratio
Source: CEIC

Since 1996, it has pledged to avoid generating volatile growth cycles by improving monetary management, notably by making anti-inflation its monetary policy goal. Financial liberalization is an integral part of this strategy. Time will tell how fast and how far it will go in the coming years.

Granting more investment freedom to local funds to go abroad so that they can seek better returns will go a long way to solving the capital misallocation and excessive cyclical volatility problems. There is no need to open the floodgates all at once. Beijing could give local financial institutions limited scope to invest in foreign equities and bonds at first; which is what QDII is all about. This will ease speculative pressure on local asset prices and strengthen the Chinese banks' balance sheets by allowing them to buy better-quality assets. The next step will be to allow Mainland companies and individuals to buy increasing amounts of hard currency for foreign investment, with an eventual goal of achieving full capital account convertibility.

The most crucial step for financial reform is to allow independent ownership and management of the banks. This should come after the legal and institutional reforms are in place and banks are recapitalized to support the needed changes. Experience has shown that bank reform is not a panacea for financial flaws unless the state cedes control of the banks completely. Privatization of the state banks should go hand in hand with financial liberalization.

The gains from this will be two-fold. The proceeds from privatization will help reduce Beijing's fiscal burden from recapitalizing the banks. More crucially, the process will introduce outside ownership and management so that banks will function as truly commercial entities to allocate capital. Simply listing banks on China's immature, speculative, A-share stock markets will not solve the ownership incentive problem. An overseas listing may be a moderate improvement, but effective management requires market discipline in the home base. Hence, the state must let go of control on the banks eventually and allow outside strategic institutional investors to participate.

Reality check on the banks

It is certain that the cushions to the banking woes that China is enjoying will not last for ever. But they are systemic issues that will not disappear swiftly cither. They should remain in place for some years, allowing China a window of opportunity to complete the necessary financial restructuring. Although China's banking system has gone through some profound changes, its reform is far from complete. As a result, China's financial liberalization has yet to unleash its full banking potential for the asset demand. A crucial part as in this is the infancy of the mortgage and personal finance market which has constrained consumer demand.

It will take longer than many have expected for banking reform to be completed, despite the WTO requirements for China to open its banking sector fully to foreign competition. This means that full capital account (and hence renminbi, or RMB) convertibility will have to wait until such reform is complete. This is because the Chinese banking system cannot handle volatile international capital flows until sound banking practices and regulations are in place. However, given China's reform momentum, its sector and country outlook remains benign.

China has made some material progress in reforming its ailing banks. NPLs have fallen steadily, as a share of total assets, GDP and new loans (Figures 2.6 and 2.7). Private analysts estimated that China's NPLs were over 50 per cent of GDP in the early 1990s. But official estimate puts them at less than 10 per cent now. Even if the true bad-debt levels were three times higher than the official estimate, they would still represent a sharp improvement.

Fundamentally, China's banking sector has gone through some profound changes since 1998, when financial liberalization and bank recapitalization efforts were launched. The process started with fresh capital injections, NPL carve-outs and organizational restructuring for the Big Four. Beijing issued RMB270 billion (US$33.3 billion) of special-purpose bonds to recapitalize the Big Four in 1998, and set up four AMCs to buy RMB1.4 trillion (US$175 billion) of bad debts from them between 1999 and 2000. Then at the end of 2003, Beijing used the country's huge foreign

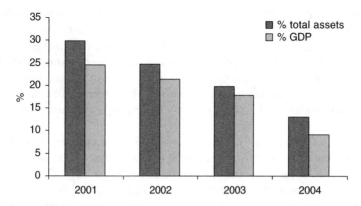

Figure 2.6 The Big Four's NPLs
Sources: CEIC, Hoover Institution, CBRC

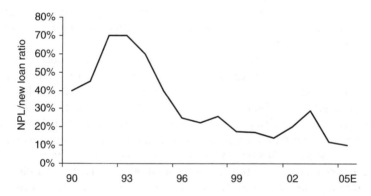

Figure 2.7 Big Four's NPL flows
Source: CEIC

reserves to inject US$45 billion into the Bank of China (BoC) and the China Construction Bank (CCB). The cash injection allowed the two banks to boost their capital adequacy ratios to over 8 per cent of asset and cut NPLs to less than 10 per cent.

China's bank clean-up efforts cost it US$260 billion between 1998 and 2003. That was about twice the amount South Korea spent on restructuring its banks after the Asian crisis and about the same amount that the US spent on cleaning up its savings and loans industry in the 1980s. Although moving NPLs off banks' balance sheets to the AMCs is not the ultimate solution to banking woes, it is the most important step to keeping systemic stability. This is because a bank is a deposit-taking institution while an AMC is not. Banking crises arise when banks in the system cannot generate enough cash flow to meet current market liabilities. Hence, when depositors panic, banks run and systemic shock follows. AMCs do not face this problem because they do not take deposits and, hence, have no market liabilities to meet. The government has sharply reduced financial risk to the economy by shifting bad loans away from banks.

The PBoC's decision in October 2004 to lift the commercial lending rate ceiling have, in principle, allowed banks to price loans according to credit risk. Crucially, the China Banking Regulatory Commission (CBRC) was created in late 2002 as an independent bank regulator, focusing on cutting banks' NPLs and improving their operations. Most of China's 128 local commercial banks (as of 2006) have independent directors sitting on their boards now, and have installed better shareholding and incentive structures that involve some market discipline. Management has also invested in a new risk-management system and tried to eliminate the conflict-of-interest problem by separating the roles of making and approving loans.

Chinese banks have also improved their technical ability since 1998 by raising accounting and regulatory standards. However, they have fallen short on developing skills for dealing with loan defaults, which include foreclosure, asset disposal, corporate restructuring and outright bankruptcy. This problem relates back to China's underdeveloped institutional and legal framework. So even if a company was closed down, the lack of a working bankruptcy infrastructure and formal commercial property rights has prevented foreclosure of the firm and resolution of its outstanding debts.

From a strategic perspective, the government's reform tactics took a sharp, arguably better, turn in 2003 when Wen Jia-bao took over the premiership from Zhu Rong-ji. Mr Zhu's policy focused on recapitalizing the Big Four in return for operational restructuring. There was never any privatization drive. After recapitalization, the banks under the Zhu regime were expected to grow their way out of the NPL problems before opening up to foreign competition. But that strategy backfired, as it prompted an extreme pro-growth policy, which created overheating in various sectors in the economy. The state banks tried to grow out of their problems by lending lavishly between 2002 and 2004, thus feeding speculation in property, cars, steel and other unprofitable industrial projects.

Mr Wen has taken a different approach since 2003. He has combined recapitalization (with renewed fund injection in the BoC and CCB) with privatization, in particular selling them off to foreign strategic investors.

The aim is to use private investors as an external force to push structural changes. The pre-listing clean-up effort has pushed down NPLs sharply.

Granted, all this does not mean that Chinese banks are now fully commercialized with sound risk management and lending decision. But the reform efforts so far have made the bad-debt situation more manageable than before. In a bid to speed up reform momentum, the Chinese authorities have opened the door to foreign strategic investors, who have responded with a strong vote of confidence.

From a trivial US$500 million cumulative foreign equity stakes in Chinese banks in 2003, overseas investors poured US$18 billion into the Chinese banking system between late 2004 and 2005, with the bulk of the investment coming in the second half of 2005 (Table 2.1). More funds will flow in, as the 25 per cent cumulative foreign ownership ceiling on individual Chinese banks is expected to be raised. The Chinese banks are also listing overseas, mainly in Hong Kong first (as an experiment before listing on the bigger developed markets), with the Bank of Communications, Industrial and Commercial Bank of China, China Construction Bank and Bank of China all listed in Hong Kong between 2005 and 2006.

Table 2.1   Major foreign investment in Chinese banks (2004–2005)

Deal date	Foreign buyer	Target bank (% bought)	Amount (US$ mn)
March 2004	ING Group NV	Bank of Beijing (19.9)	214.8
late 2004	HSBC	Bank of Commu-nications (19.9)	2,250.0
April 2005	Commonwealth Bank of Australia	Hangzhou City Commercial bank (19.9)	77.6
June 2005	BankAmerica	China Construction Bank (9)	2,500.0
July 2005	Temasek	China Construction Bank (3.6)	2,500.0
August 2005	Royal Bank of Scotland consortium	Bank of China (10)	3,100.0
August 2005	UBS	Bank of China (1.6)	500.0
August 2005	Temasek	Bank of China (9.9)	3,000.0
August 2005	Goldman Sachs, Allianz, AMEX group	Industrial and Commercial Bank of China (10)	3,000.0
September 2005	Deutsche Bank & partner	Hauxia Bank (14)	330.0

Source: Media reports

However, political, technical and incentive problems remain in the way of reform, placing a drag on its progress (see Chapter 1, '... Now you don't' section). There is a big moral hazard problem with the AMCs, which is supposed to clean up banking ailments by debt-equity swaps after restructuring the SOEs. There is also a worry that the Chinese banks may rely too much on technical solutions, such as credit-scoring models, while they do not have enough qualified personnel to spot bad borrowers and price credit properly. Interest rate liberalization and stringent loan classifications have limited help for building a strong credit culture, which is fundamental to commercialization.

Turf wars make the reform road bumpier. The decentralized structure of the banks only makes it more difficult for the reform incentive to be filtered down from the central, head office, level to the local branch level. The head office, which wants to centralize control and push down changes, often clashes with the branches, which often cave in to local officials and industrialists' demands for preferential lending. Thick politics has manifested itself in a struggle between the PBoC and CBRC.

The tussle has severely limited the ability of the CBRC to be a truly independent regulator. It was born out of political battling, when Premier Wen was consolidating his power after taking over from Zhu Rong-ji in late 2002. The PBoC, which was closely related to Mr Zhu and had multi-objectives (of which being a bank regulator was only one), had strongly resisted to separating the regulatory role from its other roles.

When Mr Wen came to power, he moved to weaken Mr Zhu's agency and installed his protégé Yan Hai-wang to form a team of experts, excluding anyone from the PBoC, to create an independent bank regulator – the CBRC headed by Liu Ming-kang. However, PBoC governor Zhou Xiao-chuan, who is a favourite of Mr Zhu, has never conceded. He uses the PBoC's mandate of keeping overall financial stability to continue to supervise and audit banks, overlapping the CBRC's work.

The PBoC–CBRC power struggle has created regulatory inefficiency. It has also dampened the outlook for a truly independent financial regulator. Political intervention in the banking system will remain an issue. These problems are aggravated by serious corruption and reflected in the poor profitability of the Chinese banking industry. For example, Chinese banks managed to generate a return-on-assets (ROA) of only 0.5 per cent in 2004, the worst in Asia, with the lowest capital-asset ratio (Figure 2.8). Their returns looked better on an equity basis, with an average return-on-equity (ROE) of 11 per cent. But banking analysts argue that was because of the Chinese banks' low level of equity (and hence capital).

Arguably, Chinese banks should carry a capital–asset ratio above the BIS standard of 8 per cent to cover their higher inherent risks. For example,

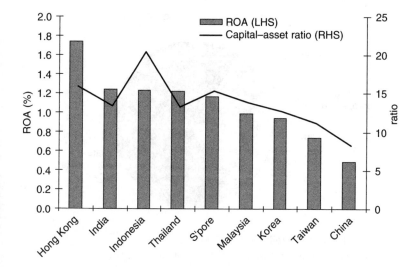

Figure 2.8   Asian banks' performance (2004)
Source: Media reports

Indonesian banks have an average capital–asset ratio of almost 20 per cent to cushion their risks. If the Chinese banks were to do the same, banking analysts estimate that their ROE would fall below 5 per cent. Meanwhile, the handicap of the AMCs is seen in the difficulty in asset disposal. They managed to sell off only half of the bad debts seven years after inception. The average cash recovery rate is about 20 per cent, and this recovery rate is going to fall as the better-quality assets have been sold off.

Despite the problems, reform momentum is strong. The CBRC has started a clean-up effort on the rural credit co-ops and postal savings since 2003. Although these institutions account for less than 20 per cent of total banking assets and liabilities today (Figures 2.9 and 2.10), their size will grow as financial liberalization spreads to the rural areas. The CBRC's effort shows that Beijing is starting to tackle the problems before it is too late.

Financial liberalization so far has already changed the banking landscape drastically. It has boosted competition among local banks. Younger and leaner commercial banks, which are estimated to account for over 20 per cent of the banking sector, in the more affluent urban areas are competing fiercely with the Big Four. Free from historic burden and more flexible in lending to small- to medium-sized firms, these new players are more adaptable to changes.

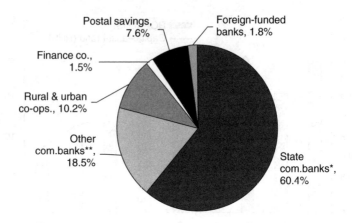

Figure 2.9   Total bank liabilities (June 2006)

* Big Four + 3 policy banks, ** Joint-stock and regional banks, city-level banks
Source: CEIC

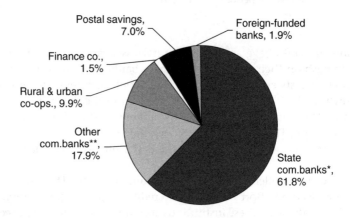

Figure 2.10   Total bank assets (June 2006)

* Big Four + 3 policy banks, ** Joint-stock and regional banks, city-level banks
Source: CEIC

The development of new funding and saving vehicles are starting to compete for business with the state banks. In the long run, as China's emerging capital markets mature, there will be large shifts of saving and borrowing from the banking sector to the capital markets. The stock and bond markets will play a bigger role in China's increasingly market-oriented economy for savers and companies to diversify financial risks.

Foreign investors will help push China's bank restructuring by providing the skills in risk management, financial product knowledge and innovation. The aim of China in selling its banks is not about money. The local banks are flooded with liquidity from both the depositors and the recapitalization funds. Rather, the purpose is to create a competitive momentum by bringing in foreign players into the Chinese system. As the obstacles for the foreign banks to take local RMB deposits and make RMB loans are eventually dismantled, the foreign players will become an immense challenge to the Chinese banks. If Chinese savings shift to the foreign banks in large amounts, the local banks' deposit base, and hence lending ability, will be eroded. Thus, the local banks are racing against time to improve.

To take reform further, China must take bold steps to allow takeovers, mergers and acquisitions and even tolerate bank failures. Beijing must also make the AMCs work effectively. Transferring SOE bad debts to the AMCs and recapitalizing the banks are the easy part of reform. The hard part is for the AMCs to sell these bad assets to debt-workout specialists to recoup their costs. This can only be done by thorough financial and institutional reforms to eliminate the incentive problems between the SOEs and the AMCs and create a liquid market for these special assets.

Eventually, the government must cede control of the banking system and allow full private ownership. In this sense, strategic foreign investors are brought in as a catalyst for this ownership transfer process. But ceding control does not mean the government has no role. It should develop an effective regulatory framework for supervising the system. Strong banks, sound regulations and minimal government distortion are the necessary and sufficient conditions for China to liberalize its financial markets fully without worrying about the stability of the state banks.

It will take some years for Chinese banks to shed the communist legacy and establish a true commercial culture. To achieve this needs a mindset change, from the old socialist mentality to a liberalized and professional attitude. This change will quicken when the older management retires (normally at 60 years old). This will mean another five to seven years away. In other words, the completion of China's banking reform will likely take longer than most observers have expected.

Since Chinese banks will not be able to handle volatile international, especially short-term, capital flows before they are fully reformed, there will be no full capital account, and hence no full RMB, convertibility until the bank restructuring process is completed. What all this means is that the business scope will remain limited in China's banking sector, despite its opening up to full foreign competition under the WTO requirements.

The 'WTO threat' to Chinese banks

Many investors are excited about the full opening up of China's banking market (effective since 11 December 2006) under WTO requirements, when foreign banks will be, in principle, allowed to provide all domestic and foreign currency services throughout China. Others argue that the flood of foreign competition would overwhelm the Chinese banks, which are not strong enough to take on the new competitors. This is a logical but not quite correct story. Indeed, the 'WTO threat' to the Chinese banks is more or less an illusion.

The reason is simple. Formidable invisible entry barriers outside the WTO's jurisdiction still exist. There is also extremely high cost in replicating the Chinese banks' franchise. All these will shield the Chinese banking system from the onslaught of the expected fierce foreign competition. However, that also means that China's banking market would be much less exciting for foreign players in the medium term than many have expected.

On the surface, China has not only been tracking its regional opening commitments required by WTO rules, but it has also exceeded them in some cases, for example, by authorizing foreign banks' access to some regions prior to the scheduled dates. However, high capitalization requirements for foreign banks' operations have acted as a major offset to geographic opening. The situation has not changed much even after the full opening of the banking market, as capitalization rules are not a visible barrier that free-trade rules can tackle.

In general, China's capitalization requirements work on a tier basis. Each tier requires a minimum amount of registered capital that allows a certain business scope and access to customers. A higher tier needs a larger capitalization amount for broader business scope and customer access. But the high capitalization requirements have often made it almost commercially unviable for many, especially smaller, foreign banks to operate and expand their business.

For example, a foreign bank must have a minimum registered capital of RMB400 million (almost US$50 million) to undertake basic RMB busness; and a branch would need a minimum registered capital of RMB200 million.[6] The scaled capitalization rules and the way they relate to customer type effectively restrict foreign banks to doing local currency business only with foreign invested enterprises (FIEs) and foreign individuals that are located in China. This is because at the higher end of capitalization where the customer type expands to include domestic residents, it becomes so expensive that it is difficult to justify returns.

A major problem lies in RMB funding. The FIEs and foreign individuals are just a small group in China with limited RMB deposits; they do not provide sufficient local currency deposits for the foreign banks to expand to include local resident business. Hence, foreign banks are forced to use the interbank market for RMB funding. But the local banks dominate the interbank market and act together as a cartel to squeeze foreign bank borrowers by offering high interbank lending rates. Obviously, this puts the foreign banks at a significant disadvantage *vis-à-vis* the local banks, which are funded by low-cost RMB deposits.

Indeed, the funding cost from the interbank market averaged 3.2 percentage points dearer than the RMB deposits between 1996 and 2006, though the spread has come down to an average of 1.4 percentage points since 2001 (Figure 2.11). Meanwhile, both the foreign and local banks face the same regulated RMB lending rate, which is set by the PBoC. With higher funding cost, foreign banks' margins are much thinner than the local banks. WTO rules are ineffective in addressing this distortion stemming from interest rate control and the Chinese banks' cartel behaviour.

There is a further restriction on interbank borrowing. No bank may borrow more than 40 per cent of its total RMB liabilities from the interbank market. Apparently, the foreign banks are at a big disadvantage because of their small RMB liabilities, the bulk of which come from RMB deposits. By restricting the source of funding, this 40 per cent rule severely restricts the foreign banks' capacity to expand into the local currency business.

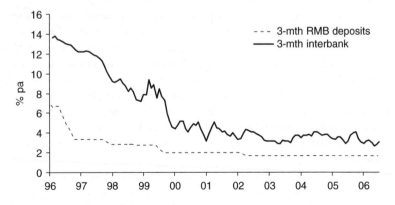

Figure 2.11 Funding costs*
* 3 month moving averages
Source: CEIC

There was also the one-branch-per-year rule[7] that effectively inhibits foreign banks' ability to expand their customer base and compete with domestic banks. While this rule has been scrapped since 11 December 2006, the licensing requirements and procedures have kept the prohibitive effects of the one-branch rule on foreign bank expansion. For example, WTO rules would not be able to get past the local delays of a foreign bank's application for additional branch/subsidiary licences if the local official in charge were just to sit on the application.

The licensing requirement is outside the WTO free-trade jurisdiction. It is a significant barrier to foreign expansion as only foreign bank subsidiaries, called foreign-funded banks and locally incorporated, are allowed to offer full retail services in China. Foreign bank branches, which are not locally incorporated, are not granted licences to do RMB retail banking. Before being eligible to apply for a full retail licence, a foreign bank must have a track-record of three years of operations and two consecutive years of profits. It is also prohibitively costly to set up a subsidiary, which requires registered capital of RMB1 billion and operating capital of RMB100 million. A branch only needs RMB200 million in registered capital and another RMB100 million in operating capital.

Due to their inability to build RMB deposits and the risk that foreign funds injected into China by foreign head offices might not be easily repatriated under China's capital controls, foreign banks also rely on the interbank market to get RMB funds to satisfy the capital adequacy rules. These rules require them to have a considerable amount of RMB on hand at all times and to have at least 30 per cent of RMB working capital deposited with up to three Chinese banks for six months.

Legislation states that the foreign and local banks would jointly determine the interest rates for these deposits at the beginning of the term. But in practice, Beijing sets the rates and discloses them only when the deposits mature.[8] In any case, the authorities set the interest rates quite low, often sharply lower than the London Interbank Offered Rate (LIBOR), according to foreign bankers in China. This effectively renders the deposits idle money with little interest income. Combined with higher interbank funding cost and the need to pay interest on customers' RMB deposits, the capital adequacy rules add further cost to foreign banks in China.

Last but not least, foreign banks will not find it easier to penetrate China's banking market even after the WTO-required 'full opening' of the Chinese market. This is because competition is already very keen among the local banks, which have tens of thousand of branches across the country. Some analysts even argue that China's market is over-banked. Chinese households' trillions of dollars of deposits are held almost exclusively in the state banks, which have vast branch networks acting as a formidable barrier to entry. It will be extremely costly, if not implausible, for foreign banks to replicate such an extensive branch network in China.

Thus, foreign banks, which still need local approval to open each individual branch and subsidiary, are unlikely to make any large-scale progress in expanding into China's national market. Even in the major cities where foreign banks are already making inroads into trade and financing services, the potentials for them to expand further within the same localities are limited in the medium term due to over-banking. The foreign banks have not only the Big Four and the joint-stock commercial banks to compete with, but they also face aggressive competition from the city-level banks, credit cooperatives and unions, which are also competing with each other and with the local commercial banks.

Foreign banks will continue to face many invisible obstacles for quite some time, despite a 'full opening' of the Chinese banking market. Arguably, while China is following WTO requirements to relax restrictions, it is also working around the rules to impose conditions that make engaging in the newly 'unrestricted' business difficult. Some market players have even dubbed China 'one country two banking systems'.

Under such circumstances, the best way to make use of the WTO opening requirements is not to open new branches, but to buy into existing local banks. This is in fact what most of the foreign banks have been doing. Even this strategy will not put much pressure on the state commercial banks, as the local banking market is already under severe competitive pressure. The state banks will be facing mostly the same players pre- and post WTO-full opening. Perhaps these players are better funded and with foreign partners, but they will not make any sudden big change in the market structure.

Implications of the curb market

Financial suppression in China has given rise to the development of informal lending, or the 'curb market' or the 'shadow banking system' or 'underground finance', as it is sometimes called. The curb market is a concern to both policymakers and investors as its unregulated activity has the potential to threaten to reduce the effectiveness of monetary policy. Some pessimists even argue that uncontrolled underground finance would eventually pull down the formal financial system and the Chinese economy. Informal lending is just another signal of doom for China's future, according to this view.

While the concern is valid, the fear of the curb market wreaking havoc on the formal system is exaggerated. On the contrary, the curb market is making positive contributions to the economy where the formal banking market fails. These include pricing credit by market forces, reducing moral hazard in lending and financing the development of the private sector.

Arguably, the 'miracle' of China's private sector development owes much to the existence of the curb market.[9] Its contributions suggest that the health and competitiveness of China's financial system, and hence the nation's economic outlook, could benefit from setting up new private banks, using the experience of informal lending as an experiment in progress. Given that the curb market remains fragmented, there is no *a priori* reason to believe that the curb market would risk China's economic future.

There is no doubt that the curb market is a form of financial disintermediation resulting from financial repression. It arises when households and companies lend directly to each other, bypassing the banking system. In some cases, such informal lending takes the form of money borrowed from relatives or friends. In other cases, lending is conducted through established informal institutions such as investment pool clubs.[10]

The concern about curb market activity intensified between 2003 and 2004, when industrial output grew robustly despite falling bank credit growth (Figure 2.12). The trend was the same for fixed-asset investment

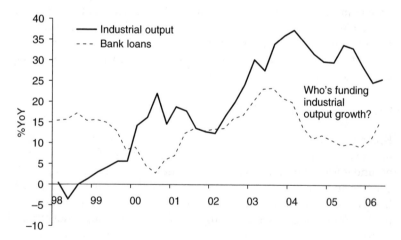

Figure 2.12 Curb market growing?
Source: CEIC

growth. If the banks were not supplying the funds, who were? Underground finance became the natural suspect. Financial market players estimate that the size of China's curb market ranged between 5 per cent and 20 per cent of total official bank loans. Anecdotal evidence also showed that interest rates in the curb market rose sharply between 2003 and 2004. This suggested that firms that were cut off from official lending channels during Beijing's macro-tightening at that period were bidding funds aggressively in the informal market.

Policymakers are thus worried that growing informal lending would reduce monetary policy effectiveness, and that the unregulated curb market could inflict systemic instability in the formal banking system. In the late 1980s and early 1990s when informal lending was active, there were several high-profile cases of intentional deceit and unintentional default that led to social instability and political tension in some localities. Further, the informal capital market competes with the formal banking system for deposits so that its uncontrolled development could cause liquidity problems for the banks.

Stories about the curb market are mainly anecdotes because there are no data for informal lending. They all start with one tenet, and that is the drainage of deposits out of the formal banking system. To fund informal lending, there must be some depositors actively moving money out of time deposits into liquid accounts within the formal banking system so that they can eventually transfer the money out to the curb market. If this transfer of funds is significant, and discounting for the amount of funds needed for consumption demand growth, by inference curb market activity must be significant.

In macro-terms, this fund transfer should be seen in the divergence between the growth of narrow money supply M1 (which includes cash and demand deposits) and illiquid term deposits (let us call this ITD, which is approximated by deducting M1 from broad money supply M2) in the banking system. In particular, we should see ITD growth slowing (as money moves out) on the back rising M1 growth (as money moves into the liquid current accounts) over time as a proxy for curb market activity growing. But Chinese monetary data show no persistent drainage of deposits from the formal banking system, in particular in 2003 and 2004 when the worry about curb market activity was at its most intensive (Figure 2.13). In the past ten years, M1 growth has surpassed ITD growth only once, in 2000/01. It either grew in tandem with or was slower than ITD.

Viewing the curb market from another angle, consider the following informal lending process. Entrepreneur Xiao Huang wants to play the

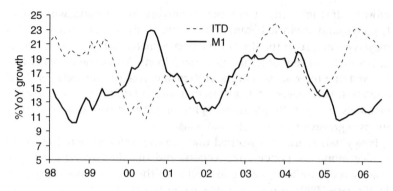

Figure 2.13   No persistent drainage of deposits
Source: CEIC

curb market to get higher returns. So he solicits deposits from friends, employees, relatives and neighbours, who give Xiao Huang their funds from the bank. Firms in need of capital borrow from Xiao Huang, who lends at much higher interest rates than the banks. He then shares the return with his fund contributors. After getting the funds, the firms deposit them back in the banks for making payments later. The net result is thus a fall in household deposits with an offsetting rise in corporate deposit accounts in the banking system.

In other words, any significant curb market activity should be reflected by a significant shift in bank deposit composition from households to corporates. But this has not been the case. While the share of household deposits in the banking system has fallen by 9 percentage points, from 58 per cent to 49 per cent over the past ten years, this can be easily explained by rising consumption growth (which absorbs liquid funds to support spending) under economic reform. Meanwhile, the share of corporate deposits has remained quite stable at 33 per cent through the years (Figure 2.14).

Without significant shift of funds from term deposits to cash and current accounts and without a big shift in deposit composition in the banking system, these macro-indicators suggest that curb market activity has not been significant. Then what was funding the robust industrial output and investment growth between 2003 and 2004 (see Figure 2.12 again) when bank credit growth was falling? Outside the property sector, a lot of that output growth was funded out of corporate retained earnings, which have become a major source of funds in recent years. The property sector got the lion's share of the bank loans during the 2001–03

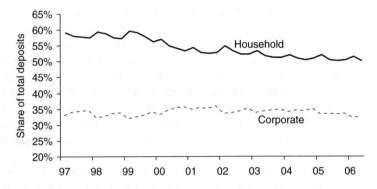

Figure 2.14 No big change in deposit composition
Source: CEIC

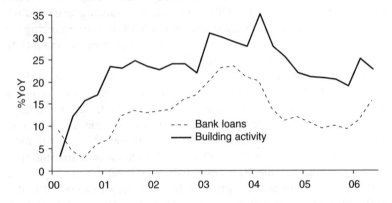

Figure 2.15 Bank credit squeezes construction
Source: CEIC

credit boom. When the credit cycle turned down in 2003 and 2004, the bulk of the negative impact was focused on the property and construction areas too (Figure 2.15). If the curb market was significant, it should have prevented the fall in building activity.

In a nutshell, the curb market remains fragmented. While it reflects the flaws of China's financial system and exposes the ineffectiveness of demand management policy, it is not the culprit for the authorities' failure in economic management. Beijing and many China observers have probably underestimated the positive effects of informal lending, which have crucial implications for China's future growth.

One positive impact is that relatively high interest rates in the curb market should help cool excessive investment growth, which has become a major headache for Beijing in recent years. An important reason for excessive investment is that capital from the formal banking system is too cheap (6.12 per cent at the time of writing versus over 15 per cent in the curb market). Though informal lending also helps some borrowers bypass the government's credit controls, such investment is different in nature from investment by the state firms funded by the formal banking system. Arguably, only those with good return potentials would go to borrow from the curb market at higher rates.

From a bank reform perspective, the curb market experience argues that developing private banks is probably as crucial as opening up to the foreign banks and restructuring the state commercial banks. At the margin, informal lending has made some significant achievement that the formal banking system has failed to do, namely setting interest rates according to market forces. This is needed for inducing market discipline to reduce the moral hazard problem in lending, and financing the development of the private sector, which owes much of its existence to the availability of informal lending.[11]

Thus, facilitating healthy development of private lending institutions, either by bringing the curb market under proper regulations or establishing private banks, would be a crucial direction for financial reform to take before complete withdrawal of government controls. Local governments have different policies towards the curb market. Some are more tolerant of its existence so that some localities have more institutionalized curb markets, while others only have piecemeal set-ups.

This difference in attitude towards the curb market can be attributed to the local government's different experience with private businesses, which is part of a structural legacy from the Mao era.[12] Those localities with more widespread and organized curb markets reflect political bargains struck between the regulators and entrepreneurs at the local level. This means that despite policies being handed down from the central authorities, local officials tend to interpret them in various ways to serve their own local interests. This local rent-seeking behaviour is just an example of the 'shang you zheng ce, xia you dui ce'[13] problem that is affecting China's reform programme. But in the case of informal lending this problem has turned out to be a blessing in disguise for the development of the private sector.

Even if formal bank lending becomes more accessible to private companies as banking reform moves ahead, the segmentation of the local credit market (where financing needs and credit profiles vary significantly between different types of borrowers) means that informal lending will continue to thrive for some time. Take Hong Kong as an example: investment pool clubs, or *hui*, were still a common funding avenue for family capital and private/small investment needs till the early 1980s. In China, the vast differences between local cultures, economic traits, financing needs and credit profiles mean that the local curb markets will have large local variations instead of national homogeneity. This underscores the common fallacy of analysing China as a single development category, which just masks the different realities at ground level.

The fate of the banking system

Financial institutions have always had a special place in a socialist economy. Lenin once described a state bank as the biggest of the big, with branches in every rural district and every factory and the most important element of the social apparatus. In China, as in any other communist regime, years after discussions began in the 1990s about privatizing the state firms, the banking system remained off limits.

However, things have begun to change, rather rapidly since 2003 when Wen Jia-bao took over as the premier. All of a sudden, three of the Big Four (except the Agriculture Bank of China) began openly making plans for domestic and overseas listings, with all three eventually listed in 2005 and 2006. Before listing, these banks had sold stakes, up to 10 per cent of total asset, to foreign strategic investors.

The government has plans to raise the foreign ownership limit to as high as 40 per cent in the coming years. Some market players are betting that a third of the total asset in China's major financial institutions could be in private hands within a few years. This would mean a significant step forward in bank restructuring. Not only would this entail new management structures, it would also mean annual audits according to international norm and by international firms, shareholder meetings and professional investor supervision. More importantly, it would mean a serious clean-up of bank balance sheets before selling shares.

Only after banks' structural flaws are fixed will full interest rate liberalization and competition be made possible. Until recently, the authorities have no incentive to remove controls on interest rates and open up the banking sector because the state banks, given their poor financial health, would falter under competition from other financial institutions. But since 2005, the government has started to liberalize interest rates, albeit partially. Liberalization will speed up as the bank cleaned-up process continues to move forward.

Meanwhile, moving bad debts off the state bank balance sheets will help resolve the state firms' debt problems. This, in turn, would help speed up privatization of the state sector. Writing down debts will enhance the state firms' value. One of the effective ways to improve state firms' financial position is using debt-equity swap. This kills two birds with one stone – cutting the firm's debt and privatizing it simultaneously. In fact, the government has tried using these swaps via the AMCs, but without much success. That is partly because of incentive problems with the banks, the state companies and the AMCs (see Chapter 1, p. 27)and partly because equity claims stayed with the AMCs and could not be sold into the open market. However, as the government disposes of state assets, albeit slowly, into private hands and as direct and indirect equity markets continue to develop, radical changes in corporate ownership and liquidity could emerge in the coming decades.

China is evolving with strong economic dynamism. As the authorities fix the banking woes, resolutions to the key problems that are troubling China today, such as capital misallocation, financial repression, corporate inefficiency, excessive investment and the lack of progress in privatization, could well emerge. Granted, such changes will not happen quickly and noticeably. But as reform momentum continues to break the communist apparatus, China will be moving towards an increasingly market-oriented economy with better health and a bigger contribution to the global economy.

3
Creative Destruction of the State

Economic reforms in the past 25 years have moved China a long way away from a planned economy, where the Communist Party (or the state) owns and controls everything from assets to business and daily life activities, to a more market-oriented system. Nevertheless, the state still owns and runs a big part of the economic system, in particular in heavy and high-tech industries and services. China's hybrid system of planned-market economy has created confusion about the role of the state sector. At times, even the local government officials do not know where the line between state and non-state assets lie. This confusion has even made it difficult for privatizing the state companies, as the lack of clear definitions for many state assets makes the officials hesitate to move.

The key question is how will the role of the state evolve in the future? Is it still distorting commercial incentives and decisions? On one hand, critics argue that the Communist Party had remained an oppressive force eroding China's future. They cite evidence that many state-owned companies (SOEs) are still a chronically loss-making burden on the economy, suffering from severe political meddling, bureaucratic problems and badly distorted incentives. On the other hand, there is also evidence that the state has supported structural changes and pushed creative destruction to replace the old inefficient SOEs and sunset industries by efficient private sector firms and sunrise industries.

As far as future development is concerned, if we look at the political and economic changes at the margin, they point to rising positive momentum and suggest that China is moving towards a better future. Crucially, the Chinese authorities have been decisive towards making market-based changes and breaking the communist policy icons, such as state owner-ship, population control and financial repression. These changes will enable the Chinese factories to dominate global manufacturing and move up the value-added ladder in the coming decades.

The confusing role of the state sector

One of the difficulties in understanding China and its economic outlook is the confusion about the role of the state in the economy; in particular the emergence of private sector incentives on the back of state sector distortions.[1] Other than being the normal government organ, with civil administrative, military, law and order, education, medical and cultural functions, China's state sector also gets involved in commercial functions. The latter is carried out by the state-owned commercial entities, whose activities cover the primary, secondary and tertiary economic sectors. This commercial aspect not only distorts economic incentives. It also creates a big confusion about the role of the state. Many of the SOEs have undergone big structural changes and have basically turned into private firms, but officially they are still classified as state firms.

The system was quite straightforward before the economic reforms. The state basically controlled all economic activities and assets in the economy. The SOEs operated the industries and services under central planning, which gave them output quotas and project assignments. No commercial thinking was involved in the production units. Banks were nothing more than the government's funding arm for its industrial policy. Their personnel were government-appointed bureaucrats, who had no sense of financial and business management. This set-up created the mindset that, to a certain extent, is still plaguing the system today, that bank loans were public funds and hence did not have to be repaid. The agriculture sector was made up of communes, producing under public quotas.

Scattered over the economy were small-scale state-owned business called 'township and village enterprises' (TVEs). They operated outside the cities and urban collectives, and were never part of the central plan. For all industries, the government appointed all managerial staff, with the lower-level personnel elected by the collectives. But because of the TVEs' lack of status in the central plan, they formed the stepping stone for the development of 'private' (or non-state) businesses later.

The planned economy has changed drastically since economic reform began in 1978. The agriculture sector has been fully privatized. All agricultural communes were broken up, with individual plots of land allocated to households (although the good intention of breaking up public landownership has not quite worked out as planned and more decisive action on land reform must be taken; see Chapter 1, pp. 36–7). The smaller-scale TVEs and collectives were gradually released from state control under economic liberalization. These TVEs have become *de facto* private firms surviving and struggling without state assistance and bank loans. But they also do not suffer from much state intervention.

Development of the private companies has sped up since the mid 1990s as economic liberalization accelerated. Without a legal framework for private enterprises, most start-ups in fact went under the guise of TVEs in the mid 1990s. The private sector, although still small, is especially well developed in the coastal provinces and cities where foreign investments have flooded in. In 2003, the latest statistics available at the time of writing, non-state companies[2] accounted for over half of all industrial enterprises in China, up from a third in the late 1990s (Figure 3.1). Nowadays, foreign companies are allowed to set up wholly owned subsidiaries without Chinese partners in most economic sectors.

By allowing the TVEs and collectives to drift away from state control and become private firms, and allowing foreign firms to set up shops in China without having a Chinese joint-venture partner, Beijing has opened up the economy and brought in market discipline to counteract incentive distortions from the state sector. This process is still pretty much work in progress. Many SOEs, big and small, have undergone big ownership changes in recent years. This structural change has blurred the line between state and non-state ownership. While many state firms were shut down after the 1997–98 Asian crisis, some others have been privatized – indirectly via management buyouts. But these privatized entities still remain officially on the books as state companies.

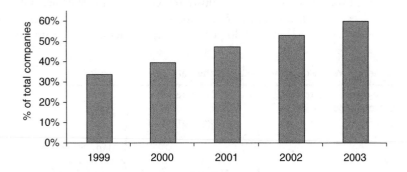

Figure 3.1 Share of non-state companies* in the economy

* Including private and foreign funded firms, joint stock companies and cooperatives
Source: CEIC

A mixture of state and private ownership has become a common phenomenon in recent years. For example, many foreign joint-ventures in the late 1990s and early 2000s were created through partnership with the SOEs. State firms have also been actively seeking investment and capital injection from private domestic investors to form joint-stock and limited liability companies. Most of the listed Chinese firms on domestic or foreign exchanges are in fact SOEs. So instead of having a full-fledged private sector, China has developed a non-state sector alongside a state sector (Table 3.1). This non-state sector includes private and mixed-ownership firms, with state ownership often accounting for over 50 per cent of the latter.

This confusion about asset ownership has made it difficult to see the role, and hence economic impact, of the state clearly. There are many small and medium-sized SOEs being privatized but still classified as SOEs officially. There are also SOEs that have sold parts of their equity to external investors through listing on the stock exchanges or as joint-ventures, but state influence in the companies remains large. Meanwhile, tens of millions of state-sector jobs have been shed in recent years, while many millions of non-state sector jobs have been created. So, on a net basis, who is feeding the workers? How big is the state, how much impact has it on the economy and how long will its influence last?

When we look at the available data for the state and non-state sectors, there is more confusion. In terms of GDP, the state accounts for less than 40 per cent of the economy (Figure 3.2). Within this 40 per cent or so state ownership, the SOEs (including both 100 per cent state-owned and state-controlled companies) account for about 30 per cent, while government administrative units make up the rest. Overall, the state is not in agriculture at all. In terms of industrial breakdown, the state accounts for 17 per cent of the output from labour-intensive industries such as trade and construction, and 30 per cent of manufacturing. That means

Table 3.1   Where does the line lie for the state?

State-owned enterprises (SOEs) $\longrightarrow$ 100% state		
Listed companies $\left.\vphantom{\begin{array}{c}a\\b\\c\end{array}}\right\}$		
Joint-stock companies	Mixed ownership $\left.\vphantom{\begin{array}{c}a\\b\end{array}}\right\}$	
Joint ventures		Many of these are still officially recorded as state firms on the books
Urban collectives $\left.\vphantom{\begin{array}{c}a\\b\\c\\d\end{array}}\right\}$		
TVEs	Non-state,	
Private companies	some 100% private	
Agriculture		

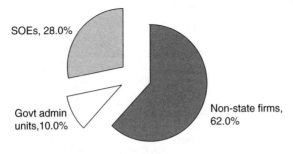

Figure 3.2 Output distribution*
* 2003, the latest data available at the time of writing
Source: CEIC

the state produces over half of the output from the heavy, high-tech and services industries, including government services.

However, the picture for the size of the state is different in terms of employment and asset-ownership. The share of SOE employment in total employment in the economy has dropped sharply and steadily since the 1990s (Figure 3.3), reflecting significant downsizing of the state sector under economic restructuring. The government administrative units now account for only 6 per cent of the total employment, while the SOEs account for 8.6 per cent. This suggests that the flourishing non-state sector has created the bulk of the new jobs and has taken up much, if not all, of the surplus labour in the creative destruction process (Figure 3.4). Meanwhile, the state share in fixed assets has remained significant at almost 60 per cent of all assets in the economy (Figure 3.5).

Things do not seem to add up here. The state share of employment, including government administrative units and SOEs, is less than 15 per cent of total jobs in the economy. But its share of output is almost 40 per cent of GDP. Meanwhile, the government owns 53 per cent of the total asset in the economy. The data is all over the place and does not give a consistent picture for the size and impact of the state in the economy.

In fact, this is not as puzzling as it seems. The government has focused on capital-intensive production under its economic liberalization programme. Thus, it has retained control of many big industrial, high-tech and services firms and its fixed-asset investment share in the economy has remained large. Meanwhile, it has withdrawn from the labour-intensive industries such as manufacturing and left the development of these industries in the hands of the private sector. Hence, the state share of employment has fallen.

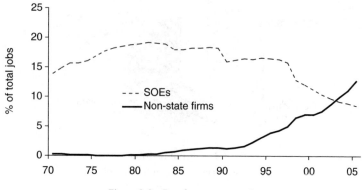

Figure 3.3 Employment trends
Source: CEIC

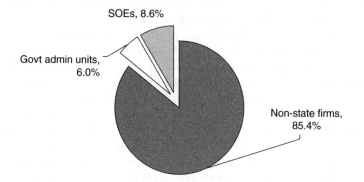

Figure 3.4 Employment shares*
* 2005, the latest data available at the time of writing
Source: CEIC

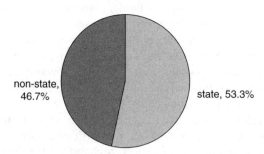

Figure 3.5 Share of fixed assets
* 2005, the latest data available at the time of writing
Source: CEIC

So which is the most significant factor for gauging the size of the state sector: output, employment or investment share? In fact, each of these measures reflects a different aspect of state ownership and so represents a different way of assessing the role of the state in the economy. But from a theoretical perspective the value-added aspect is the most relevant for examining the state's impact on the economy. Hence, the GDP share, as depicted in Figure 3.2, is perhaps the most useful factor for assessing the role of the state.

The shrinking role of central planning

This means that the non-state sector is now larger than the state sector and hence should have a bigger impact on economic activity. More importantly, the steady decline of the state sector, in terms of its absolute size, output and employment shares in the economy (Figures 3.6 and 3.7), reflects Beijing's resolve to pursue creative destruction to make way for the rise of the non-state sector and private firms.

The state sector has shrunk especially fast in recent years. In 1998, the 91,000 or so SOEs accounted for 55 per cent of all industrial enterprises in China. But by 2005, the number had fallen by half to 47,000, with their share falling to just 17 per cent of the total. A similar declining trend is seen in the output and employment shares of the state in the economy. The state's share in total industrial output fell from over 80 per cent in the early 1980s to about half in the 1990s and to less than 40 per cent by 2005; its employment share has fallen from over 20 per cent in

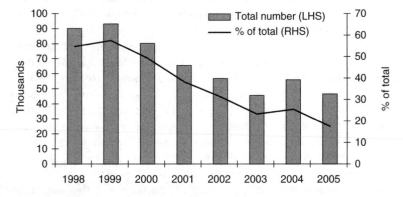

Figure 3.6　SOEs and state-controlled firms
Source: CEIC

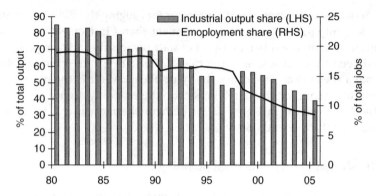

Figure 3.7   State output and employment shares
Source: CEIC

the 1980s to less than 10 per cent now. In effect, the size of the state sector has been cut in half since the late 1990s.

The decline of the state sector was a result of serious economic restructuring under former premier Zhu Rong-ji in the mid 1990s. Many SOEs were closed down or sold off to domestic investors, especially in the coastal provinces, to boost 'private' sector growth. Nevertheless, many of these privatized state firms are still classified as SOEs in the official data. Why?

The downsizing of the state sector had resulted in tens of thousands of SOE closures and millions of job losses. But in the absence of any formal bankruptcy laws, the SOEs were not officially closed down and workers continued to get subsistence wages from local governments. Hence, the true jobless, if these quasi-unemployed were counted, would have been much higher than the official 30 million job losses due to the industrial restructuring. Industrial plants and equipment were either discarded or sold or given to existing or new enterprises.

The point is that the downsizing of the state sector and the industrial restructuring have been real and significant. But still the government controls the most important and largest economics sectors, such as banking and finance, telecoms and utilities, and has controlling stakes in large manufacturing firms. In fact, it still wants to create the Fortune 500 equivalent of Chinese firms. So, is Beijing still actively interfering in resources allocation and investment decisions, which some argue is detrimental to future growth? How much offsetting impact does the market have on this state distortion and China's growth outlook?

To understand the relative impact of the state and the market on China's economic future, we have to distinguish between the micro- and macro-economic aspects. While progress on industrial restructuring and economic reform has been slow at the micro-economic level, the progress on the macro-front has been significant. Although most SOEs are still operating under the old mindset and bureaucratic environment with distorted incentives, the planners at the top level in Beijing have all but disappeared. In fact, central government bureaucrats do not do much planning these days. Instead, some are involved in economic forecasting, while others have become regulators and managers of the economic process rather than setting production targets and quotas.

Yes, China still sets five-year plans, but the process is more like a brain-storming session for setting broad policy objectives and development directions. These changes are even reflected in the bureau names. For example, the former State Planning Commission is now called the State Development and Reform Commission (SDRC). Former industrial ministries have been disbanded, changed into regulatory agencies incorporated in the new Ministry of Commerce.

The Chinese system today has changed drastically from the old communist days. Before reform in 1978, the 'economic plan' dictated all activities and resources allocation from the national level down to the local village level. Output volumes, employment, investment decisions and daily life activities were all set out by the central planners.

The TVEs and collectives were, in the planners' eyes, unimportant elements. So, they were not a formal part of the budgetary system and got no government funding. But they face the same constraints as the private firms, including no bank loans for operations and development. They also face the same output quotas and price controls as all other SOEs.

After over 20 years of reform, however, the TVEs and collectives have been freed from central control and have become *de facto* private firms. Bank lending to nonstate businesses has been rising to facilitate the development of the non-state sector (Figure 3.8), though it still amounts to a small share in total lending for the time being.

Beijing started shutting down or privatizing the SOEs in the mid 1990s. The move was an admission of the fact that most state firms were chronically unprofitable with distorted incentives. The remaining SOEs are free from day-to-day control by the planners. To a large extent, they can make their own production and business decisions. Firms are now responsible for their losses, but in return they can also keep their profits. In other words, the SOEs have mostly dropped out of the government's budget. If this liberalizing trend continues, they will become a lesser burden to the public in the future.

The government's control on investment and its planning role have been drastically liberalized. As the SOEs are restructured and sold off, they have been taken off the state budget. Given Beijing's practical

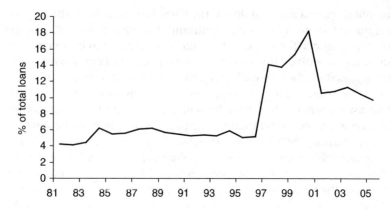

Figure 3.8   Non-SOE loans*
* National banking system data
Source: CEIC

initiative for change, it will likely relinquish more control in the coming years. On the surface, all investment projects over a certain budget still have to be approved by the relevant national and provincial planning officials. And banks cannot lend to any projects without state approval.

In reality, except for strategic and heavy industries, such as telecoms, steel and infrastructure, which are strictly bound by annual investment plans and budget approvals, the approval process for most investment projects is more like a watchdog. The bureaucrats merely want to ensure that investment criteria and fund requirements are met and that the projects are in line with broader national objectives. For the future, the authorities are planning to scrap official approvals for investment in most sectors. They will only control large strategic SOEs and priority sectors as defined by the SDRC.

The government is also dismantling some of the classical communist planning icons, notably government subsidies and price controls. Commercial subsidies have been cut drastically over the years. SOEs are now given profitability guidelines and are asked to cut costs and losses. As part of the price liberalization programme, the SOEs are given autonomy to adjust prices to achieve these goals. The government has also begun to take away the SOEs' social welfare burden, such as schooling, hospitals, housing, pensions and other administrative liabilities, that have been funded out of the SOEs' revenues.

As a result, direct state subsidies to the loss-making SOEs have fallen sharply from almost 10 per cent of GDP before economic reform to less

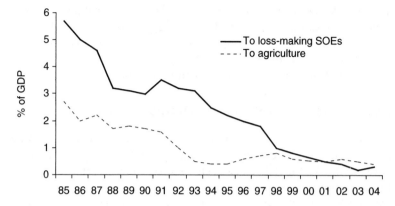

Figure 3.9   State subsidies as a share of GDP
Source: CEIC

than 0.5 per cent now. Farm subsidies have also been cut sharply to a similar extent (Figure 3.9). It is true that many SOE subsidies have just been moved from the state budget to the banks, which take on the saviour role by extending cheap loans to the loss-making SOEs who would not be able to repay them.

But this is a problem of the past. Very little of the indirect subsidies from the banks have gone to finance new losses from the SOEs. Banking reform, when properly implemented, should eventually take care of this problem. Overall, the creative destruction of the state sector and the removal of social welfare liabilities from the SOEs have raised state firms' profitability (see below for more discussions).

The destruction of price controls is more impressive. In the pre-reform period, the state set nearly all prices in the economy, from the farm- and factory gates to wholesale to retail levels. But today, the state controls only about 10 per cent of all prices in the economy.[3] These include energy, utilities, some staple foods and some services such as health care, transport and telecom. Virtually all industrial and manufacturing prices and most commercial services prices have been liberalized.

Overall, there has been a sharp decline in the role of the state in the macro-economy. Many of the classical communist controls on economic activity have been scrapped. However, at the micro-economic level, the state's *de facto* influence is still dominant, even in the most liberalized sectors, such as textile, brewery, white goods and retail (see the last section below). In fact, the state still holds significant shares in the joint-stock and listed companies, and has control on many urban collectives and TVEs. Moreover, the communist mindset of power, public ownership, government subsidies and the like still remain deep-rooted in many parts of the system, even though their physical presence may have been eroded. These old forces will continue to clash with the progressive forces in fighting to shape China's economic future.

Chinese corporate profit and competition puzzles

All these changes suggest that the state sector has ceased to be a big problem for China's economy. Barring any major policy mistakes and negative shocks, the state is not likely to be an oppressive drag on China's future growth, as some have argued. The large state-owned 'black holes' that siphon off ever-increasing amounts of fiscal resources are disappearing, thanks to the creative destruction of the state sector and reform within the bureaucratic system.

High levels of bad debt and social liability are certainly issues China has to deal with, but they are historical problems rather than new ones. The structural changes in the economy have delivered results: the vast majority of the SOEs have become profitable on a flow basis, meaning that overall new business conducted by the SOEs is profitable. Nevertheless, there is still confusion in assessing China's overall profitability.

On one hand, macro-proxy for Chinese profit still shows a margin squeeze and some see collapsing profit as a symptom of Chinese economic woes and futile reform efforts, with a disaster waiting to happen. On the other hand, corporate data show a steady margin recovery. So which one is true – a disaster that will sink the economy or a profit recovery indicative of a positive future?

In a macro-sense, the wedge between consumer price index (CPI) and producer price index (PPI) can be taken as a proxy for aggregate profit in an economy – with the former being a proxy for aggregate sale price and the latter being aggregate cost. From this perspective, Chinese profit has been falling for some time (Figure 3.10). Critics argue that falling profit was an indication of reform failure, with economic growth being propped up by public investment and exports.

There are two problems with this assessment. First, there is strong evidence of creative destruction driving structural improvement in the Chinese economy. Not only has the number of private companies thrived at the expense of the SOEs, but the private sector has become an employment engine in recent years (Figures 3.11 and 3.12). This shows that economic fundamentals underpinning the profit picture are much

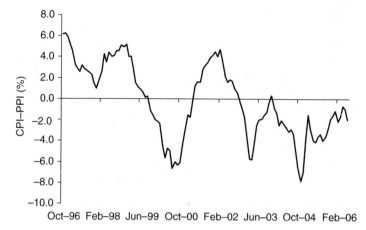

Figure 3.10 Chinese profit squeeze?
Source: CEIC

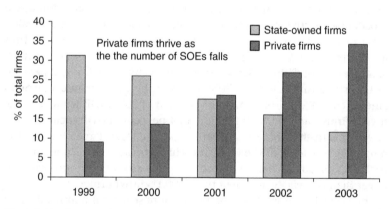

Figure 3.11 Creative destruction
Source: CEIC

sounder today than before. Second, in a technical sense, the macro-profit proxy may not be appropriate for China. The proxy works best when there are few price and cost distortions. But despite the decline in state intervention in prices and costs over the years, incentive problems still persist in China and they distort both price and cost trends.

However, looking at the industry data, even official data show that almost one third of the SOEs were still losing money, as 11,112 Chinese SOEs out of a total of 34,280 reported losses at the end of 2004. Doesn't

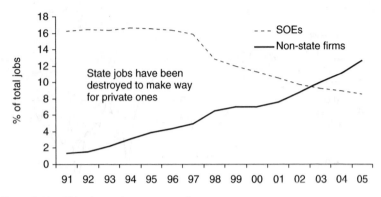

Figure 3.12   China's employment trends
Source: CEIC

this argue that China's structural reform and creative destruction have been illusive? Not really. One should not see the Chinese data in isolation. To get a better assessment, one should put China's situation into a broader perspective, for example by comparing it with other economies.

Let us compare the Chinese loss data with that of the 6,213 US firms listed on the New York Stock Exchange and NASDAQ. At the end of 2004, 32.4 per cent of Chinese SOEs lost money, compared with 36.2 per cent of US listed firms in the red. Total losses of the Chinese industrial SOEs amounted to RMB67 billion, or 0.5 per cent of 2004 GDP, while losses of the US firms totalled US$114 billion, or 1 per cent of GDP. Including services firms in the Chinese data will make the losses larger, but not too much larger relative to the US losses. This is because the Chinese industrial SOEs already account for more of the state sector economy, which is larger than the aggregate size of the 6,000 US listed firms.

The point is that while China needs more structural reforms to right the system, the loss data *per se* tell us nothing about the structural progress. The fact that almost one third of the SOEs still lose money is not an indication of reform failure. They do not look unusual by comparison, as an efficient economy like the US also has over one third of its firms making losses.

Meanwhile, corporate data from the Chinese National Bureau of Statistics (NBS), which includes all SOEs and non-state firms with annual sales revenue over RMB5 million, show that Chinese total profits have been recovering, albeit slowly, since early 2005. The profit-to-cost ratio has held up quite well (Figure 3.13), suggesting that cost controls have underpinned profitability.

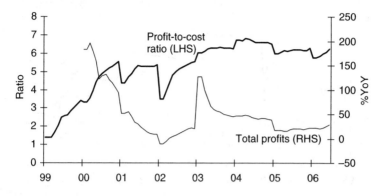

Figure 3.13   Chinese profitability
Source: CEIC

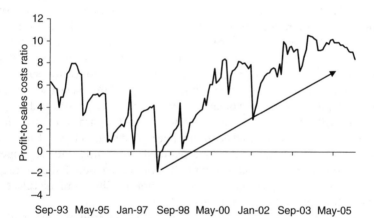

Figure 3.14   Profitability of 5,000 principal enterprises

Data collected by the NBS are a rather reliable profitability indicator because companies have to pay taxes on their reported profits. Hence, they have no incentive to overstate their financial conditions in their reports to the government. Further, the People's Bank of China's (PBoC) survey of 5,000 principal industrial enterprises shows a similar profit recovery picture since the late 1990s (Figure 3.14).

In a nutshell, there has been real improvement in Chinese corporate profits after significant downsizing and consolidation, especially since 2000. The number of loss-making SOEs has also been falling steadily

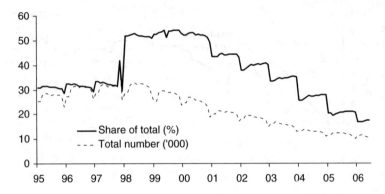

Figure 3.15   China's loss-making firms
Source: CEIC

(Figure 3.15). Continued structural changes will solidify the foundation for future corporate profit growth. Another reason for the SOEs' turnaround is their new focus on capital-intensive higher value-added industries. State protection for these industries, in the form of barriers to entry, has also bolstered their profits. Nevertheless, protectionist measures are not a solution. Reform momentum needs to speed up to cleanse the system and put the economy on a long-term sustainable growth path.

Competition in China's marketplace is another irony confronting many observers. A planned economy like China should have little competition, as the state would have planned everything and developed monopolized industries according to its political agenda. But despite its economic planning background, competition in China's marketplace is one of the fiercest known among corporate chiefs.

The reason for China's highly competitive environment is market fragmentation and regional autarky. While China does have its monopolized SOEs, these are only protected at the provincial level. Each province has its monopolized automaker, steel producer, telecoms provider and the like, but local protection does not go beyond the provincial border. In terms of regional development, each province acts as an independent state pursuing its often protectionist agenda by cherry-picking local industries to compete in the local and national markets.

Local protectionism started to break down during the decentralization process in the 1980s and 1990s, with the central government dismantling interprovincial trade barriers, eliminating local tariffs, taxes and cross-province import bans. On the back of this local trade liberalization, every province wanted to extend its local industrial influence across the border. Thus, everyone set up television factories, breweries, auto plants, garment factories and the like across provinces, creating huge competition and excess capacity. The availability of cheap funds from the state banks only aggravated the competitive pressure by boosting capacity and over-investment.

Keen competition, meanwhile, has acted as a crucial discipline on restructuring the SOEs. Industry studies on Chinese markets have shown low market concentration levels even by developed market standards. The top five firms account for less than 15 per cent of the national market share in some highly competitive sectors, such as beer. Even in heavily regulated sectors, such as telecoms, cars, aviation steel, energy and media, for which many developed economies would only sustain a national monopoly for each sector, there are a few major players competing fiercely in China.

China has also been breaking down the barriers to foreign entry at a rapid pace. The average import tariff rate has fallen steadily, from over 40 per cent in the early 1990s to 9.9 per cent in 2005 (Figure 3.16). The declining trend is going to continue under WTO requirements. Meanwhile, the network of quotas and restrictions on foreign firms trading and distributing in China has been gradually dismantled. Except in strategic industries, such as banking and aviation, Beijing has eased or lifted most licensing requirements on schedule under the WTO. In foreign trade, it only intends to keep those import licensing restrictions that are on controlled chemical products, such as those that can easily be turned into narcotics and ozone-destructive-materials.

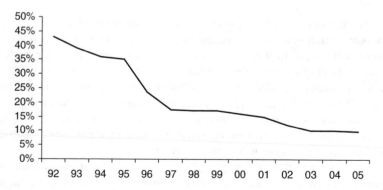

Figure 3.16 China's average import tariff rate

Source: *Xinhua News*

The future of state-owned enterprises

China has embarked on a privatization programme since 2003. The leadership wants to keep some of the large strategic state firms and let go of the small ones – a policy dubbed as 'zhua-da fang-xiao' in Chinese.[4] However, the management structure of China's SOEs is very complex and their ownership is vague. That makes privatization difficult. The basic problem is that there is no clear ownership definition for the state assets. The bureaucrats do not know what to sell and who will be in charge of the sale process.

In principle, the state owns the SOEs. But the state itself is a vague concept in the privatization context. This is because there is no single entity that oversees and manages the state companies (see below). Until recently, the SOEs took directives from a range of functional ministries and the provincial and city governments. The SOEs were managed by state-appointed bureaucrats, who mainly worked with Party cadres and trade unions and had little commercial sense.

Despite the ownership confusion and slow changes, China has been trying to reform its SOEs. Beijing is taking a three-prong approach to changing the SOEs with the aim of operating them along western commercial lines:

- It wants all SOEs legally incorporated as joint-stock firms, with shareholder ownership structure.
- For those SOEs that Beijing wants to keep under control, it will assign a single entity to oversee and manage their operations.
- The rest of the SOEs will be fully privatized.

Some changes, such as the introduction of the contract responsibility system, which gives decision-making autonomy to the SOE managers, were bottom-up approaches. Others, such the creation of the State-owned Assets Supervision and Administration Commission or SASAC, were top-down approaches originating in central government initiatives. But overall, changes have been much slower than the change in the macro-economic environment in which the SOEs operate. Most state employees are still working under the management structure that was put in place some twenty years ago.

That no major SOE reform progress has been achieved can be blamed partly on China's glacial policy making and partly on resistance from local bureaucrats who want investment in their provinces to continue at full speed. But SOE reforms have also been hindered by turf war between

SASAC and the Ministry of Finance (MoF) over who should receive and control the SOE revenues. As an investor in the SOEs, SASAC would very much like to manage them. The head of SASAC, Li Rongrong, is seen as having an ambition to turn his agency into an imitation of Singapore's state investment company Temasek. However, the MoF argues that it should have control of the funds since it had paid for the losses and reorganization of the SOEs over the years.

Improving the usage of the SOE funds is important for both macro-economic management and structural reform. A crucial reason for why monetary policy has been ineffective in curbing China's excessive investment growth is because those investments have been funded mostly by SOEs' retained earnings. Chinese banks play only a minor role in funding the investment binge.

The World Bank[5] estimates that Chinese firms, not households, are the country's biggest savers. Since SOEs do not pay any dividends, almost all of their earnings are reinvested, disregarding the rate of return. In recent years, retained earnings were the biggest funding source for new projects, accounting for half of all investments. But much of this money has been used inefficiently. SOEs stuffed with plenty of cash have little concern for shareholder value. Their excessive investment generates low rates of return and overcapacity.

Under this situation, draining banking system liquidity will do little to curb investment growth. Flooded with funds and lacking a profit motive, the SOEs have little incentive to improve efficiency. Thus, an effective way to change the SOEs' extravagant habits, the World Bank argues, is to reduce the amount of funds at their disposal. This can be done by extracting some of the SOEs' profit by making them pay dividends, thus forcing them to spend/invest the rest more wisely and improve capital allocation. It would also reduce the cash available for the SOEs to speculate in the asset markets or to expand into non-core wasteful business lines. From a regulatory efficiency perspective, it is important for SASAC and the MoF to reach an agreement on how best to supervise the SOEs' accounting system and thus work out a way to centralize the usuage of SOE revenues.

Arguably, corporate reform is the slowest among the various structural changes in China. While downsizing and shedding of surplus labour from the SOEs have been real and swift, privatization has been not. Thus, the next step in pushing corporate reform forwards should be overhauling the state assets management system to institutionalize and speed up privatization. The creation of the SASAC in March 2003 was a major step towards this, though only time will tell how successful it will be in its job.

In a broad sense, SASAC is a crucial departure from China's previous chaotic efforts, when hundreds of government ministries and bureaucratic agencies scrambled for decisions on the daily operations of the SOEs. At a stroke scoop, SASAC is entrusted with formal ownership and management of all non-financial state enterprise assets. The central SASAC in Beijing is also responsible for creating the regional SASACs, guiding them through the work of improving the transparency and centralization of SOE budgets.

In fact, SASAC was specially created to address the problems of the debt-ridden SOEs. As of mid 2006, it had a portfolio of 167 of the largest centrally owned SOEs. They included firms in telecoms, civil aviation, oil and gas, cars, steel and chemical, with a combined asset of RMB6 trillion (or US$750 billion). SASAC aims at selling off most of the assets in its portfolio, and just keeping about 80 of the largest SOEs under its management by 2011. It is looking to list, and eventually fully internationalize, Chinese corporate giants such as Petro China, CNOOC, Baosteel, Sinopec, China Telecom, China Unicom, Lenovo, Haier, TCL, Air China and China Eastern Airlines.

SASAC should, in principle, help improve the overall corporate governance system of the SOEs through an efficient board of directors, and push privatization ahead by clearly defining asset ownership and being in charge of the asset sale process. It should also enable China to address the problem of chaotic decision-making. Since SASAC plays an investor role in the SOEs, the government should have better control over governance through a more effective centralization of decision-making initiatives under the agency.

Under the Bureau of Enterprise Reform principle, SASAC is responsible for supervision and administration of state-owned assets. It appoints and removes or makes proposals for hiring management personnel in the SOEs. It draws up plans for reorganizing and restructuring the SOEs. It also oversees the fund-raising activity for and division, merger and declaration of the bankruptcy of the SOEs. It makes hiring-and-firing decisions for the SOEs, decides on the transfer of state-owned equity and implements SOEs remuneration guidelines. Last but not last, it is charged with preserving and increasing the value of state-owned assets.

However, doubts still remain about SASAC's effectiveness since inception. There are difficulties for SASAC in penetrating the SOEs' operating activities, due to the thick bureaucratic barriers at the SOEs. SASAC itself is also trapped in the old 'power-is-king' mindset. This is a typical communist legacy – as people are paid neither well nor properly, they are deprived of any commercial sense and tend to focus on amassing power to secure their privileges.

There are also doubts about whether SASAC has given its board of directors enough power to carry out its functions, or whether it has managed to exercise its ownership rights effectively. The old aristocratic mindset is reflected by the lack of transparency in SASAC's decision making. This can be seen in its sudden unexplained reshuffling of top management in four of China's state-owned telecom carriers in 2004, the lack of proper public consultation on its policies and the lack of interministerial coordination at both the central and provincial levels.

To improve its effectiveness and credibility, there are a few things SASAC should do. It should focus on addressing the fundamental problems for privatization and corporate governance reform, which is asset ownership and pricing. As discussed above, despite all the structural changes in the SOEs over the past two decades, many SOEs remain in the grey area between collective, private and state-owned. Corporate ownership structure must be clearly defined for the management of state-owned assets to be effective. To push changes in this regard, Beijing has some broad policies in place such as 'letting some SOEs grow further while retracting some others' (you-jin you-tui), and 'grabbing the big SOEs and releasing the small ones' (zhua-da fang-xiao).

On asset pricing, SASAC is responsible for preserving and enhancing value for state assets. Many state assets have been sold to managers at excessively low prices, due to various problems of bribery and theft. This, in turn, creates political and social tensions. SASAC's job is to price state assets properly so that the smaller SOEs will get fairer pricing and not fall victim to the economic restructuring process. In improving asset pricing, SASAC's role in reorganizing the SOEs and restructuring their capital should effectively improve the firms' balance sheets.

SASAC should also strengthen the process of debt-equity transfer from the SOEs to its portfolio for restructuring/disposal. In this aspect, SASAC's work can augment the AMCs' efforts to restructure the SOEs through debt-equity swap. This is because transparent and efficient debt-equity transfers by SASAC should facilitate the debt-asset swaps by the AMCs, and both should enhance asset value of the underlying firms. Further, SASAC should be given the legitimacy to perform its intermediary function in the SOE bankruptcy payment procedures to banks, which should be the first receivers of repayment under the new bankruptcy law passed in 2006. Effective implementation of this function should also help reduce banks' non-performing loans.

Despite the slow reform pace, the creation of SASAC to manage state assets and facilitate privatization is, in fact, another sign of Beijing's trying to break the communist policy icons of public asset ownership and political intervention in business. Following some OECD guidelines on SOE corporate governance reform, SASAC launched seven pilot SOEs in 2004 by allowing them to operate on western business practices, with foreign managers and chief executives being part of a more transparent corporate governance system. The pilot scheme has been extended to 14 SOEs in 2006 and 30 in 2007.

By reducing Party cadres' interference in business, Beijing is sending a forceful signal that it wants fundamental changes in the corporate sector. Like the experiments with scrapping the *hu kou* system and legalizing private lending rights (see Chapter 1, p. 33), this corporate reform initiative is still in its early stage. But the impact will be far-reaching if implemented properly at the national level.

On a grander scale, the SOEs should open up to market discipline through the globalization process, international listing and inclusion of larger foreign management teams and more independent foreign directors on the SOE boards. SASAC is examining other models of state-owned companies both in Asia (such as Singapore's Temasek Holdings, Japan's now defunct *keiretsu* and South Korea's *chaebol*) and the western world (France's State Asset Management Bureau and similar agencies in Finland and Norway). Temasek is working with SASAC on Chinese SOEs reform. It appears to be an inspiring blueprint for China in terms of transparency improvement and corporate governance mechanisms, though Temasek's own corporate structure and transparency are, arguably, still questionable.[6]

One of the biggest debates over the future of the SOEs is how to speed up privatization under SASAC? How big a share of China's biggest state-owned conglomerates can be sold to private investors? What is the limit of foreign ownership for these SOEs? As the current trends goes, Beijing is likely to relax the foreign ownership limits gradually. For example, the authorities are considering raising the limit for an overall foreign stake in Chinese banks to 40 per cent from 25 per cent.

In the medium term, not all SOEs should be privatized. Those strategic industries such as banking, telecoms, civil aviation, steel, insurance, construction and energy must go through significant restructuring before they can be exposed to full foreign competition. Arguably, state intervention is needed to control the opening-up process to avoid sudden shocks to the system. Beijing's biggest challenge for the future is to transform the state sector without risking massive social unrest. The authorities are pursuing this balance by setting social stability as their top policy priority. Hence, changes are being made, but not at as fast a pace as many critics want to see.

Industrial evolution

What is the future for the Chinese factories under this framework? Since the mid 1990s, China's role in the global economy has been a factory to the world. It has imported increasing amounts of energy and raw materials and combined them with low-cost local labour to make cheap consumer and industrial products for the developed markets. This process has fuelled China's industrialization and economic transformation. But there have been doubts recently about the sustainability of this business model, as Chinese labour costs are rising and its huge demand for world resources has pushed up commodity prices and other business costs.

Despite the cost concerns,[7] it is still too early to conclude that China would lose its comparative advantage in labour-intensive manufacturing in the short term. More likely, China will climb the value-added ladder and its factories will remain the world's factories in the next two decades. The formidable challenge for the developed economies is that China will make sophisticated and high-value goods at lower costs, thus increasing the spectrum of goods under competitive stress.

The most crucial factor that gives China's factories a long-term comparative advantage in tradable goods is the vast hinterland behind its production lines. At present, China has some well-known industrialized regions such as Guangdong and the Greater Shanghai region, and industrializing areas such as Shandong and Hebei. Yes, labour costs are rising in these areas. But no, labour costs will be kept relatively low for long as urbanization brings in cheap labour from the rural regions and as industrialization spreads inland. There are many low-cost regions that would take another twenty years to reach Guangdong's present level of development.

Thus, it is wrong to see China as a single development model because there are important local differences. Further, what seem to be white elephant projects now are, arguably, part of Beijing's long-term plan to push industrialization into the underdeveloped parts of the country. For example, the empty toll roads and even airports in the poor inland areas of Shanxi and Sichuan are part of the basic infrastructure being built in preparation for industrial development.

Despite the rising cost of production, China's cost advantage remains significant at the factory level. Combined with Chinese firms' high tolerance of low return on investment, this gives China strong competitive power for a long time to come. The state plays a crucial role in shaping Chinese business expectations, which directly affect the suppliers' low investment return tolerance. Since it will take time to free China's system from the hands of the state, the old communist mindset and state intervention will remain.

This means that Chinese factories will continue to accept excessive investment and low rates of return in the medium term. The mindset change could easily take two to three decades, if not longer. This means that developed markets will have to face return compression stemming from the Chinese in the coming decades. Meanwhile, China's rising demand for energy and raw materials will continue to boost commodity prices, raising overall business costs.

In the world system, everybody will be facing a double whammy – investment returns compression and rising costs – under these circumstances. But China's higher tolerance of lower profitability will allow it to 'tough it out' much longer than the developed markets' factories will be able to stand. Beyond a certain threshold, developed market firms will be forced to relocate or outsource to China. This is another reason why the global outsourcing trend to China (and other lower-cost bases) is irreversible.

For China, production costs become a challenge in the existing industrialized areas, other underdeveloped regions in the country will be ready to step in. Compared to other low-cost economies, such as Vietnam, Myanmar and Bangladesh, China has developed a critical mass for manufacturing and this advantage will become more evident in the coming decades. Thus, China's role as the world's factory will continue in the next few decades, despite competition from economies with similar or even lower costs.

What is more, Chinese manufactures are not complacent. They are climbing the value-added ladder all the time. This means that they will be raising the bar for world competitors by producing high-value and increasingly sophisticated products but at lower costs. This is already happening in the motor-parts industry, for example. Just a few years ago, China could only make poor-quality and costly motor-parts that the world market shunned.

Critics used to argue that the precision engineering required for the best parts was well beyond the reach of inexperienced Chinese companies and their low-cost workers. But such a pessimistic view has been proven wrong. The product quality of Chinese car-parts makers has improved drastically in just a few years. Now major western car makers, such as Volkswagen AG and Daimler Chrysler AG, are buying billions of dollars of Chinese-made motor-parts, including brakes, fuel pumps, steering systems and wheels. The trade data also underscore China's moving up the value chain. In 2005, China recorded its first trade surplus

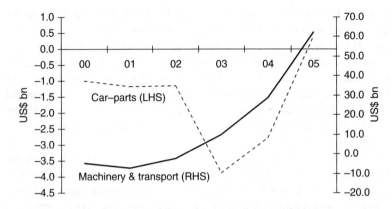

Figure 3.17 High-value goods trade balance
Source: CEIC

for motor-parts. The overall trade balance for high-value goods such as machinery and transport equipment has turned positive since 2003 (Figure 3.17).

These gains show how China continues to evolve as a manufacturer, posing new challenges for rivals in Europe, Japan and the US. The performance of the motor-parts industry is also indicative of the future for the Chinese factories. Instead of dwelling on making simple consumer goods, such as furniture and textiles, they have spread out quickly to dominate more labour-intensive parts of the consumer electronics business, and recently moved into a broader range of industries.

This is indeed a natural evolution of Chinese factories, as the country's comparative advantage changes gradually. With local wages in the key industrial regions rising, Chinese manufacturers are seeking to improve efficiency and reduce reliance on cheap labour. The only way to do this is to move into high-value products, such as motor-parts, and shift out of traditional exports, such as toys and textiles.

While China still dominates labour-intensive manufacturing, there is a big push, both from the domestic and international fronts, to make Chinese companies globally competitive; and they cannot just do it with cheap labour. The world's biggest car firms have continued to flock into China, looking for growth in China's emerging market to make up for the lack of growth in their mature domestic markets. They, in turn, often demand their parts makers to be able to supply them directly in China.

In response to this increasing demand, major western motor-parts makers, such as Robert Bosch GmbH of Germany and ArvinMeritor Inc.

of the US, have made significant investment in Chinese factories to make parts for the local market as well as for exports. The higher standards that global companies have introduced, combined with the international growth of the local motor-parts makers, have spurred innovation and pushed smaller Chinese companies up the technology ladder. For example, Huaxiang Group, based in the coastal city of Ningbo, started out in 1982 making plastic caps for medicine bottles. Now it makes moulded plastic for car interiors, with about 20 per cent of its business coming from exports.

China will remain factory to the world due partly to its climbing up the value chain, which will enlarge the range of products that it can make at lower costs, and partly to its willingness to accept low returns and even endure losses for long periods of time. Due to these low returns, the need for survival has led some analysts to predict a wave of mergers and acquisitions (M&As) in China's industrial sector in the coming decade. The stock market reform should facilitate M&As future activities.

Despite the strong rationale, M&As in China may not happen as fast as many think. The government has made big efforts to foster consolidation in the car, steel, aluminium, textiles, retail civil aviation and media sectors. But success has been limited so far, except in the railway and telecoms sectors where new entrants have not been allowed. In banking, deregulation in the mid 1980s led to the emergence of dozens of regional and city banks around the country. The sector has started to consolidate only recently due to the insolvency of some regional banks. But China remains over-banked, with tens of thousands of state bank branches spreading across the country and competing with thousands of local and foreign banks. There has been basically no consolidation in the brokerage industry and the trust and investment industry.

Why do Chinese firms refuse to rationalize? The lack of an efficient capital market is the big problem confronting M&As in China. It can take a very long time for companies to secure permission from the regulators to issue the new shares that are often needed for acquisitions. It is also very difficult to get the green light from the authorities to issue bonds for funding M&As. Meanwhile, the dominance of the old communist mindset, which lacks commercial thinking and profit incentive, is also to blame.

The stock market reform that is under way should eventually provide the government with an exit from business and commerce, which is of the utmost importance for promoting economic reforms. But capital market reform will likely take a long time to complete (see Chapter 1, pp. 34–5). Then there is the issue of how much and how fast the government is willing to let go – all to do with the old mindset again. Many local governments will want to hang onto their equity stake because that is their political influence in the Chinese companies. As a result, state ownership and intervention will continue to hold back the rationalization of Chinese industries in the medium term.

What about the private sector?

Excluding the listed and joint-stock firms, collectives and TVEs which are still controlled or influenced by the state, the true private sector is still very small in China. Official estimates put the private sector at no more than 30 per cent of the economy. Other estimates of between 50 per cent and 70 per cent are confusing the non-state sector[8] with the true private sector. In terms of the stock market, of the 1,300 or so A-share companies listed on the domestic exchanges and the 230 Chinese companies listed in overseas markets, less than 40 are controlled by the private sector.

Even the four most liberalized sectors, retail, brewery, textile and white goods, are still dominated by the state. It is true that a few large retailers, such as Gome, Suning, Yongle and Wumart, are controlled by the private sector, but they account for only a small share of the overall retail sector. The retail sector was first liberalized in the early 1980s, and is now deemed fully deregulated. But deregulated does not mean privately owned, as government incumbents are still dominant in the sector. Of the 66 retailers listed on China's stock market, only one, Suning, is controlled by the private sector. There are also many family-run stores across the country. But state-owned retailers, mostly department stores, still dominate the retail sector and occupy prime locations.

Most large textile companies are either under CNPC, Sinopec or the National Textile Council (formerly the Ministry of Textile Industry). Foreign companies, including those from Hong Kong, Taiwan and Japan, have opened a large number of textile factories in China, but many of them are suppliers to the SOEs and the state firms are still very important in the sector. In the white goods sector, top players such as TCL, Konka, Haier, Hi-sense and Sichuan Changhong are all state-owned. There are some private sector players, such as Skyworth, Kelon and Gree, but they are not dominant players.

The brewery industry was one of the earliest deregulated sectors. Ownership restriction in Chinese breweries was lifted in 1978. But most domestic breweries, spirits makers and wineries are state-owned. The largest three breweries (Tsingtao, Yanjing and CRB) are controlled or majority-owned by the government. Except for Harbin, which was acquired by Anheuser-Busche in 2004, the government owns majority shares in all other breweries. Similarly, the largest spirits makers and wineries, such as Kweichow Moutai, Yibin Wuliangye, Dynasty Fine Wines, Great Wall and Yantai Changyu, are all state-owned.

Meanwhile, the biggest sectors in the economy are either 100 per cent or majority-owned by the state. They include oil, petroleum, mining, banks, insurance, tobacco, telecoms, steel, aluminium, power, civil aviation, ports, railways, highways, cars, health care, education, chemicals and cement.

The point of all this is that, despite massive creative destruction of the state sector over the years, China's economy is still subtly dominated by the state. Though the physical role of the state is declining and the SOEs' day-to-day operations may be freed from direct government meddling, the state remains influential via intangible means such as way of thinking and habitual inertia. The private (and the non-state) sector only plays, and will remain, a secondary role in the medium term.

What is more interesting is that the bulk of the private sector still behaves like the state sector, at least for some years ahead. This irony is unique to China, and is poorly understood by many observers. The reason is simple. Many Chinese entrepreneurs are ex-government officials. They are still very much bounded by the communist mindset, are only just learning about commercial and profit motives and are still ignorant about proper business dealings and standards. This has a lot to do with China's young capitalism.

In the past twenty-five years, China did not really have a true business cycle. Despite all the talks about boom-and-bust cycles, China in fact only went through slow growth and very strong growth (Figure 3.18). This means that business opportunities have been plentiful, and the biggest rewards have gone to the most aggressive, and arguably unscrupulous, entrepreneurs. In other words, most Chinese entrepreneurs do not understand business cycles because they have not experienced any. This is also the reason why business consolidation has been slow even in the most liberalized sectors. Most Chinese entrepreneurs want to tough it out and hope to win by aggressively expanding their scale during the slow periods.

Adding this attitude to the *guan-xi* factor, or the private firms' reliance on close connections with the state sector for business, creates a prefect recipe for the private sector firms to behave like their SOE counterparts. Why? This is because insider dealing through political connections is a key part of the business process for many private firms in China. Since they survive and prosper on the fringe of the state sector, these private firms are influenced by state sector performance and decisions. They

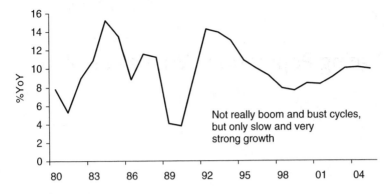

Figure 3.18   China's real GDP growth
Source: CEIC

also have to budget accordingly for the state firms' capital expenditure and production schedules. The government's influence on the private firms via contract awards and even personnel appointments in the private sector are thus crucial in determining the private sector's behaviour, at least in the medium term.

In a nutshell, China's state economy has undergone some significant changes, with Beijing showing willingness to break away from some classical communist policy apparatus. There has been painful downsizing in the state sector, and SOEs have been exposed to intense competition from both inside and outside the state sector. Nonetheless, the government still owns, directly and indirectly, a large share of the economy. The average SOE has turned profitable in recent years after decades of losses, thanks to the wrench of restructuring. But it is still saddled with historical debt burdens and distortions from state interference.

The Marxist legacy is still deep-rooted in many parts of the system. This will continue to impede structural reforms and the future growth of the true private sector. But all is not lost. Current policy and development trends are evolving to allow China to solve these problems in the coming years. The improving commercial legal framework and the recent reshuffling of SOE ownership should both give new impetus to the privatization process.

4
Ageing Population: What's New?

Demographics are becoming a big challenge for China. As the population ages, the returns on different factors of production – land, labour and capital – will change, as their relative scarcities will change. This will have far-reaching implications for China's investment returns, economic policy and growth outlook. The introduction of family planning policies in the 1970s, with the implementation of the 'one child' policy in 1979, has led to a sharp slowdown in population growth in the following decades. With the 'baby boomers' now in their 40s, China is facing an unprecedented ageing process.

The United Nations (UN) has estimated that under the 'one child' policy, China's population (1.3 billion today) will peak at 1.45 billion by 2030 and fall thereafter. There will be over 300 million pensioners by then, or 21 per cent of the total population. While there are almost six working-age people for every retiree today, the ratio will drop to two workers per pensioner by 2040. Some fear that China's ageing population is a time bomb waiting to wreak havoc on its economy. China's ageing process resembles that in the developed economies such as Japan and the US but takes place at a level of income many times lower.

It is natural to ask how China is going to pay for its pension liability, what the impact on the fiscal balance will be, and what the implications on China's return on capital, living standards, economic policies and growth outlook will be. There is no doubt that China's pension costs are high, but its 'pension crunch' is still some decades away. There are ways for Beijing to tackle its large pension liabilities, including adjustments to the pension system, diversion of tax revenues, issuing debt and selling assets.

Hence, the ageing problem is not imminent and not doomed as some think. But the ensuing labour shortage problem means that China's economic model should shift to high value-added production, away from labour-intensive low-end manufacturing exports and towards more consumption-oriented. The inevitable long-term effect of an ageing population and a declining workforce on return on capital and GDP growth will be negative. This implies economic policies will have a bias towards capital formation for raising labour productivity to sustain living standards over the long term.

From population boom to bust

After the Communists came to power in 1949, Mao Zedong's economic vision was to build up China with a large capital base via heavy investment and mobilization of the massive rural population into a productive labour force. He believed that a big population was identical with a strong China. Hence, a population expansionist policy was pursued to encourage large families. This population pro-growth policy had led to persistently high birth rates for almost thirty years (Figure 4.1). Between 1949 and 1957, China's gross birth rate averaged 33 births per 1,000 population. After a temporary drop between 1958 and 1961, due to the disruptions from the Great Leap Forward movement, the birth rate went up to 43 per 1,000 population and stayed at over 30 until the early 1970s.

Meanwhile, improvement in social policy and health care raised life expectancy, cut infant mortality rate and thus contributed to a fall in the gross death rate. The Communist regime also ushered a period of stability after 1949, bringing to an end decades of civil wars, domestic uprisings and foreign invasion. This allowed families to settle down and

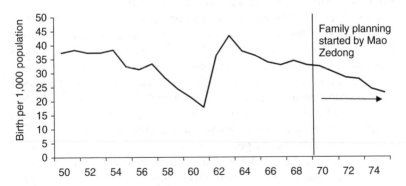

Figure 4.1 Gross birth rate (1950–75)
Source: CEIC

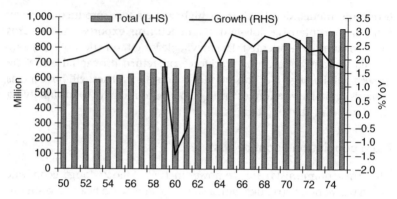

Figure 4.2   China's population (1950–75)
Source: CEIC

to raise children. The combination of political stability, a high birth rate and a fall in the death rate caused a population boom in China. Total population jumped almost two-fold from 540 million in 1950 to 924 million in 1975, equivalent to an annual rate of increase of almost 3 per cent in the period (Figure 4.2).

The Chinese authorities began to adjust their population in the 1970s as global fears of surging energy and food prices intensified. The slow pace of economic growth also exposed the burden of a rapidly growing population. Hence the government introduced family planning in 1973, and implemented the 'one child' policy in urban areas in 1979. Still effective today, the family planning policy advocated later marriage with late child bearing and fewer children per family. It is carried out via both the healthcare system and financial incentives.

Official family planning units are set up to give out information on contraception and offer cheap contraceptives and/or birth control operations, including induced abortion, through the healthcare system. The government also uses financial incentives to encourage small family sizes. A fine, called a 'social fostering fee', of RMB30,000 is levied on each additional child over the one-child minimum. Couples with more than two children are not entitled to free maternity care, and there are no free education and social security benefits from the state for the additional children.

Since the mid 1980s, the population control policy has been somewhat relaxed, with rural couples being allowed to have a second child if the first one is a girl. Members of minority groups are allowed to have three children, and urban couples have the option of having a second child without penalty if both of the parents are from a one-child family.

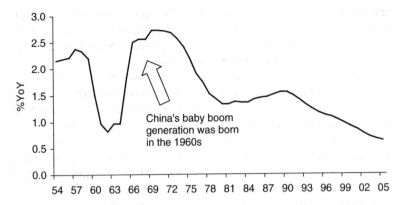

Figure 4.3   From population boom to bust*
* 5-year moving average
Source: CIEC

The family planning policy has been extremely effective, with the birth rate falling precipitously from over 30 per 1,000 population in the early 1970s to just 9 in year 2000. The fertility rate[1] also dropped from 6.06 to 1.85, well below the replacement rate of 2.1 that is needed to prevent the population from declining. On the back of a steady death rate averaging 6.5 per 1,000, China's population growth slowed sharply to less than 0.6 per cent a year now from over 2 per cent in the early 1970s (Figure 4.3). After rising by 71.1 per cent from 540 million in 1950 to 924 million in 1975, the total population rose by only 41.6 per cent in the 30 years between 1975 and 2005.

There are regional differences in birth rates, with urban rates considerably lower than the rural rate. There is also a gap in the birth rates between the backward interior provinces and the well-developed east coastal regions. These differences reflect not only official policies, but also the cultural and financial pressures of urban life in the more developed regions. The average marriage and pregnancy ages have risen in the wealthier cities, with many couples choosing to lead a 'DINK' (or double-income-no-kids) lifestyle.

If the current trends continue, the United Nations Population Division (UNPD) projects that China's population would peak at 1.45 billion by 2032, and begin to fall thereafter. Meanwhile, the China's National Bureau of Statistics projects that the country's population would peak at 1.54 billion some time between 2040 and 2045. While the estimates vary among the forecasters, the bottom line is that China's total population will peak in the next 25–30 years. This leads directly to the ageing population problem, which has important implications for China's workforce, the burden of the dependent population (those who are younger than 15 years old and older than 60 years old) on the economy and future growth.

China's 'baby boom' generation was born in the late 1960s (see Figure 4.3). This means that by 2020, these baby boomers will be reaching retirement age so that there will be fewer people entering the workforce than retiring. The UNPD estimates that this ageing trend will be more pronounced by 2050, when for the first time in China's history retirees will make up the largest of the five-year age categories. This sounds like a distant issue. But what is more important is that China's working population (age 15–60) as a share of total population has already reached its peak, at 68 per cent today. The share of working population is expected to fall steadily to less than 60 per cent by 2030 and to 52 per cent by 2050 (Figure 4.4), according to the UNPD.

As the baby boom generation moved into the workforce in the late 1970s and 1980s, the dependency ratio[2] fell to 0.47 dependants per worker today from 0.54 in 1990 and 0.83 in 1975. The low dependency ratio today means that a big portion of China's population is economically productive. If the UNPD forecast is correct, China is currently approaching a demographic 'golden age', when the dependency ratio is at the lowest (or saddle) point (Figure 4.5).

As the working population shrinks and the old population increases, China's dependency ratio will rise after the saddle point. Due to the

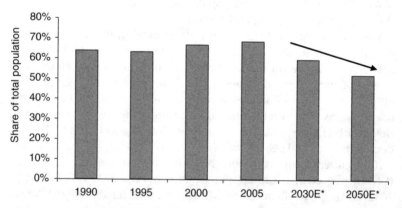

Figure 4.4   China's working population*

* Age between 15 and 60 years old, UNPD forecast
Sources: CEIC, UNPD

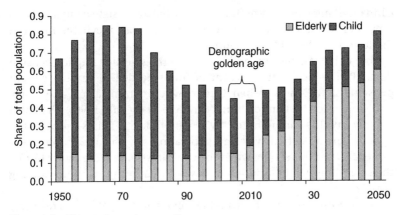

Figure 4.5   China's dependency ratios
Source: UNPD

population control policy, most of the rise in the dependency ratio will come from the elderly group (see Figure 4.5). By 2050, the dependency ratio is expected to rise again to the 1975 level of 0.8 dependants per worker. This will take up more economic resources and put a heavier burden on the workforce of sustaining the ageing population in future years.

The pension puzzle

What is special about China's demographics is that it is facing developed-country demographics and social liabilities but with a developing country per capita income level of slightly above US$1,000 a year. This has led to questions about whether Beijing has enough resources to sustain economic growth and an ageing population simultaneously. Others also wonder who will be paying for the army of retirees?

An ageing population may not be a problem if there are enough young workers to replace the retiring ones. But China does not seem to have the working population necessary to support the ageing. With a rising dependency ratio, Beijing should act now to provide for the growing number of elderly before it is too late. But the current pension system is severely underfunded, with the size of the shortfall estimated at between RMB4 trillion and RMB7 trillion (US$480 billion–US$850 billion), or 45 per cent–75 per cent of GDP.[3]

Adding this pension shortfall to the need for bank recapitalization, China's total contingent liabilities for keeping the financial system afloat easily surpass 100 per cent of GDP. That is why pessimists see

China walking with a fiscal time bomb, irreparable state companies and a pension debt. They cannot help but predict an inevitable financial implosion for the Middle Kingdom.

China's biggest pension problem lies in the so-called implicit pension debt (IPD), which is the amount of funds needed to pay the current pensioners.[4] IPD arose when China switched from a 'pay-as-you-go' (PAYG) pension system to a funded system in the late 1990s. The PAYG scheme pays the current retirees with current taxes. This is equivalent to saying that the current working population pays for the current pensioners. Under this set-up, when the current workers retire in the future, their pensions will be paid by the taxes levied from the future working population.

In an economy with a shrinking labour force and an increasingly greying population, the PAYG system simply cannot generate enough payments to pay for the pensioners. On the other hand, a funded system, such as Singapore's Central Provident Fund or Hong Kong's Mandatory Provident Fund, pays worker pensions out of a fund built up during their working lives. Under this scheme, both the worker and the employer have to contribute to a pension account for the worker, which can only be withdrawn on retirement. In other words, a worker's retirement is self- and fully funded.

In the past, caring for the aged was not a big issue for China. The numbers of retirees were far fewer than the numbers of workers so that retirement benefits could easily be met by a PAYG system. Such a system was also part of the Communist Party's social contract in piecing the society together – workers would work for state companies for their whole life; in return, all their retirement needs would be met by the state via state-owned enterprise (SOE) pensions. However, the PAYG system cannot last as China's life expectancy rises, birth rate falls and working population shrinks. Sooner or later, China will not have enough young workers to support the retirees.[5]

Aware of the problem, Beijing began switching from the PAYG system to a funded system in 1997, when it adopted a three-tier scheme proposed by the World Bank. The first tier is a compulsory defined-benefit state pension pooled at provincial level. It is funded by employers' contributions, which range between 13 per cent and 16 per cent of wages. The next tier is a mandatory individually funded defined-contribution plan, with employers contributing 3 per cent and employees contributing 8 per cent of wages to each individual account. The third tier is a voluntary, supplementary plan. Beijing used the northern province of Liaoning as a testing ground for this new scheme in early 2001.

The pilot project was successful, with some RMB1.3 billion accumulated in 4.8 million accounts within six months after inception. The government is rolling out the Liaoning model nationwide gradually. This three-tier system effectively spreads the burden of retirement payments between the government, SOEs and employees, thus preventing China's pensions system from collapsing under an ageing population. The funded scheme is also a milestone in institutionalizing China's private savings, which reached RMB32 trillion[6] (US$4 trillion), or 175 per cent of GDP, in mid 2006. Before this new pension scheme, bank accounts were the only institutional glue for China's household savings.

The new pensions system has made state pension coverage mandatory for all urban workers, not just state and collective workers. The coverage has indeed been gradually extended to include many private, foreign and joint-stock companies and self-employed workers. While the change of the pensions system is still work in progress, the urban pensions system had already covered 155 million workers, or a third of the total urban workforce, in 2003.

More importantly, by transferring pension responsibility from the SOEs to social insurance agencies under the Ministry of Labour, the new system cuts the ties between the SOEs and pension payments. This is like tearing up the Communist Party's social contract in ruling the society, and giving individual decisions more economic freedom. This is another crucial sign of Beijing's resolve in breaking up the classical communist apparatus in the economy.

Despite its merits and importance, the trouble with the new system is that moving from the old scheme to the new leaves a big pensions liability funding gap, which is what creates the IPD. When today's workers set aside money under the new scheme to pay for their own retirement, they are not contributing to pay the current retirees and those senior workers who are nearing retirement but have never paid into any pension plans. The SOEs are stuck with these transitional liabilities, which are stretching their finances that are already in a dire shape. Under the 1997 pensions-reform plan, SOEs were required to continue to pay existing pensioners, while also paying into the individual worker accounts under the funded system. Some SOEs have to pay up to a quarter of their entire wage bill to meet their pension obligations.

Without additional funds to plug the IPD hole, pensions reform will be hampered. Many SOEs have cheated by moving funds destined for current workers' pensions to pay today's pensioners. This has caused serious distortion in pensions reform. The central government has tried to tackle the problem by topping up payments out of tax revenues. But this

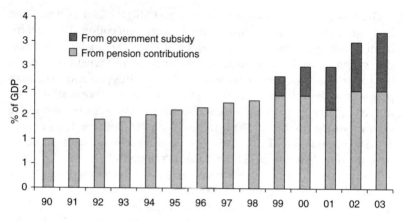

Figure 4.6 Social security fund composition
Source: CEIC

is not a solution because it only transfers the SOEs' pensions liability to the fiscal deficit. China needs new, not transference of, funds to plug the pensions hole. Indeed, the situation has not improved despite the central government's help. According to the State Council Office for Economic Restructuring, the shortfall in pension funding since 1997 have accrued to over RMB200 billion (US$26 billion). Overtime, the shortfall will grow exponentially as the dependency rate rises.

The extent of the future pensions problem depends crucially on the ability to generate pension-designated savings today; and to invest those savings at a good rate of return to augment the growth of the pensions pool. However, the current low worker coverage ratio relative to the number of pensioners already in the system means that China is not yet generating enough pension savings to meet its potential liabilities in the future.

Under full coverage, worker contributions are estimated to be more than 12 per cent of GDP. However, actual contributions under the current coverage amounted to only 2 per cent of GDP (Figure 4.6), which is not even enough to pay for the current pensioners. Hence, the social security fund has been forced to 'borrow' from individual fund accounts to meet its pensions obligations and the government has been topping up the funds through subsidies funded out of current tax revenues.

Meanwhile, the rate of return on pension savings has been extremely low. Even after government subsidies, the accumulated pension balances in individual accounts are barely increasing relative to the income level

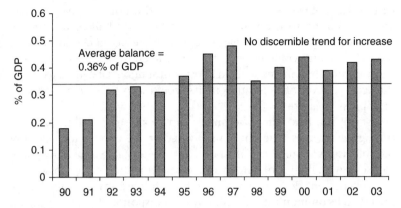

Figure 4.7 Cumulated pension fund balances
Source: CEIC

(Figure 4.7). This is mainly because the social security fund holds domestic bonds and bank deposits, which earn a dismal rate of return averaging 2–3 per cent a year. This is far less than the rate of GDP growth.

There is unlikely to be any sharp rise in the return structure in the short-term. This is because the underdeveloped domestic capital market will continue to restrict investment alternatives. This also means that the social security fund will remain dependent on investing in bank deposits, the return of which will remain low for as long as the system is flooded with money and interest rates remain low and controlled. All this argues for broader financial liberalization and capital market reform as a crucial leg for pensions reform (see below).

In principle, the government can fund the pension debt through raising taxes (including the pension contribution rate), or borrowing, or asset sales, or a combination of the three. But the first two options are not practical and not fair. Funding the current pension payments out of taxation and public borrowing will effectively put the financing burden on the shoulders of both current and future workers. They will have to save for their retirement as well as paying higher taxes for repaying the government's borrowing when these debts mature in the future. The current pension contribution rate of over 20 per cent from employers has already caused complaints and resistance from the business community. Further increase in the burden would only undermine business confidence.

Another way of plugging the pensions hole will be adjusting the pensions system by enrolling more workers or lower pension benefits.

Part of the problem to date is that only one third of the urban workers are contributing to the pensions system but over half of retirees are receiving state pensions. This gap accounts for the lack of pension savings today. So if China could take greater efforts to enlist more workers in the pension contribution net, it could boost contribution. Of course, reducing the relative level of pension benefits would also be a viable, though unpopular, measure.

Last but not least, the government can tackle the pensions problem through asset sales. The question is whether the government has any saleable assets? Surely, not all state assets are saleable, especially those bad SOEs with high debt burden and low profitability or even losses. But the government does own some assets with good market value. They include telecommunications, oil, power, transport and media agencies. As of 2003, central and local governments held sole or majority share of some 150,000 non-financial enterprises, with an estimated book value of over RMB10 trillion, or about 80 per cent of GDP. Privatization since 2003 should have shrunk the pool of saleable assets, but not by much as the privatization effort has remained limited so far.

Since a large number of the chronic loss-making SOEs were shut down during the industrial restructuring process in the past two decades, the remaining ones are relatively viable and hence should command reasonable sale prices. Even if the sale prices were less than the book value of the assets, the government could potentially realize some 50 per cent of GDP-worth of funds in a concerted privatization effort.

Meanwhile, Beijing has huge foreign exchange reserves amounting to over RMB8 trillion (over US$1 trillion) at the time of writing, and overseas assets worth more than RMB2 trillion. The government also owns all the country's land and natural resources that potentially have great value. Finally, if privatized, the market value of the services industries will likely command a premium over their face value suggested by the GDP estimates, due to keen foreign investor interests in them.

The point is that while the situation in China's pension system is not ideal, it is not likely to crush the financial system in the immediate future. China's pensions crunch is some 25–30 years away. Many things may change in the interim period to ease the ageing problem, such as a change in the immigration and population growth policies.

Further, the Chinese government owns many assets that are growing in value. Rising reform momentum under WTO membership, combined with the need to cover the pensions debt, means that the government will sell state assets on a large scale in the coming years. This, in turn, supports the urgent need for capital market reform because the pension funds will need assets required for investment generating a decent return over time to meet their future liabilities.

In other words, capital market reform is not only crucial to facilitate bank restructuring, but is also a linchpin of pension reform. The current capital market is not deep enough to fulfil these needs. Under the new pensions scheme, pension funds have to invest at least 50 per cent of their money in bank deposits and treasury bonds. A maximum of 20 per cent can be invested in corporate bonds, and no more than 30 per cent in securities funds and equities.

While this allocation sounds reasonably balanced between safe (but lower-return) and risky (but higher-return) assets for pension fund investment, this strategy is not feasible at this time. This is because China's underdeveloped capital market is not capable of supporting any major institutional investors, such as pension funds. The local RMB6 trillion or so stock market capitalization is misleading, as two-thirds of the shares are held by the state and state-related entities. The process to release the state shareholding is slow so that the situation is not going to change much in the next few years. The bond market is illiquid with poor-quality papers, and overall capital market reform is moving very slowly. The vast majority of players in the capital market are speculators rather than long-term institutional investors.

Thus, China's pension funds will still be limited to invest mainly in cash and government bonds in the short term. If China is to fund the army of retirees adequately over the coming decades, it must step up capital market reforms. It will also need to privatize the pension fund management business. Faced with pressure to protect, and enhance, the value of pension fund assets, the government will have no choice but to outsource management of its fast-growing pensions pool to professionals. Given the infant local asset-management business, this implies huge opportunities for foreign money managers in the medium term.

China is making some initial progress on liberalizing the capital market and fund-management business. For example, to boost the quality of assets in the domestic securities market, authorities are allowing the local subsidiaries of foreign companies to list on the Shanghai Stock Exchange and to raise funds by issuing RMB-denominated bonds in the domestic market. The government will transfer some of the estimated RMB4 trillion in state-held shares to pension plans via stock-index funds modelled on Hong Kong's Tracker Fund, where stocks are packaged into trust fund units and sold to the public. It is also setting up independent fund-management companies by inviting foreign asset-managers to participate.

Don't jump for joy just yet. The pace of change is still painfully slow. Despite the promise of many policy proposals and pioneer projects to fix the system, pressing problems have yet to be resolved. For example, the increasing costs of pensions and the limitations of the system (such as insufficient money to pay for the IPD and cheating by some officials on the new funded-pension scheme) mean that there is neither a fully funded system nor a clear way to pay for the transition costs of such a system. All enterprises, including foreign ones, will thus bear a somewhat heavier pension contribution burden than they would have to if surplus funds were available. Under this situation, it is likely that those more successful companies may face higher pressure to make more pension contributions to help top up the system for some years to come.

Despite this drawback, successful implementation of the funded pension scheme should increase China's economic efficiency by enabling companies to transfer, or change, workers more easily than before. This will increase labour market mobility, which has been a thorny issue hampering structural reforms. Companies, especially the foreign ones, can in theory shed excess labour without fearing that they would not be taken care of, since the pooled account is part of a provincial or city commitment to a pension of at least 20 per cent of the local average salary. The increased labour mobility should also permit more qualified workers to transfer jobs should opportunities arise.

Finally, China's seemingly large IPD, estimated at between 45 per cent and 75 per cent of GDP, is not that large by international standards. The US has an IPD of around 110 per cent of GDP, Italy 240 per cent of GDP and Brazil 190 per cent of GDP. The real danger in the system is a Japanese-style quagmire, where misguided muddle-through would erode growth momentum to zero.

Nevertheless, China's cash- and asset-rich government still has room to handle its population crunch through policy adjustments and reforms, with capital market reform being the centrepiece of the whole programme. Overall, privatization is the only way out of the financial mess facing China today. The government needs to allow more market discipline to guide the system. It is not an overnight job, but there is no reason to conclude China is in a dire financial state just because tough reforms take longer.

The real story about labour shortage

If the pensions crunch is not an imminent problem, what about labour shortage? With an ageing population, a shrinking labour force causing shortages is natural. But the story is a little more complicated than this. Certainly, ageing population is a long-term factor that affects China's labour supply. But the problem today is in fact not really a shortage as such.

In autumn 2004, the Chinese government reported for the first time that factories around Shanghai and the Pearl River Delta (PRD) in southern China, the nation's two great export powerhouses, were suffering from severe labour shortages of some 2 million workers. Entrepreneurs in these manufacturing hubs complained that they had big difficulties in hiring additional workers and expanding capacity. Some industry surveys conducted in the Guangdong Province in 2005 also showed that although a third of the manufacturers there had raised wages and benefits to attract and retain workers, there was still a shortage of over 1 million workers. In early 2006 at a job fair in Fuzhou, more than half a million positions designed to attract farmers to move to work in urban areas were left unfilled.

All this sounds strange, as China is approaching the demographic 'golden age' (see p. 100) with the labour force still expected to grow for another decade or so before it will start to fall. So, labour shortage should not occur so soon. Of China's 1.3 billion population, some 900 million are classified as agricultural. Among these, almost 800 million are registered in rural villages and the rest are registered in small towns. Within the rural population, there are about 500 million people in the working-age range between 15 and 59 years old, according to government census.

Some analysts estimate that China only needs 100 million people working on the farms to support current agricultural output levels. This means that four-fifths of the 500-million strong working-age rural population are surplus labour with either insufficient work or no work at all. This surplus labour can be hired elsewhere. Many of them do find jobs elsewhere, notably in manufacturing and services in more developed areas, such as Guangdong, Fujian, Zhejiang and Jiangsu provinces, as migrant workers. Indeed, Chinese census data show a 'floating' rural population of 100 million. This still leaves about 300 million working-age rural labour unemployed or underemployed;[7] that is 300 million potential new workers for manufacturing and services. So where is the shortage?

What is going on is a combination of a labour market maturing process and labour immobility that is pushing up costs. China's labour market is maturing, albeit at a very slow pace and in an uneven pattern, with some cities maturing faster than others. Manufacturing wage pressures are on the rise in the cities with a fast-maturing labour market. This wage trend will continue over the longer term as a natural economic evolution process.

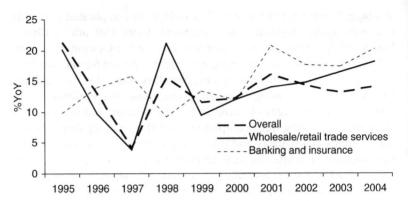

Figure 4.8   Skilled labour earnings outperforming market
Source: CEIC

Skilled labour has been in short supply since early 2002, and wages for them have been rising faster than the overall wage growth since then (for example, see banking and insurance and trade services in Figure 4.8). But the perceived shortage of unskilled labour is unprecedented.

The root of the problem lies in the structure of the labour market and labour demand. Given the abundance of young workers, most textile, toy and electronics manufacturers pick and hire only young rural workers. In fact, they hire mostly young female workers, who are more painstaking, dedicated and willing to work for lower wages than males are. A Ministry of Labour study in 2004 found that some 75 per cent of the factories surveyed hire only females between 18 and 26 years old. In the more manual labour-intensive sectors such as construction, there is a similar focus on hiring young men in the same age group. How many in the 100 million floating rural workers are between 18 and 26 years old? No one knows, but presumably it is a large share. According to Chinese census data, about 100 million rural residents are in the age range 18–26.

However, the disturbing trend is that the remaining supply of men and women under 26 years old is dwindling. This is largely a result of China's strict population control policy since the late 1970s, which has led to a declining growth rate in both the population and the labour force since the 1980s. According to census data, there are about 185 million rural residents, or 23 per cent of the total, in the young working-age group between 15 and 29 years old. If 100 million are already working in the cities, there is not much young surplus labour left.

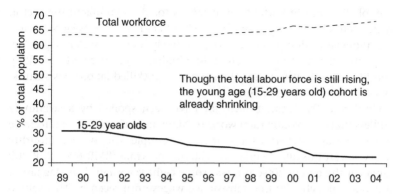

Figure 4.9 A shrinking young workforce
Source: CEIC

Further, not all of the remaining young workers are available for working in the factories. There are those who want to remain in farming. Others are full-time students, or taking care of the elderly, disabled and/or parents. It is thus not surprising that manufacturers are finding it difficult to hire young workers. In fact, the numbers in the 15–29 age cohort are already shrinking (Figure 4.9), even though the working-age population has not yet peaked. Most of the growth in the workforce has come from the older workers, as the baby boomers move through the age brackets.

The preference for young workers has further restrained labour supply. In addition, thanks to the growing economy and technological advancement, there is a rising demand from companies for technical labour in research, management, computer services, information system and the like. In 2006, for example, over one third of the unfilled jobs in Guangzhou and Shenzhen were estimated to be technical positions for young workers.

On the other hand, manufacturers have themselves to blame for creating a short labour supply. They have been mean with worker welfare. Most of them are used to a workforce willing to work for 12 hours a day and live in crowded dormitories for a monthly salary of RMB600. If they hire workers in their 30s or older, that means dealing with families, housing and healthcare needs and, hence, higher cost. The poor working conditions have become a problem as the younger workers have moved up the education ladder. They are demanding higher pay, better employment terms and better working conditions.

China has also seen a sharp rise in the proportion of students going beyond the nine-year compulsory education ending in junior high school. This has important implications for the manufacturing sector, which relies heavily on junior high school graduates for its labour force. The more education people get, the less likely they will seek low-pay factory jobs. Instead, they are demanding higher wages and better working conditions. This also means the supply of unskilled labour has shrunk. Hence, labour costs are rising.

Until recently, Chinese factories have been spoiled by a seemingly endless supply of young rural workers. Many manufacturing regions have not seen wage increases for years. For example, the average monthly salary for an unskilled worker was about the same (RMB 600–RMB 700 range) at the end of 2004 as it was some eight years ago. This stagnation was made possible by low subsistence wages until recently. This subsistence wage is the migrant workers' income from farming, which represents the opportunity cost for them to move from the countryside to work in the cities. In other words, the subsistence wage represents the minimum for manufacturing wages because workers will not move from their farms to the factories if they cannot earn more than their farm income.

So if farm incomes are low or stagnant, there is no need for factory wages to rise to lure workers. And this was what happened. Between 1992 and 1996, Chinese farm incomes rose 150 per cent to RMB200 a month from RMB80. But then there was no growth in the following years. As of 2001, monthly rural incomes were still hovering at about RMB212, barely increased from the levels of five years ago. That was why the subsistence wage was low and also stagnant.

The farm sector suffered badly between 1996 and 2002, when China's economic growth fell sharply under former premier Zhu Rong-ji's austerity programme to fight inflation. Agricultural prices fell by an average of one third during that period, as a result of weak domestic demand and rising agricultural yields. But what was a disaster for the farm sector had turned out to be a big boon for the export manufacturers, who enjoyed a combination of rapid overseas, especially US, market growth and cheap wages at home.

Chinese farmers' fortunes have changed since 2002. Farm prices have recovered strongly since then, boosting farm income growth due to a sharp rise in grain prices and agricultural subsidies paid directly to farmers as well as the cut in agricultural taxes. In 2004, the government issued new rules to extend the duration of the land contract for farmers to improve incentive and productivity. Many migrant workers then left their city jobs and returned to their villages.

Farmers also got additional subsidies from the central government due to a grains supply shortage. Between 2002 and 2005, Beijing stepped up

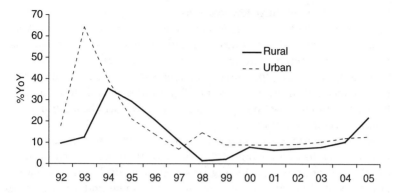

Figure 4.10 Urban and rural income growth
Source: CEIC

efforts to help farmers by cutting taxes and raising subsidies. This resulted in fast rural income growth, which has outpaced urban income growth since 2005 (Figure 4.10). All these factors have combined to boost farmers' subsistence wages, hence pushing up the wages of the city workers.

China used to be in a situation where there was essentially an unlimited supply of labour. In economics terms, China's labour supply curve was flat or perfectly elastic. This means that as factory and construction demand for workers rose, there was a seemingly infinite reserve of young rural workers willing to work at the prevailing wage. Not anymore; China's labour supply curve has turned into a normal upward-sloping one. This means rising wages are needed to lure more supply of labour. With rising farm prices and incomes, and a tighter supply of single, under-26-year-old workers, the marginal cost of hiring new young workers is rising.

Labour-intensive growth model maturing

The days of cheap wages and stagnant wage growth in China are probably gone for good. Farm prices are expected to have embarked on a secular upward-trend and labour market dynamics are pointing to a tightening supply of unskilled workers in the coming years. Many of the available unemployed and/or underemployed workers are older and have families. This means that they are not as readily or as cheaply mobile.

The inevitable upshot of rising labour cost will squeeze profit margins, but the short-term impact on China's competitiveness will still be limited. An increase in export-oriented manufacturing wages from US$80 a month to US$110 over the next few years, as seen by many observers, would not make a dent on China's cost advantage *vis-à-vis* other Asian economies such as India, Indonesia and Vietnam. Further, China has many other medium-term advantages, such as infrastructure support, huge domestic market potential, stable political climate and proximity to suppliers. But in the longer term, China will inevitably lose competitiveness to other low-end export economies. That will be a natural economic development process.

In the long term, these demographic and labour market trends suggest that China's low-cost labour-intensive growth model is maturing. A direct implication is that slowing, and eventually declining, population growth will drag on future growth. Many medium-term estimates assume a perfectly elastic (or horizontal) labour supply curve for China so that its labour-intensive growth model can be sustained without any frictions.

However, China's large pool of surplus labour is mostly unskilled and in the 35–59 age cohort. This sets apart China's future growth path from its experience in the past twenty years, when a seemingly unlimited supply of young and low-cost workers fuelled the boom in export manufacturing and urban services. An ageing population and short supply of young low-cost workers could cut China's trend-growth rate by 0.5 to 1 percentage point in the next decade.

From the demographic and labour market perspectives, there are two conflicting forces working in the system that make China's future growth path unclear. On one hand, a large part of the increase in productivity and output growth was due to gains from reallocation of labour over the past two decades, in the form of large inflows of rural workers into the urban areas. Hence, it is possible that as these labour flows slow down in the coming years, due to a shrinking pool of desirable young workers, the economic growth rate will fall.

On the other hand, there should be big growth gains from better capital allocation in the coming decade, as China further liberalizes and privatizes the economy and fixes banking problems. The ultimate upshot of China's future growth rate rests on the relative strength of these two forces, *ceteris paribus*. What is certain is that China has followed the growth development pattern of its Asian neighbours (Figure 4.11), with robust growth from a low base and eventually will move up the value chain on a slower growth trend.[8]

What this also means is that China's rapid trade expansion should be slowing down in the coming years. Chinese export growth has consistently outpaced the Asian region by an average of eight to ten percentage

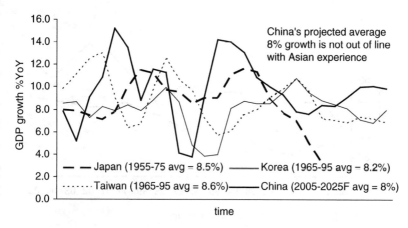

Figure 4.11 China's growth is not out of line
Source: CEIC

points since the early 1990s. That is mainly because of China's role as the primary base for low-cost outsourcing in labour-intensive goods, such as toys, textile, low-end electronics, assembly and appliances.

While the trend of outsourcing to Chinese factories will likely continue, the product mix will have to move to higher value-added goods as rising wage costs and a shrinking pool of young migrant labour take a toll in the low-end industries. Granted, this shift is probably still some years away, as China's comparative advantage in labour-intensive industries remains strong in the medium term. But China should be reacting to its demographic changes by moving into the higher-value and higher-tech industries, just as its Asian neighbours have done.

An ageing population also means less saving and more consumption in the economy. Indeed, cyclical, structural and political forces are converging to shift China's economic model towards consumption-driven (see Chapter 6 for more). Mainstream savings and consumption theories, such as the Permanent Income Hypothesis and the Life Cycle Hypothesis, suggest that consumers have a stable consumption pattern in their lifetime. They borrow to fund consumption when they are young, save when they are in their peak earnings years, and then draw down savings to fund consumption again during their old age. In theory, an ageing population with more pensioners should mean more consumption and less saving in future years.

As for China, the number of retirees is rising, but the number of children (and hence the young population) is falling for future years. These are

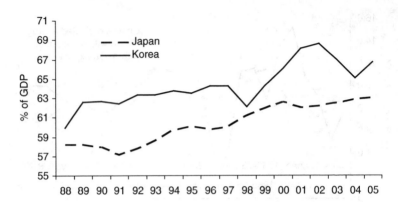

Figure 4.12   Japanese and Korean consumption
Source: CEIC

offsetting forces on consumption behaviour – more retirees will increase spending but fewer young people will reduce spending. With China's population average age rising from 33 years old now to 46 in 2050, it is arguable that China is moving into its peak saving years. This seems to suggest that Chinese consumption will fall.

However, if experience of other Asian countries is any guide, evidence seems to argue for higher Chinese consumption, despite the country moving into its prime saving years. Both Japan (with a median age of 43 years old) and Korea (median age of 35 years old), the two economies known to have an ageing population and moving into their prime saving years, have private consumption rising as a share of GDP (Figure 4.12). Their high consumption share (over two-thirds of the economy) should persist, or even rise further, as the ageing population effects become more pronounced in the coming decades.

Ageing, capital return and economic policy

Demographics are also posing daunting challenges to China's future growth dynamics in terms of investment returns, structural reform and economic policy. The cause–effect sequence runs as follows. Ageing population leads to a shrinking labour force, which reduces the marginal product of, and hence the return on, capital. Investment will thus fall due to lower return. This means a vicious chain effect – when labour falls, investment falls which, in turn, leads to decline in output and living standards.

The only way to keep or raise living standards on the back of an ageing population is to raise productivity. This needs fundamental structural reform. It also needs more capital formation. But capital formation will not rise unless capital return rises. This has an important policy implication. To raise the return on capital in the face of a shrinking labour force, China has to keep a loose monetary policy bias in the long term, as low interest rates are needed to stimulate investment. The government will also have to give tax incentives and improve technology to help enhance the return on capital in the long term.

These implications also apply to Europe whose population is also ageing. But they have even greater relevance to Japan, whose population started falling in 2006. Behind the BoJ's pledge to keep interest rates very low after it ended quantitative easing and ZIRP (or zero interest rate policy) in mid-2006, there was this tight demographic constraint on monetary policy. Meanwhile, Japan's acceleration of structural reforms since 2001 indeed reflects its vision to put in place long-term solutions to tackle the demographic challenge. The lesson for China is that with a proper response it can still enjoy sustainable growth even in the face of adverse demographics.

The impact on the economy, investment and living standards of an ageing population can be seen in the neoclassical Cobb-Douglas production function,[9] which states that output is a function of capital and labour inputs and technological changes. The first point to note is that as the population ages, the returns to different factors of production – land, labour and capital – will change. This is because the factors' relative scarcities will change. Secondly, the return on any factor of production is its marginal product, or the increment to output from an extra unit of that factor being added, holding the amount of all other production factors constant. The extra revenue added by an extra unit of capital is the return on capital.

The neoclassical school of economics argues that an ageing population should depress the return on capital. This is because, according to the structure of the classical production function, changes in the factors of production being used have feedback effect on each other. Labour is more productive when more capital is added, and capital is more productive when there is more labour. This is simply the flip side of the law of diminishing returns.[10] Thus, adding capital raises the marginal product of labour and hence the return on labour, which is wages. By the same token, adding labour raises the return on capital.

Here comes the problem with ageing population and a shrinking labour force. If adding labour will raise the return on capital, then lowering labour, as ageing population will do, will lower the return on capital. If the return on capital is lower, investment will fall and so will the capital stock. When both labour and capital fall, output falls too. In an ageing economy like China, where the labour force is shrinking faster than the population, the standard of living will inevitably fall. The chain effect becomes vicious – ageing population will lower the return on capital, which will lower the capital stock and lower the living standard, *ceteris paribus*.

However, the political economy school argues that things do not have to be so grim because other things are not constant. The government and society can respond to demographic changes to prevent the fall in living standards. The key is to raise productivity, so that the economy can produce at least the same amount with a smaller labour force. The political economists use the following simple relationship between output and inputs (capital and labour) to explain their argument.

Output (Y) can be expressed as $(Y/L) \times L$ (i.e. $Y = (Y/L) \times L$), where L is labour and Y/L becomes output per unit of labour input, or productivity, which depends largely on the capital stock. To relate this to the ageing population problem let us do the following. If P is population and if we divide both Y and L by P, the output/input relationship under the political economy school's interpretation then becomes $Y/P = (Y/L) \times L/P$. Y/P is just output per capita, but it is also a proxy for the standard of living. Y/L is productivity and L/P is the labour participation rate.

This simple mathematical manipulation has important meanings. It states that living standard (Y/P) is equal to productivity (Y/L) times the labour participation rate (L/P). The key point to note in this simple model is that the relationship between the labour force and the population is not stable. In fact, this is a major flaw in standard growth models, which usually assume the number of workers (in the labour force) equals the number of consumers (in the whole population). But this is simply not true.

With an ageing population, China's labour participation rate (L/P) is going to fall in the decades to come. To keep living standard (Y/P) constant, productivity (Y/L) must rise to offset the fall in labour participation. How can productivity rise? From an investment perspective, one way to do that is to raise the return on capital. This will increase capital formation to boost labour productivity and ultimately national output or GDP.[11]

Both the neoclassical and political economy schools of thought have relevance to economic policy tackling the ageing population problem.

An improvement in the technology level in the economy will raise returns on both labour and capital, as reflected in the neoclassical production function. Thus, government policies to enhance overall productivity will help keep the living standard, despite a shrinking labour force. Policies that favour the income distribution towards capital will also raise the return on capital, which will enhance capital formation and, in turn, raise labour productivity and output under the political economists' framework.

Granted, labour will lose out to capital in a relative sense under those capital-enhancing policies, as the share of income going to labour will be lower. But labour need not lose in an absolute sense. Since increasing the capital stock also raises the marginal product (or productivity) of labour, the return on labour (i.e. wages) should also go up. Thus, if the tilt of income distribution towards capital generates a large increase in the capital stock, wages will rise on balance. Note that technology advancement will also help boost wage growth.

Meanwhile, a shrinking economy and/or falling living standard will benefit no one. Thus, labour is better off with a smaller share of a bigger pie than with a larger share of a smaller pie, as the former could still be larger than the latter in absolute terms. This is especially true when the burden of sustaining an ageing population is considered. In an economic sense, growing the pie is Pareto-optimal,[12] as everyone benefits from a better reallocation of resources.

The private sector will not react to the problems of an ageing population by increasing investment because the marginal product of, or return on, capital falls in the first place when the labour force falls. Thus, the government needs to step in and change the incentives in the economy to allow capital deepening to occur. This is why the drive for structural reform is so crucial in an ageing society. The need to enhance the return on capital, so as to encourage capital deepening to raise productivity, indeed constrains China's monetary policy to a loose bias over the long term. This is because low and stable interest rates are needed to boost capital formation. Meanwhile, preferential tax policies for investment and structural policy to promote technological advancement can also boost investment in the long term.

Japan offers an example for China in terms of reactions to an ageing population. Japan's problem is more imminent than that in China, as its population started falling in 2006. Though slow, the Japanese government is reacting to the adverse demographic implications by creating better technology and tilting income distribution towards capital. It has changed the tax system in favour of investment with capital gains tax cuts, and more reliance on consumption tax to fund the government budget. It has also broken the barriers to reform and pushed structural changes to reduce economic distortions and enhance the productivity of the country. The implications for China are clear – these capital-deepening and productivity-enhancing measures will be able to deliver sustainable growth even in the face of adverse demographics.

5
Socio-economic Disintegration: Myth and Truth

China's future is doomed, according to those who see its social, economic and political structures coming apart at the seams.[1] Their logic is simple – China cannot, and does not know how to, handle its structural changes. This incompetence will manifest itself in rising unemployment, falling income growth and rampant corruption. Frustrated and deprived farmers and workers would be pulled together to rise against the state. Saddled with a huge financial burden from the bankrupted state-owned enterprises (SOEs), bad banks and a big fiscal black hole, the state would not be able to respond. Systemic disintegration would follow.

Admittedly, the critics rightly see many of China's socio-economic and political problems, and there are no arguments about the important details that they have pinpointed. There have been more mass protests in China recently, including strikes, demonstrations, sit-ins, traffic-blocking, building seizures and people taking to the streets.

Official data show that such 'large-size' incidents rose ten-fold to 870,000 cases in 2005 from a decade ago. Average group size in protests has also risen from fewer than ten in the mid 1990s to over fifty in recent days. In the first six months of 2005 alone, there were 350 large-scale protests, 17 of which involved more than 10,000 protestors, injuring almost 2,000 people, killing over 100 and inflicting RMB40 billion (US$5 billion) worth of economic losses in the country.

The problem with these bearish views is that they have concentrated mostly on yesterday's problems and failed to see the dynamics in the Chinese system. Even without the recent improvement, China's fiscal problem will not get out of hand. On the social unrest problem, the reported incidents, though more frequent and widespread, remain largely unorganized.

Many pessimists have also failed to see that these social tensions were cyclical, but not structural, in nature. This means that the system does not suffer from inherent social instability. The student demonstrations in the late 1980s and social upheavals in the 1990s were associated with periods of economic slowdown. This is a common phenomenon in tough times aggravating social and political pressures. There is no evidence of any organized national uprisings against the state.

Fiscal handicap aggravating social problems?

Some pessimists argue that the Chinese government was in big financial trouble, as falling revenues, rising public spending, soaring unemployment, unpaid pensions and bad banks would force a fiscal breakdown. These will also bring social tensions to the boil and eventually cause economic disintegration. Since everything boils down to money, let us deal with the fiscal issue first. There is no doubt that the worry about China's fiscal problem is real. But to see it as likely to explode and bring down the country is an exaggeration.

The volatile economic conditions in the 1990s seemed to underscore this extreme bearish view of China's future. The combination of a sharp economic slowdown and fundamental restructuring under Beijing's economic reform had shrunk government revenues sharply. Meanwhile, the push to jump-start the economy and boost infrastructure programmes had pushed state spending through the roof. The result was rising public debt issuance and a 3.6-fold jump in the fiscal deficit between 1990 and 2002, when the deficit peaked (Figure 5.1).

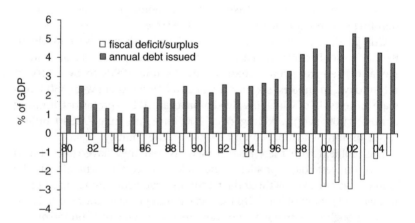

Figure 5.1   Rising fiscal deficit and public debt
Source: CEIC

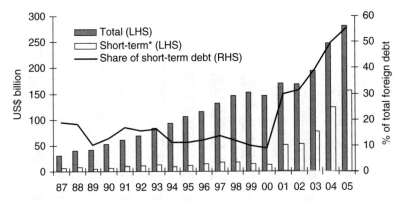

Figure 5.2 Foreign debt trend worsening
* 1 year or less in maturity
Source: CEIC

Sceptics also have the external debt picture to worry about. China's external debt has not only risen over time, suggesting that the Chinese economy is increasingly relying on external funding. Its short-term debt portion has also risen sharply to over half from less than 20 per cent in the late 1980s (Figure 5.2), raising fears that China's foreign debt structure has become unstable and subject to fickle foreign sentiment. Further, there is a hidden debt that adds to the fiscal stress. In recently years, Chinese officials have been reporting about US$20 billion a year less in short-term foreign borrowing than recorded in the data from the Bank for International Settlements. Even allowing for the usual sloppiness in China's statistics, this discrepancy suggests a large amount of unauthorized borrowing by Chinese companies. Lastly, there is a huge contingent liability stemming from the shortfall in social security funds for the unemployed and pensioners. This shortfall amounts to RMB4–7 trillion (US$480–US$850 billion), or 45–75 per cent of GDP, according to various estimates.

More troubling is the Chinese authorities' complacency towards the fiscal deficit, as signalled by Beijing's willingness to tolerate a rising budget deficit in a robust economy between the late 1990s and early 2000s. This raises doubts about Beijing's commitment to fiscal prudence. The concern is that if the government finds it acceptable to run a large fiscal deficit at a time when the economy is growing at 8 per cent a year, it is hardly likely to have the will to rein in spending during periods of slower growth. That raises the spectre of public spending spiralling out of control.

Official data show that spending amounted to RMB1.9 trillion (or 17 per cent of GDP) in 2001, up from RMB682 billion (or 11.2 per cent of GDP)

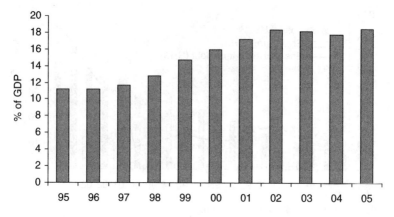

Figure 5.3   Government spending to GDP ratio
Source: CEIC

in 1995. That was supposedly all in the name of salvaging the economy after the Asian crisis and the bursting of the global technology bubble. But no one knows for sure if that was the real reason or if the bureaucrats were just caught up in a habit of runaway spending. Indeed, government spending remained large, at over 18 per cent of GDP since 2001 (Figure 5.3). What is certain is that without spending controls, any tax reforms aimed at boosting fiscal revenues are not enough to solve the deficit problem.

The potential of this developing into a fiscal crisis is well illustrated by Argentina's descent from boom to bust in the 1990s. Like China today, Argentina was a model reformer in the 1990s, and the darling of international investors. It boosted growth by fiscal expansion, attracted massive capital inflow and eliminated foreign exchange risk by pegging its currency to the US dollar. But it differed from China by borrowing even more heavily from foreign countries to fund local economic expansion. This made Argentina vulnerable to financial shocks when there was a fall in the foreign appetite for Argentine investments.

That was exactly what happened in 1999 and early 2000, when international money managers made a last dash into the US stock market, causing a sharp drop in the capital available to Argentina and other emerging markets. As the country struggled to keep its foreign funding, interest rates soared, crushing the economy under a huge mountain of debt. The government's attempt to regain investor confidence by implementing a series of fiscal and regulatory reforms came too late. The

Argentine economy collapsed in December 2001, when the government defaulted and abandoned the currency board system.

The Argentine experience is a relevant lesson for China. It shows that overall capital flow to developing economies is primarily determined by global liquidity. But a country's economic performance can affect what share of this capital flow it gets. Since China is getting the bulk of foreign capital flowing into Asia, its ability to sustain investor confidence is crucial. As and when the flow of international capital tightens again, China's fiscal and debt conditions will come under international scrutiny. Though its huge foreign reserves and still low external debt mean that China is still a long way from catching the Argentine disease, there is good cause to be concerned about the potential for crisis should the fundamentals worsen in China.

In the coming years, China will be further opening up her domestic markets and financial system to foreign competition under the WTO requirements. Together with the public spending programmes that are at the heart of Beijing's growth and bank bailout strategies, it is almost certain that domestic and external debt levels will rise further. A more open economy will not only ease the way for capital flight if investors lose confidence but it will also make China more likely to be adversely affected by any unfavourable changes in the international financial environment.

The fiscal risk is there, but it should not be exaggerated. Fiscal revenue growth has improved steadily since the late 1990s (Figure 5.4) following the government's application of the new VAT and income tax laws, and

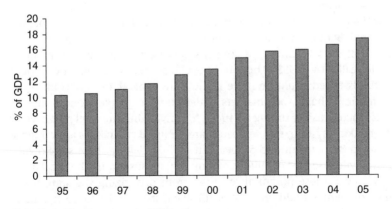

Figure 5.4 Fiscal revenue to GDP ratio

Source: CEIC

as the economy recovered from the shocks of domestic policy tightening and regional crisis between 1994 and 1998. Fiscal revenues rose to 17 per cent of GDP in 2005 from just 10 per cent in 1995. Reflecting this improvement was a decline in the fiscal deficit since 2002 (see Figure 5.1 above). Moreover, the growth of public debt has tapered off since 2002 (also see Figure 5.1 above), and China's total public debt has never got close to the critical threshold of 50 per cent of GDP that would raise concerns among the international community.

China's structural ability to contain its fiscal risk also remains strong in the short term. The country's US$300 billion foreign debt is only about a third of its US$1 trillion strong foreign reserves. Total short-term foreign debt, maturing in less than a year, is only about 17 per cent of the foreign exchange reserves. This means that the Chinese system is not held hostage by the foreign creditors – even they demand immediate repayment, China has more than enough reserves to honour all of its foreign debt obligations.

There are also ample funds available in the form of household savings sitting idle in the banking system. They amount to over US$2 trillion and will continue to grow as long as there is a lack of alternative investments. The bad-debt-burdened state banks are under pressure to repair their balance sheets. So they are wary of using the deposits to make fresh loans. This means that Beijing could easily tap into this big pool of savings by issuing treasury bonds to the public and the banks, and use the proceeds to boost economic growth, recapitalize the banking system and dispel social grievances. Given the low level of public debt (at about 17 per cent of GDP in 2005), it can easily finance spending through borrowing for some years.

If the potential revenues from privatizing the Big Four state banks are counted, Beijing's finances look even better. Some market estimates suggest that sales in Chinese state bank stakes after they are recapitalized could realize over US$50 billion (or over 2 per cent of GDP). The amount of funds raised could be more if the state bank shares are sold in the domestic A-share stock markets under buoyant market conditions. So, other factors aside, timing is crucial for privatizing the Big Four. Beyond the banking system, state-owned shares of listed companies are valued at between 30 per cent and 50 per cent of GDP. Selling these state-owned shares will raise tens of billions of renminbi for sustaining the fiscal book.

However, these potential revenues from privatizing the state banks and companies could prove to be illusive if structural reforms fail. More crucially, looking deeper into the situation reveals a serious fiscal financing gap in the medium term. The official debt and budget data do not include Beijing's contingent liabilities – costs that are not debt and expenses now but could become so in the future. These include RMB270 billion special bonds issued in 1998 to recapitalize the Big Four, RMB1 trillion in bonds issued by the four asset management companies, or AMCs (guaranteed by the Ministry of Finance), to fund the purchase of bad debts from the banks, and a further RMB1.8 trillion in bad debts which they are still owed.

In a nutshell, China's fiscal situation is not ideal. The pessimists may have been overly bearish but the fiscal problem is a valid concern and the Middle Kingdom is facing a potential risk of a fiscal bust in the longer term if the government sits on its hands over the problem. But this outcome is not unavoidable and the authorities are not sitting on their hands.

A clear resolve to tackle the country's fiscal difficulties will help China to avoid suffering a fate similar to Argentina's. Beijing must pursue a two-pronged approach to both raise fiscal revenues and cut wasteful spending. Fiscal reform is part of the structural reform programme for dispelling any misunderstanding about the government's policy direction and avoiding the socio-economic disintegration that some die-hard pessimists are seeing.

Unemployment is not the real problem

Now let us turn to the structural side of social tension. Rising unemployment is commonly cited by the crisis-mongers as a fertile ground for China's social problems to grow out of hand. Indeed, official data show that China's registered jobless rate has risen steadily since economic reform started (Figure 5.5). There were over 8.4 million registered unemployed in mid 2006, up 32 per cent from mid 2001.

Some private sector analysts argue that the official jobless rate was deceiving, and that the actual unemployment was much higher at some 25 per cent–30 per cent of the workforce. This would imply that close to 100 million people, or almost 10 per cent of the whole population, were out of work. Indeed, the volatile economic conditions in the 1990s and early 2000s seemed to reflect the Chinese authorities' inability to handle the structural changes and resultant rise in unemployment. If this situation is true and continues, it will only create an ever-increasing amount of social problems.

A deeper look at China's employment and demographic trends suggests that this bearish argument does not stand up to scrutiny. The official jobless rate does underestimate the unemployment situation, but the 25 per cent–30 per cent jobless rate overstates it. The official data problem stems from China's lack of a proper bankruptcy law. China's

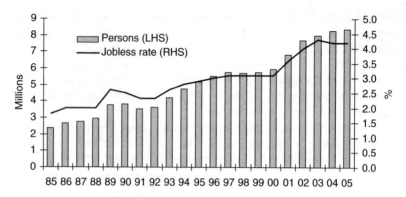

Figure 5.5   Urban unemployment
Source: CEIC

registered jobless rate only covers the urban residents who have registered for unemployment at job centres where they can get new job information and some training benefits. It does not include those state-owned enterprise (SOE) workers who were laid off during the industrial restructuring process. They totalled about 30 million between the late 1990s and early 2000s.

These workers were never included in the official jobless data because they were never formally classified as unemployed. Without a functioning bankruptcy law for the SOEs, state workers were kept on the books of the defunct companies and got a subsistence wage from the state. By the state's definition, these workers had only 'left their job units', or *xia gang*. Unfortunately, there is no reliable data for the number of *xia gang* workers. Perhaps a proxy for it is the difference between the economically active population and official employment. These data are available from the official and census records. By this estimate, the number of *xia gang* workers stood at 13.8 million in 2005. Adding this to the 8.4 million of registered unemployed worker brings the adjusted unemployment to 22.2 million in 2005, or 11.1 per cent of the urban workforce. This was more than double the official jobless rate of 4.2 per cent.

Adjusting for the *xia gang* workers gives a more realistic jobless picture of China (Figure 5.6). The underlying jobless rate is probably above 10 per cent, but unlikely to be as high as 25 per cent–30 per cent. The important point here is that, despite adding the *xia gang* workers, the adjusted jobless rate peaked between 2000 and 2003, and has been falling since then. The turn of the jobless trend after a 15-year increase suggests that more jobs had been created to absorb the surplus labour as the economic

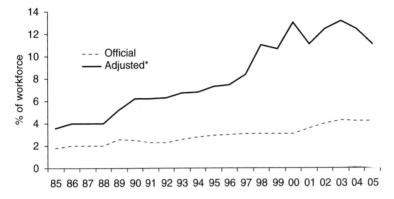

Figure 5.6 China's realistic jobless rate
Source: CEIC

restructuring process deepened. The cyclical recovery of the economy, which bottomed in 1998–99, had also had a more pronounced impact on lowering unemployment as the underlying structural framework improved.

The improvement in the labour market is reflected by urban real wage growth, which has risen strongly, averaging over 10 per cent a year in 2004 and 2005. All this underscores the cyclical nature of China's social discontent, which rose during periods of economic slowdown and falling income, as in the late 1980s and late 1990s, but subsided during economic recovery periods (Figure 5.7). The current trends show the underlying force for stirring social troubles is in fact easing, not intensifying, in the coming years.

If unemployment were a fertile ground for brewing social problems, there should be slum areas scattered all around China's big cities. But this is not the case. The city environment in Beijing and Shanghai is in sharp contrast to cities like Mumbai, Mexico City, Jakarta and Lagos (in Nigeria), where persistent social unrest is well known to visitors. While there is uncontrolled growth of slum areas within these other cities, with millions of destitute and marginalized people living in informal housing with no access to daily utilities and sewerage, there is an apparent lack of slums in China's major cities. What Beijing and Shanghai have are flourishing city centres leading to orderly, though not necessarily affluent, residential areas which then fade out into farmland.

Cynics say that the Chinese authorities just suppress the slums through onerous local registration requirements and restrictions on mobility so

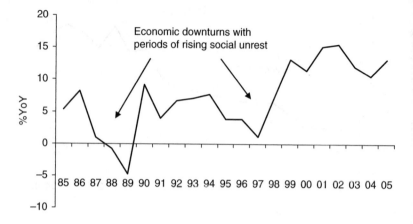

Figure 5.7   Real urban wage growth
Source: CEIC

that the rural poor just cannot simply move into the cities as they want. While this is plausible, government restrictions do not effectively stamp out slums if the economic situation is really bad. After all, China's rural population is not that immobile. Despite the official constraints, there are over 100 million migrant workers from the farms working in the cities and towns. Many other countries have also tried similar stringent constraints to bar rural–urban migration, but they do not work. Slums are pretty much a common scene in almost all large cities in the developing world.

So what is behind the lack of slums in China that makes its socio-economic system more stable, despite the thorny unemployment problem? Income growth has been a fundamental stabilizer for the Chinese society. After two decades of rapid growth, China's per capita GDP is much higher than those slum-plagued cities in the developing world mentioned above, except in Mexico. But Mexico has a more serious income inequality problem[2] than China (Table 5.1).

More importantly, China's migrants do not just move to the cities and idle about. They are working migrants. China's structural reform has led to a booming non-state sector creating millions of new manufacturing and services jobs that attract surplus workers from the farms. Hence, China's rural migrants move off their farms to be employed by the factories in the cities and towns. This is quite different from the rural migrants in many other emerging economies, who move to the cities which then cannot generate enough jobs to absorb them into the community. This cohort of unemployed thus becomes the natural source of social tension.

Table 5.1 Per capita GDP*

	(US$ per year)	Gini coefficient
Mexico	10,186	54.6
Nigeria	1,188	50.6
China	7,204	44.7
Indonesia	4,458	34.3
India	3,344	32.5

(China is either richer or has lower income
inequality than other countries; slum problem is absent
in China.)

* On purchasing power parity basis
Sources: International Monetary Fund (2006), Wikipedia

A big problem with many developing economies is that their farmers are being forced off their land by political and interest groups, or by unfair land distribution that makes some farmers unable to make a living. Thus, millions of rural residents just venture into the cities to try their luck. If they cannot find jobs, they should return home. But they have no farms to go back to. China is different again in this respect in that its equitable land distribution has helped keep farmers at home. The breaking up of the collective farms in the 1980s and the improvement in rural land-use rights in the 1990s and in recent years did just that. By giving every family a claim on agricultural land, it allows underemployed labour at least to make a subsistence living from farming.

Yes, there are incentive problems with implementing rural reform (see Chapter 1, p. 36),but they mainly deter Chinese farmers from making long-term investments rather than barring them from making a living. China's half-baked rural reform has helped keep its rural population from just packing up and flooding into the cities. The stable land claim has even attracted many rural migrants back home after some years of work (and saving) in the cities. Gradual improvement in the rural reform process will make the farmers better off in the long-term, and thus ease the problem of massive migration to the cities. All this compares favourably to the mass of rural dispossessed in many other developing economies.

Last but not least, China's demographics will help prevent its unemployment from swelling through a rising rural population. The average rural family in China has 1.5 children, due to the population control policy established since the 1970s. This compares favourably with many other developing economies, where every family has at least three children. China's rural population is shrinking over time, and its smaller family size makes the 'feeding' problem more manageable than for many of its developing neighbours.

Further, the large number of Chinese rural migrants actually returning to their rural homes because of the stable land claim, is in stark contrast with the situation in most emerging economies, where the rural population flows into the cities and never leaves. In China, there is significant two-way traffic. This does not mean that all rural migrants go back home in their 30s, when they are no longer wanted by the factories. However, many of them find that while their savings from working in the cities do not add up to much in the cities, they are a fortune back in the countryside. So many just take their savings, return to their villages and start a family.

What about the farmers?

Arguably, the biggest source of China's social problems lies in the rural sector, where 800 million rural residents are facing stagnant income growth, high taxes and a rising wealth gap. The volatile growth conditions in the 1990s coupled with intensifying industrial restructuring indeed created rising rural discontent, especially in the late 1990s and early 2000s. A simple extrapolation of this trend, as made by many critics, easily leads to the conclusion there will be an eventual day of reckoning when the rural economy will break down, creating a huge flow of poor and angry migrants flooding into the cities and causing social and economic disintegration.

Keeping socio-economic stability among its 800 million-strong rural population is a daunting challenge for the Chinese authorities. The widening income gap between rural and urban earnings has created a sense of inequality and acted to disrupt social harmony. Rural income averages no more than 38 per cent of urban income since 1992 (Figure 5.8). In 2005, Chinese farm income averaged RMB3,900 per head per year, only about 37 per cent of urban income of RMB10,500.

Moreover, the rural–urban income gap has been rising over time. In 1990, per capita farm income was close to half of that in the cities. It fell to about 40 per cent in 1997 and 37 per cent in 2005. Both rural and urban income growth fell sharply between 1994 and 1997, when Beijing cracked down on the runaway economy. But falling agricultural prices between 1997 and 2002 had damaged farm income growth further in the subsequent years, dragging its average growth rate down to 5 per cent a year versus 8.4 per cent of urban income growth (Figure 5.9).

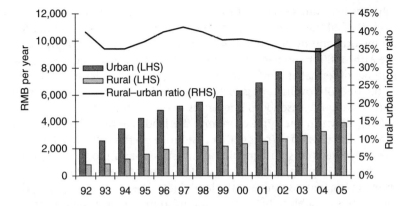

Figure 5.8 Rural–urban income divide
Source: CEIC

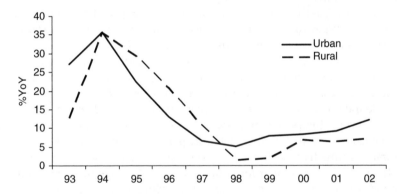

Figure 5.9 Rural and urban income growth
Source: CEIC

The dismantling of state social services in the 1980s and 1990s also made the rural households worse off, intensifying their feeling of being left behind by economic progress. A worsening fiscal deficit had forced the central government to cut spending, including those on free public medical and educational services in the rural areas. For example, between 1980 and 2005, the government budget for health and medical costs fell from 36 per cent of total spending to about 15 per cent.

In addition to the cut in central funding, the cash-strapped local authorities also squeezed the farmers in its financing of various spending. The share of medical cost financed through enterprise-run health insurance schemes fell from 43 per cent to 25 per cent in the 15 years to 2005. As a result of all these cut-backs, an average patient's out-of-pocket burden on medical and health costs rose from 20 per cent of total spending in the early 1980s to 60 per cent in 2005. There was also a sharp rise in the number of formal and informal rural taxes, fees and levies in the 1990s. At the time of slow income growth, this withdrawal of social service support acted to increase social grievances in the countryside.

Deep down in the rural economy, the land tenure problem created more social tension. When China first broke up the collective farms in the early 1980s to spur agricultural investment and productivity, each family was given a plot of land with a long-term (15-year) lease. But they were never given assurance of the land rights. Despite the long lease, the land was still subject to sudden administrative redistribution by the local officials. This uncertainty about ownership only deterred farmers from making long-term investment and defeated the original purpose of breaking up the collective farms.

Worst of all, as the Chinese manufacturing and property boom got under way in the 1990s, many local governments confiscated land from the farmers without reasonable, or even any, compensation. Hence, throughout the 1990s when China's export manufacturing was building up a critical mass, the rural community was left behind with sluggish income growth, a shrinking social safety net and rising social tensions.[3] Such an environment would indeed be conducive to socio-economic upheavals down the road.

However, China's economic dynamics for the rural population have changed for the better since 2003. In particular, Chinese farmers and rural migrants have seen big improvements in their economic fortune. These changes are secular in nature. They should make the rural livelihood better in the coming decades, thus containing the risk of social unrest. The rising wealth gap will remain a challenge facing the Chinese authorities and socio-economic issues could become the Achilles heel for China's growth if they are mishandled. But their medium-term risk should not be exaggerated.

Rural earnings have turned around. These include farm income and migrant wages. After falling for many years, grain and many agriculture prices surged in 2003 and 2004. By mid 2004, farm prices exceeded the 1997 level. This underscored the sharp rural income growth since 2004, when it outpaced urban income growth by a big margin (Figure 5.10). Granted, a cyclical fall in farm income growth would bring back much hard feeling and social grievances. But there are reasons to believe that this rural earnings recovery is more than just a cyclical improvement, as secular forces are unfolding to raise farm income on a long-term basis.

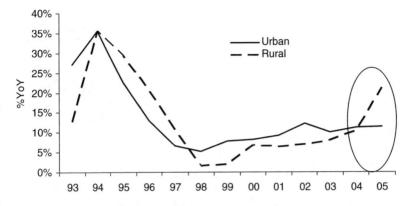

Figure 5.10 Rural income growth recovery
Source: CEIC

Falling supply of agricultural land on the back of rising demand for better-quality farm products forms the fundamental basis for a secular improvement in farm income. Despite its huge land mass, China has one of the lowest ratios of arable land to total land area of any major country. This limited arable land stock has been shrinking due to industrialization, which competes with agricultural demand for land use. With exports growing at an average rate of 28 per cent year on year since the late 1990s, manufacturing has grown in leaps and bounds, intensifying the land demand competition.

Meanwhile, housing reform, urbanization and financial liberalization, which boost property demand and landownership, have led to a residential construction boom since 1998. This has added to the industrial demand for land, thus intensifying the competition for land use on the back of a limited stock of arable land. As a result, China has seen a sustained drop in sown acreage since the late 1990s (Figure 5.11). The small rise in agricultural land use in 2004 was temporary, due to a moratorium on land conversion and official subsidies aimed at pushing grain production to help the farmers. With commercial and residential demand for land continually rising, the supply of arable land is expected to continue to fall in the coming years.

Meanwhile, the shift in China's food demand pattern will boost future farm prices, and hence farm income. As China gets richer, the share of food spending in total urban consumption falls.[4] But as overall income rises rapidly, the food consumption pattern has also shifted towards higher-calorie food products, such as meat and dairy products, and

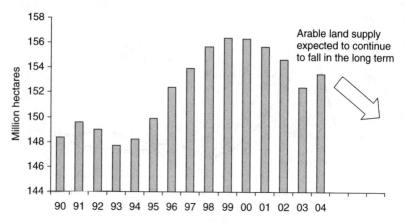

Figure 5.11   Sown area dropping
Source: CEIC

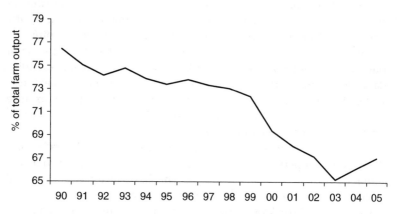

Figure 5.12   Share of grain output
Source: CEIC

processed foodstuffs such as snack items and fast food. This also means a rise in the derived demand for foodgrains and cooking oils.

An arable land supply squeeze combined with a demand shift towards higher-value food products has also prompted a shift in agricultural production pattern. There has been a marked shift away from land-intensive low value-added activities, such as grain production, to higher value-added activities, such as animal husbandry, dairy farming, and fruit and vegetables (Figure 5.12 and Table 5.2).

Table 5.2 China's agricultural output growth (2000–2005)

Milk	211.7%
Fruit	40.9%
Corn	31.5%
Cotton	29.4%
Sugarcane	26.9%
Meat	26.4%
Rapeseeds	23.4%
Vegetables	16.3%
Beans	7.4%
Wheat	−2.2%
Rice	−3.3%

Production has shifted to focus on less land-intensive and higher value-added products

Source: CIEC

The government's measures to raise grain production in 2004 and 2005 (as seen in the rise in grain output share in Figure 5.12) through high subsidies and restriction on land conversion were a short-term policy to boost farm income after years of sluggish growth. It is unlikely to reverse the secular market forces of falling arable land supply, falling grain output and rising demand for better-quality foods. These trends will continue to boost farm produce prices and rural income in the years to come.

Government policy also helps improve farm income. Since 2003 when Beijing started to push rural consumption as part of the policy shift towards boosting domestic consumption to replace investment and exports as the key economic growth driver, it has been cutting farm taxes. Fiscal revenue growth has also been rising in recent years, enabling the government to cut taxes and increase rural infrastructure spending to boost rural income. With farm income poised to embark on a secular ascent, this policy shift should help reverse the farmers' feeling of being left out in the economic expansion and thus ease the threat of rising social grievances.

The government has also acted on solving the land tenure problem, though more work still needs to be done. In 1998, it started granting 30-year leases to farmers to replace the original shorter (15-year) leases. In 2003, it enacted the Rural Land Contracting Law to provide more secure tenure arrangements for farmers, to bar local officials from redistributing farm land arbitrarily and to allow farmers to trade their land rights.

Though implementation of these laws is not trouble-free, with violation by local authorities still common, the move shows that Beijing is not sitting on its hands. The implementation problem is largely a legacy of

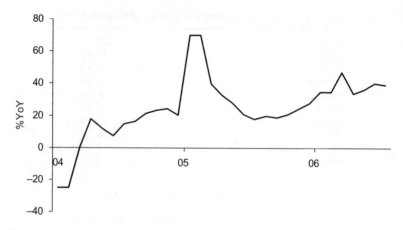

Figure 5.13   Farm sector investment*
* Farming, forestry and animal husbandry
Source: CEIC

the old Marxist attitudes (see Chapter 1, p. 26) but not the result of lack of reform resolve, as some critics argue. Despite their insufficiency, the government's initiatives have achieved some of the intended effect on stimulating agricultural investment (Figure 5.13) on the back of rising food prices and farm income. Farming, forestry and animal husbandry investments rose by an annual average rate of 40 per cent in 2006, after rising 32 per cent in 2005 and only 8 per cent in 2004.

Sceptics would argue that the hundreds of millions of migrant workers who left their farms to seek work in the cities could become a catalyst for social unrest. They are known to have been exploited, underpaid or even unpaid after months of hard work. While the government will have to act to protect human rights, demographic trends suggest that the wages for the migrant workers can only go up in the coming years. From the pay perspective, this source of social discontent should be contained.

Studies show that most light manufacturers hire only young women workers between 18 and 26 years old. Even heavy work, such as construction, also only hires young, unmarried workers under 30 years old. China may have 200 million 'surplus' rural workers, but not all of them are in the age range of 15 to 29 years old. The rural working population in this young age cohort is about 185 million. But some 100 million are already engaged in factory work, mostly as migrant workers in the cities and towns. Much of the remainder could be actively working in the fields, studying, caring for the elderly and parents, and so on.

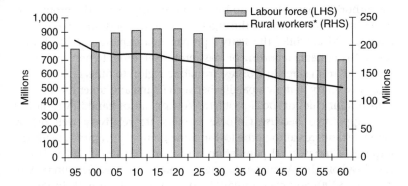

Figure 5.14 Labour force and young workers
* 15–29 years old
Sources: CEIC, UNPD

Hence, the supply of young, preferred, employable workers is very limited as compared with the huge demand. More importantly, the supply of these workers in the 15 to 29 age group is falling (Figure 5.14), according to the United National Population Division (UNPD) projection. This will create a supply squeeze in the coming years, even before the labour force hits its peak. Most of the growth in the labour force will come from the older (over 30 years old) workers as the baby boom generation makes it way through the age brackets.

These demographic trends show that Chinese manufacturers and services providers are going to face a shortage of young, preferred, employable workers in the long term, despite the massive population. This means wages are going to rise persistently for the workers, regardless of whether they are migrant workers or not.

Indeed, migrant workers' wages are already on the rise. Data from the Ministry of Labour show that the marginal wage for new migrant workers has risen since 2004, from RMB600 a month to RMB900. This rising trend is going to be sustained, as companies will have no choice but to pay more and improve workers' benefits for hiring and retaining them. This means that the livelihood of rural migrant labour will continue to improve.

Overall, Beijing is well aware of the challenges posed by social unrest, especially in rural areas. It has been using a carrot-and-stick approach to handle the issues. Sometimes, it allows moderate levels of discontent to be aired by adopting a somewhat permissive and sophisticated strategy. On some occasions, senior leaders even sided with the protestors to show sympathy and support.[5] But in other more troubling and persistent cases, the authorities have shown no hesitation in suppressing the protests by mediating with or arresting the organizers and key personnel behind the incidents. Meanwhile, the Party's propaganda department has kept a tight grip on media reporting of mass protests in order to prevent 'media contagion' from spreading unrest from one region to others.

Those who try to draw a parallel between China and other low-income countries for clues of social problems getting out of hand in China will be disappointed because Chinese farmers are relatively well off by regional standards among the low-income group. Per capita agricultural output of China's rural population was about US$400 in 2005. This is way ahead of other Asian developing economies, such as Vietnam ($195), Pakistan ($290) and even India ($215), and is on a par with Indonesia and the Philippines.

More importantly, China has a more equitable land distribution system than many of the developing economies, and this helps keep Chinese farmers happier than their counterparts in the other developing countries. As a result of the break-up of the collective farms in the 1980s, each Chinese rural family was given an average of half a hectare of land with a 30-year lease, despite the implementation problems. Production quotas and most of the controls on agricultural prices were scrapped. Each family farm has been functioning as a private business, producing according to market demand conditions and keeping its earnings. China's state farms now account for less than 3 per cent of agricultural output. The fact that almost every family in China has their own plot of land stands in sharp contrast to the common pattern of landless peasantry in the developing world. In Asia, only Vietnam has a similar equitable land distribution pattern.

China has over 100 million rural migrants working in manufacturing, construction or services industries in cities and towns. This group of working migrants is much bigger both in relative and absolute terms than in other developing regional economies. Just as overseas remittances help stabilize and contribute to the Filipino economy, income transfers from the cities give a boost to China's farm sector and help stabilize the socio-economic framework.

A melting pot for corruption

Last but not least, the corruption problem in China could still be the straw that breaks the camel's back. Corruption acts to worsen unequal distribution of wealth and disrupt social harmony by raising social discontent. In an economy like China, where the state still dominates the resources allocation and decision-making process, it should not be surprising that corruption remains part of daily life.

China's corruption problem seems to be getting worse by the day, as an increasing number of high-profile corruption crimes have been busted and reported in recent years. Since 1998, for example, China's courts have reported an average of some 35,000 corruption crimes a year, with annual fines and recovered losses amounting to over RMB4 billion. These were up sharply from the early 1990s, when the average number of corruption cases reported were only in thousands and the amount of funds involved was much smaller. Cynics argue that the reported cases were just the tip of an iceberg.

The central authorities seem to be stepping up their anti-corruption efforts in recent years. In the 18 months between 2005 and mid 2006, the Chinese Communist Party held a three-phase internal education programme involving 70 million Party members, the largest such programme in the Party history, to re-educate them about member duties and corruption. Beijing has also made it clear that the fight against corruption is not only about what kind of party the members want to build, but also about the Communist Party's survival and its continued dominance.

The anti-corruption campaign has intensified since 2004, with investigations into Party officials' behaviour and commercial cases being stepped up. In 2004 alone, the Central Discipline Inspection Commission handled close to 170,000 corruption crimes and penalized – jailed or even handed down death sentences – over 170,000 Party members, including many senior provincial and ministerial officials. Even the judicial officials could not escape the purge. Hundreds of judges were convicted for corruption that year. Commercial crime was also being addressed with increased urgency. Hundreds of thousands of employees, branch managers and heads of departments of financial and commercial institutions were punished for fraud, fund embezzlement and other corruption-related crimes.

In 2006, the authorities reported more high-profile anti-corruption cases as a means of showing their resolve to 'clean up' the Party. Many high-profile cases were reported even in the international media. Severe punishment terms were handed down to those convicted senior officials at that time, including two Beijing vice mayors, a deputy commander of the naval forces and a deputy director of a provincial railway bureau (For example, see *Far Eastern Economic Review* (2006), *The Economist* (2006) and *South China Morning Post* (2006).) In June 2006, an audit of the Agricultural Bank of China uncovered US$6.45 billion in irregularities, leading to the firing of 64 employees and disciplinary action against more than 1,300. Over US$1 billion was involved in the bank's serious criminal cases and US$3.5 billion in irregular loans.

On a positive note, the recent sharp increase in the reports on corruption crimes reflects an improved legal system and media freedom in China. In the 1980s China's legal system was so inadequate that it was virtually unrecognizable to any visitors from the developed world. The inadequacy of the system and the ignorance of the people had combined to make it implausible for the average Chinese citizen to press charges when abuses occurred. However, the legal framework for civil and commercial law has improved leaps and bounds through the years, though the work of legal and institutional reform is far from over.

Meanwhile, China's media is getting more freedom and becoming more aggressive in reporting corruption crimes and official scandals, while the public is exposed to these reports via various media reports and the internet. The result of these changes is clear: a better legal system, improved public confidence in individual rights, and repeated anti-corruption campaigns driven by the top authorities all add up to a sharp rise in the official cases and public reporting.

Although judicial reform has been taking place alongside the anti-corruption drives, its impact on the system is still limited. More generally, political reform to boost government transparency, upholding the rule of law and ensuring an independent judiciary and free press will go a long way to reducing corruption. However, all this will remain largely ineffective in the Chinese system in the short term because its hybrid (state–market) economic nature makes the environment a perfect melting pot for corruption. The trouble is that the state sector is the fundamental source for corruption while the private sector is a dominant force allowing corruption to persist. How so?

Contrast a highly competitive business with a state-sector business. It is difficult to find much corruption in the business of a manufacturer who makes shoes, toys, television or any light consumer goods for export. If there is any at all, it will be very slight. Credit this to market forces. There is no room for corruption in a highly competitive business, where cut-throat competition wears profit down to the bone. Under-the-table payments go into raising the cost of goods. That means inefficient pricing, cutting into the profit margin and risking the firm's going out of business.

However, corruption is commonly found at the other end of the scale – public works. And this is not unique to China, but is found all over the world. The culprit for that is the lack of competition within public works.

Table 5.3 Bribery in business sectors

Survey question: how likely is it that senior officials in this country would demand or accept bribes, e.g. for public tenders, licensing in the following business sectors?

Business sector	Score
Public works/construction	1.3
Arms and defence	1.9
Oil and gas	2.7
Heavy manufacturing	4.5
banking and finance	4.7
Civilian aerospace	4.9
Real estate	3.5
Telecoms	3.7
Power generation/transmission	3.7
Mining	4
Transportation/storage	4.3
Pharmaceuticals/medical care	4.3
Forestry	5.1
IT	5.1
Fishery	5.9
Light manufacturing	5.9
Agriculture	5.9

A score ranges from 0 to 10, where 0 represents very high perceived levels of corruption, and 10 refers to extremely low perceived levels of corruption

Source: Transparency International

For example, when a government department puts out a road-building project for public tender, the government is a monopsony,[6] or a single buyer. This monopsonistic power allows the officials in charge of the project to engage in rent seeking – in the form of bribery here – to profit themselves from the tendering process. For those companies which are bidding for the project, they do not go out of business if they pay a bribe because they could recoup the bribery cost by charging it to the public purse. There is insufficient competitive pressure in the public works business to discourage the bribery incentive.

In fact, this is what the survey by the international corruption watchdog Transparency International found.[7] It showed that public works was the most corrupt business sector around the world and light manufacturing goods the least corrupt business (Table 5.3). The bottom line is that corruption is predominantly a public-sector phenomenon. It impinges on the private sector because it is mostly the private sector that pays the bribe while the public sector takes it. The lack of competition in public works just facilitates bribery. Thus, corruption arises mostly when the private sector is involved in public-sector projects or when public officials intervene in the workings of a private-sector market.

Granted, it is often private-sector businessmen who offer to pay the bribes. But they only do so because they believe they cannot win public works contracts without bribing the officials and because they know they can recoup the bribery cost in the contract payment they charge. While that makes them as guilty of corruption as the public officials, the fact remains that corruption can only exist in the first place because the public purse has loose strings. Public officials know they can take advantage of the situation to make the private sector enrich them. More fundamentally, corruption exists because there is not enough competitive pressure on constraining bribery behaviour in the private sector.

Thus, corruption in any economic sector exists in inverse proportion to competition in that sector. This inverse relationship in fact extends to the country level. Typically, an economy with greater competitive forces, as approximated by the Heritage Foundation's economic freedom index,[8] tends to have less corruption, as measured by the Transparency International's Corruption Perception Index[9] (Figure 5.15). Singapore and Australia are ranked among the cleanest and most competitive economies in the world, while India and Indonesia are ranked among the most corrupt and restricted economies by the international watchdogs.

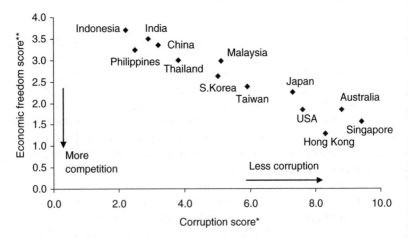

Figure 5.15 Economic freedom vs corruption

Sources: **Heritage Foundation, *Transparency International

China is not the worst, but is among the group with an opaque economy and significant corruption.

The relevance of this analysis to China's corruption problem is that China is caught halfway between a command economy and a market economy. This hybrid economic system is the most fertile ground possible for corruption – plenty of public-sector projects and enterprises where cost is not subject to market discipline, and plenty of private businesses to tap into this corruption hotbed and quietly steer a share of the proceeds to the public officials who lay a trap for them. There is a limit on the extent to which administrative and political reforms can fight corruption. They cannot wipe it out as long as China is stuck with a hybrid economic system.

Judicial reform in China also has its limits under the current economic framework. There is an inherent conflict-of-interest problem in the system. Top court officials are mainly appointed by, and are thus accountable to, the local party and government. But because local economic interests are often at stake where there are disputes and lawsuits, there is often serious interference by local officials in judicial proceedings that favour special interests with political connections.

Thus, corruption and the fight against it always create political tension between central and local governments. The fight is further aggravated by the problem of appropriation among the ranks. In China, there is an historic sense of entitlement that goes with high office. In cases of corruption, the issue is primarily about proportion. Lower-level officials attract punishment when their expropriations become disproportionate to what they have produced for the higher levels. Since individual

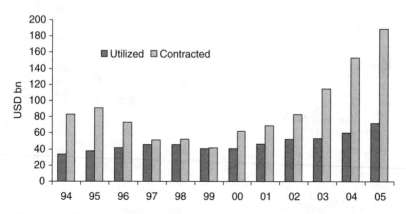

Figure 5.16   FDI inflows to China

Source: CEIC

judgements of the higher ranks determine the process of indictment, the hierarchical pyramid makes investigation and adjudication very political.

But the international community seems hopeful that China is doing the right things to tackle the problems for the future. The confidence is seen in foreign direct investment (FDI) inflows to China. Actual untilized FDI inflow has remained steady through the years (Figure 5.16), except during the Asian crisis when international capital withdrew *en masse* from Asia. More interestingly, contracted FDI inflow, which reflects foreign sentiment more than actual commitment to invest in China, has risen sharply in recent years. If corruption is a serious concern, international investors should have chosen to invest in other markets rather than China so that both actual and contracted FDI inflows would fall.

China's FDI flows have also compared favourably with the regional economies, partly indicating that there is more foreign confidence in China to sort out its corruption problem than in many other Asian economies. China's net FDI inflow is the second largest in Asia after Singapore (Figure 5.17). Remember Singapore is ranked by the international watchdogs as one of the 'cleanest' economies with the strongest competitive forces operating in the system. But China is ranked as opaque, lacking competition and corrupt. Strong FDI inflow to China is thus a vote of foreign confidence in the Middle Kingdom to improve its economic conditions, transparency and corruption records.

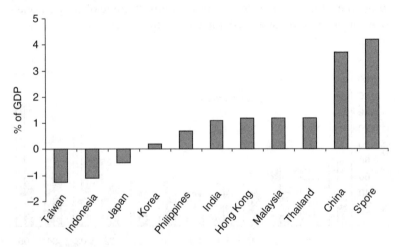

Figure 5.17   Net FDI flows*(a vote of foreign confidence)

* 2001–2005 average

Source: CEIC

Facing the corruption challenge

Corruption is indeed deeply rooted in China's fast-growing hybrid economy. Its fabric is tightly woven from various economic and political interests. Thus, it is very difficult to articulate things to assess whether the corruption problem is improving or worsening. But most agree that the anti-corruption battle cannot be won in just a few years, or even in some definitive timeframe.

In the medium term, corruption is perhaps part of China's economic maturity process. It is even a crucial precursor to an open marketplace, as the transition from a suppressed system to a market system unleashes the hunger for enrichment – fast and even at the expense of others. Every economic evolution goes through this stage from a low base; China is no exception. On the ground, it is equally difficult to determine whether the Communist Party has really stepped up anti-corruption activities or just produced another propaganda campaign. But the overall signs are pointing to a stronger and more objective legal process being put in place.

At the top, the Party's efforts to fight corruption focus on its immediate political and economic interests. Since reform began, the biggest victims of corruption include the people, the Party and the state. From the establishment of the Contract Responsibility System in the early 1980s to the recent surge in domestic mergers and acquisitions, rent seekers have made every effort to 'steal' the state assets. They have diverted rural land, developed property, industrial assets and their earnings away from public ownership and put them into the hands of politically connected private parties under the disguise of economic restructuring and privatization.

The majority of the Communist Party's disciplinary cases in recent years have involved economic crimes related to asset conversion, especially property and land sales, which in turn involves collusion among local party officials, developers and banking authorities. These malpractices have contributed significantly to the twin problems of bad loans and overheated property investment, as both are being driven by the promise of illicit private gains and real commercial potential.

The downfall of Shanghai's top Communist Party leader in September 2006 highlighted the difficulty of rooting out corruption under the current system. Chen Liang-yu, then Shanghai's Communist Party Secretary and one of the 24-member strong Politburo, was sacked for his role in a major corruption scandal involving over RMB3 billion (US$400 million) misappropriated funds from Shanghai's social security fund. He was charged with using the funds to help relatives in criminal ventures and of covering up illegal activities by aides. Mr Chen was the most senior official brought to book since 1995 when a former senior party leader in Beijing Chen Xi-tong (unrelated to Chen Liang-yu) was forced out of office and jailed on corruption charges. The move against the Shanghai party chief was a welcome sign that even top party officials were not immune from the government's crackdown on corruption.

However, Mr Chen's downfall also showed that despite years of effort to eradicate corruption, it had remained a cancerous growth eating into the heart of the Communist Party. The root of the problem lies in the system set-up, where the combination of controlled and market systems acts as a melting pot for brewing corruption by giving senior officials much unchecked power that is not commensurate with appropriate remuneration. This backdrop has created a serious moral hazard problem for officials to abuse their board powers of administrative discretion for personal gain.

Fundamentally, Beijing still has much to learn in using the legal system properly to fight the embedded anti-corruption battle. The way Mr Chen was removed highlighted the supra-legal status of the Communist Party, which is part of the system's problem. He was sacked according to party rules after a month-long investigation by the party's central disciplinary commission directly from Beijing. This mode of investigation dates back to imperial days when special investigators were sent from the capital to deal with local misconduct. However, this old way of doing things reflects the flaw in the system that local authorities lack the power and incentive in going after their corrupt superiors.

The leadership should be applauded for initiating an internal probe to root out corruption. However, given the inherent incentive problem under the current system, the authorities' efforts to eradicate corruption will likely have limited effects. As long as the Party remains above the law, there is a lack of credibility in its professed goal of developing a legal system based on the rule of law. And without such a system, the battle against corruption will not be won.

A way to strengthen the anti-corruption campaign is to streamline China's anti-graft agencies, especially the Central Commission on Disciplinary Investigation (CCDI). A powerful body with the authority to discipline practically all Party cadres, the agency reports directly to the ruling Politburo Standing Committee in Beijing. While there is nothing wrong with an anti-graft agency reporting directly to the highest power, but the CCDI's credibility is in doubt due to its opaque operations and potential conflict of interest problem. For example, the current head of the CCDI also serves as a member in the Politburo Standing Committee, and he is also a long-term ally of the President.

In a nutshell, the negative views on a pending collapse of China under the weight of corruption and the resultant social discontent are mostly a remnant of economic downturns in the 1980s and 1990s. When the economy was stagnating, prices were falling and millions of workers were being laid off, it was easy to extrapolate the instability trend into the future. But evidence suggests that social discontent in China was more cyclical in nature than structural.

Things do not stand still, and they have changed for the better. A steady-growth trajectory will smooth out cyclical social grievances over the long term. With a secular rise in rural incomes and better leverage opportunities in the cities (due to financial liberalization), housing and non-durable consumption will continue to rise. The resultant rise in living standards is the best cushion against the build-up of social tensions. The government does have the fiscal resources to manage any socio-economic challenges, though its fiscal position is not perfect.

However, the problems stemming from unequal income distribution and corruption cannot be taken lightly. A real progress in fighting corruption will only be possible if the system is able to empower the police and judicial authorities to launch independent and fair investigations of the alleged crimes. The point is that, as things stand, only the Party with the blessing of its senior leaders can order investigation against serious corruption. This is not sufficient to tackle the problem effectively.

The challenge for China is to make officials accountable for and transparent in their dealings. A free press with powers within the limits of the law to expose abuse of power will help. But the current system is not yet conducive to these fundamental changes. For example, although not part of the country's official law enforcement or judicial establishment, the CCDI often passes records on suspects to prosecutors and the courts and even give instructions on the kind of punishments to be handed down. This only reinforces how top Party organs still preside over the country's legal and judicial systems. The need for making changes will remain a big challenge for Chinese authorities in the years to come. If mishandled, corruption and income inequality could be the Achilles heel for China's economic future.

6
Sustainable Growth or Short-term Rebound

Despite the structural changes that have been taking place in China, its transition to a market-based system remains incomplete. Much still needs to be done on financial and corporate reforms; the government's role in economic management needs to be redefined; private and intellectual property rights need to be enhanced; and the current rule-by-law framework needs to be replaced by actual rule-of-law.

Sceptics are right to wonder whether China could continue market-oriented reforms, walk the fine line between speeding up reform and keeping overall growth steady, and still be able to balance the tension between reform and social discontent. The outcomes of these policy manoeuvres will decide China's economic future. Crucially, China's growth-reform experiment remains untested. No former communist economies have made any successful transition from a planned regime to an economically robust market-oriented system.

Experience of other Asian tigers do not necessarily mirror what China's economic future will hold, as some of China's growth transition dynamics are unique. In a nutshell, China's economic future will depend on whether Beijing can expand its bold experiments in scrapping communist controls on national policies. Only then can the whole system embrace market forces and the Chinese people get more freedom and rights in areas other than economics. With solid reform momentum and creative destruction of the state, odds seem to favour a stronger and better China in the future.

System needs market discipline

For the Chinese system to move forward, it needs a good dose of market discipline to piece the hardware (capital, technology, infrastructure and so on) together with the software (business practices and ethics, and the like). The dispute in late 2005 between property buyers and developers in Shanghai over the buyers' withdrawal from residential deals clinched during the pre-sale period highlighted the lack of market discipline in China's asset market.

The incident is reflective of the problem in the overall system. On one hand, the property dispute serves to remind optimists of the inherent risks in China's asset market. On the other hand, it underscores the importance of market discipline to the country's market reform. The authorities will have to step up market-oriented measures to correct the distortions.

There were both demand- and supply-side factors to the property dispute problem. The demand problem came from the property buyers. In late 2005, more than 2,000 people who bought flats in Shanghai between 2004 and 2005 were negotiating with the developers who sold them these homes. They wanted the developers to take back the properties and return their payments less a pre-agreed penalty sum. The buyers also notified the banks that they would end the mortgage loans and stop paying instalments to the developers. But the developers refused to budge in the beginning.

How could this bizarre situation happen? To push sales, the developers had agreed in the pre-sale contracts to take the properties back and return the payments less an agreed 3 per cent (of the flats' value) as a penalty if the buyers chose to get out of the deal later. The problem stemmed from the property market correction in mid 2005 and 2006, which had inflicted heavy losses on many buyers even before the flats were delivered. So they wanted to back out by paying the 3 per cent penalty.

These contracts amounted to a 'put' option[1] on property transactions with a 3 per cent put premium. But what sounds like an advanced financial idea in property transaction had turned out to be a speculative boost, creating moral hazard among the buyers. This is because by limiting the buyers' downside to only 3 per cent, these property puts had encouraged buyers to take undue risk, knowing that the developers and the banks would take all the market risk.

This put option had indeed spurred property speculation activities in Shanghai. And the willingness of the developers to draw up such contracts were rooted in the political nature of China's property market. Property development and sales have played a crucial role in the local governments' efforts to boost GDP and tax revenue growth, which are key performance indicators affecting the officials' political fortune. The incentive for local governments to boost property prices (as an effort to boost land sales revenues and tax intake) was especially strong under Beijing's pro-growth directives between 2000 and the first half of 2004.

Against this backdrop, the role of the property put was to boost property demand at the expense of prudent investment decision. This attracted massive investment, first from local funds in Shanghai, then from out-of-province funds and eventually foreign funds, in the property sector. The property put had thus fostered a speculation hotbed, which masked the market fundamentals.

A sign of an overheated property market in Shanghai was seen in the rising 'property velocity of money'. This measures the number of times per year that money changes hands – in terms of property transactions. This concept is borrowed from the 'income velocity of money' in economics. The income velocity is simply the number of times money changes hands per year in the economy. It is calculated as nominal GDP divided by money stock. The logic is that if money changes hands faster than money and real economic growth, inflation rises, creating distortion in the economy.

Similarly, the property velocity of money is the nominal value of residential property divided by money stock (M2 is used here). This velocity was accelerating between 2000 and 2004, only to fall off sharply in 2005 when the government cracked down on property speculation with various restrictive measures (Figure 6.1). This evidence suggested that money was changing hands like a hot potato in the property market, underscoring rising speculation, inflating property prices and creating distortions in the market, from the turn of the millennium.

Then there is the problem of the developers (the supply side). Other than just drawing up the property put options to create excessive imprudent demand, they even engage in tactics of creating phony market

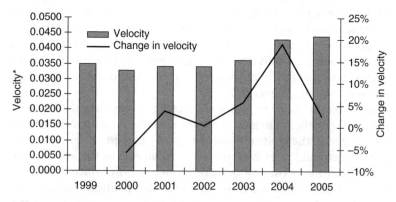

Figure 6.1   Property velocity of money*

* nominal residential property value divided by M2
Source:CEIC

conditions to lure buyers. For example, there were media reports of some Shanghai property agencies hiring labourers to line up outside residential show flats in order to create a false sense of excessive demand.

Crucially, developers' incentive was distorted by the land sales system, which did not allow market forces to set land prices. According to *Xinhua News*, until recently more than 70 per cent of land sales in China were carried out behind closed doors; over 20 per cent were given free to developers in cases where the local authorities were keen to develop certain sites for political or other reasons. Only about 5 per cent were auctioned. This gave the developers below-market land cost, allowing them to reap enormous development profits, and boosting their incentives to develop land as quickly as possible and use gimmicks to create excessive and phony demand for property. Although the land sales system has improved recently, with open auctions being increasingly used in land sales, old habits die hard in the short term.

The disputes were finally settled by the developers agreeing to cut their sales prices to compensate for the buyers' losses due to the market decline. But this was still not right. The contract terms should not have been drawn up to create moral hazard in the first place. Since the buyers got away intact this time, this means that the incentive problems remain in the system. Enforcing market discipline is the only way to correct them.

The authorities should learn from this incident to handle similar property disputes better in the future and to consider the signals they should send to the market. Ruling against the buyers will invoke market discipline on the demand side, which is what the Chinese market needs. But the developers should not be allowed to get away with breaching contracts. Crucially, the authorities should implement open auction for all land sales to eliminate the developers' incentive problem. Now that property sales prices are set by the market, it is only right to allow the land cost to be set by market forces too.

The government should also consider the effect of externality from the public sector on assessing land value. Public goods such as infrastructure projects, city improvement and development policies often have positive spill-over effects on the surrounding land and property values. This appreciation in land value should be taken into account when implementing land auctions.

In a nutshell, the property dispute might be a blessing in disguise, as it opens up the opportunities for improvement by exposing the flaws of the property market and the current land sales system. The signal is clear that Beijing should take market discipline more seriously in the reform programme.

What's right with China?

Economic inefficiency in China can clearly be reduced because the visible hand of the government to direct, and distort, resources allocation is still heavy. Hence, it is easy for critics to find faults in the Chinese system and pick on the remaining inefficiencies, including the wasteful state-owned enterprises (SOEs), the broken banking system, the impaired institutional and legal frameworks, and the social/income inequality. Those who dwell on these criticisms are offering little value in understanding and assessing the evolution of China's economics. This is because they are missing the big picture as well as the economic dynamism of China.

Despite the system's deficiency, China must have got some big issues right to allow itself to leap forward in such huge strides for over two decades. And if the right policies are pursued, to which the signposts seem to be pointing, China could even become the world's largest economy before 2050, according to some market players. To see what China has done right, examine its total factor productivity (TPF)[2] growth. Various academic studies[3] have found that strong TFP growth, averaging 3 per cent–4 per cent a year since 1978, has contributed significantly to China's strong economic growth, although accumulation of the physical capital stock and human capital were also important factors.

China's sustained rise in productivity often compares favourably with those of the other Asian tiger economies.[4] That remarkable performance is, in part, a result of a low base in the pre-1978 era from which Chinese growth started off. More crucially, it is a result of the prolonged structural efforts that have gradually purged economic inefficiencies in the system.

Of course, China's reform path is not a smooth straight line. There have been hiccups, with the volatility in productivity growth contributing to volatility in economic growth. Basically, there have been three periods of productivity surges coinciding with three reform episodes and creating large GDP growth fluctuations (Figure 6.2).

The first productivity boom took place in the early to mid 1980s, when agricultural reforms broke up the collective farms, liberalized agricultural prices and thus created strong market incentives for the farmers. The second productivity surge came about in the early to mid 1990s, when the late paramount leader Deng Xiao-ping's south China trip resulted in a wave of economic liberalization. His pro-market reform marked the start of the creative destruction process replacing many of the old inefficient state firms and industries by the more efficient sunrise non-state economic entities.

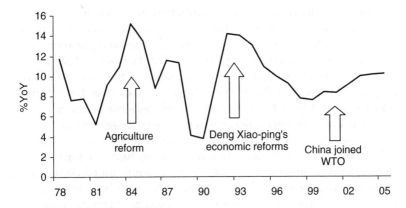

Figure 6.2   GDP growth and economic reform
Source: CEIC

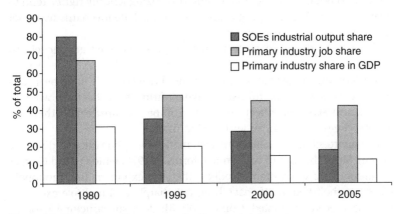

Figure 6.3   Declining reliance on agriculture and state sector
Source: CEIC

The third wave of productivity gains began in the early 2000s, when China joined the World Trade Organization. WTO membership has not only offered China greater access to the world market but it has also acted as an external discipline on China to push domestic structural reforms forward and to break down the entry barriers to state industries and the service sector where inefficiency is at its most prevalent.

These reforms basically have boosted China's productivity through resources reallocation, both from agriculture to industry and services, and from state-owned to non state-owned sectors (Figure 6.3). The latter is a strong evidence for creative destruction, in which the authorities have allowed inefficient state firms to fail so as to make way for the emergence of the efficient market-driven non-state and private firms.

Research on industry data[5] shows that the TFP of Chinese industrial enterprises has grown more than twice as fast as that of the SOEs, and at least 60 per cent faster than that of the indirect state-controlled firms. Further, reallocation of labour from the SOEs to the non-state sector has added 0.5 percentage points to overall growth per year[6] since reform started.

By loosening the government's economic grip on the system, structural reforms have shifted resources allocation and decision making towards a more market-oriented process, thus creating significant efficiency gains. Arguably, what prompts this profound policy shift is a change in the heart of the central leadership. They have become pragmatic in pushing for constructive changes by breaking away from the ideological logjam. Since the mind change is new, bold reform moves, such as breaking the control on population movement and privatizing lending rights, tend to be undertaken first on a pilot basis and intermediate mechanisms are set up to smooth the transition process.[7]

This pragmatic approach to policy changes has given greater rein to market forces, which started with agriculture and then extended to the secondary and tertiary sectors over time. Price controls have been dismantled step by step, non-state-owned firms have been allowed to merge, and SOEs have been forced to compete against each other and against the non-state firms and foreign firms.

This approach has gradually injected market discipline into the domestic system. Since the start of economic reforms in 1978, which ended China's inward-looking self-contained policy, the state-export trading monopoly has been abolished, tariffs have been cut sharply and multiple exchange rates have been eliminated. Combined with domestic structural reforms, Beijing's decisive effort to open up to world trade and investment has attracted massive FDI inflows (Figure 6.4). China has become the world's largest FDI recipient since 2005. The surge in contracted FDI is a signal of rising foreign confidence in China's reform and economic outlook.

Creating incentive compatibility along the way of structural reform has been key to allow China to deliver efficiency gains. Starting with the breaking up of the collective farms in the 1980s, private economic incentives have been implanted gradually in the system. Despite the lack of political reforms, the attraction of economic gains has aligned the incentives of the local officials to act as 'partners' of rather than 'predators' on private entrepreneurs. Even China's partial privatization programme has ignited private incentives to boost investment and spending.

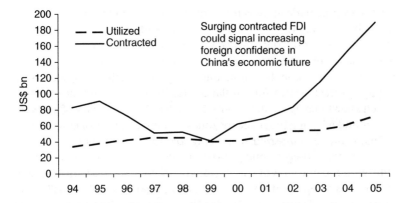

Figure 6.4 FDI inflows to China
Source: CEIC

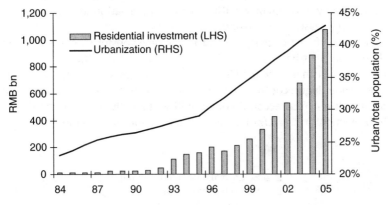

Figure 6.5 Urbanization and residential investment
Source: CEIC

For example, in urban housing, the government retains ownership of land but grants property rights up to 70 years to the private sector. Since housing privatization started in 1998, investment in residential housing has soared (Figure 6.5), contributing to investment and ultimately GDP growth. This trend will continue for a long time to come, as the huge pent-up housing demand is just starting to be released by housing reform and financial liberalization. The latter, also in its early stage of development, will increasingly loosen households budget constraint on demand for assets.

China's pragmatic approach to privatization and granting of property rights has re-established private ownership, and hence private economic incentives, under the state-owned socialist system. Its privatization began with market liberalization, followed by transfer of user rights and the right to income through contracting with private individuals, such as the family contract system for farmland and the SOE performance contract which allows management buyouts. In the late 1990s, a policy of 'grabbing the big and releasing the small' (or zhua-da fang-xiao) led to a large number of small and medium-sized SOEs being sold to private hands.

The impact on economic growth of this approach has been remarkable, with income growth rising strongly on the back of a shrinking state sector. This is representative of the unleashing of 'animal spirits'[8] in the private sector (Figure 6.6). Despite this, economic incentives must be improved further into the future. Strengthening farmers' land rights and advancing privatization in the core industries remain two important unfinished tasks. Further privatization also needs to move with greater transparency and equality, with proper compensation arrangements to be set up to ease social tension.

From an efficiency perspective, the key question for China is whether these gains can be sustained? This is equivalent to asking if the reform momentum can be sustained in the future. The signposts, such as attempts to ease population control, financial repression and public ownership, and to liberalize capital account convertibility gradually, point to continued improvement in the reform incentives and economic structure.

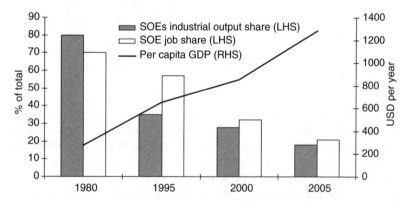

Figure 6.6   Income rises as SOE dominance falls
Source: CEIC

If implemented properly on a national scale, these measures will take China into a new solid economic growth era in the long term. In the medium term, China will likely see reform dividends paying off to create a sweet spot of growth laying the grounds for long-term economic prosperity. There are two aspects to this mid-term growth outlook.

First, the external discipline from China's WTO commitments will continue to bite. China will have to speed up domestic restructuring by deregulating and opening up key state industries and service sectors under the WTO framework. The government has already stepped up efforts to restructure the country's ailing banks and SOEs. It has also started to embark on capital market reform.

WTO membership will also push China to improve its underlying legal and institutional frameworks, as WTO commitment involves standardizing a large number of commercial laws and regulations. This should help make China's regulatory environment more stable and transparent in the future. Granted, all these expected WTO effects depend on China's willingness to let go of control and truly open up. Signs are clear that central leadership is serious about restructuring China and would use the WTO as an external discipline lever to deepen economic reforms.

Second, China will continue to reap efficiency gains from resources reallocation. As Chinese producers move up the value chain and globalization integrates China deeper into the world economic system, China will have to speed up in reallocating resources from the state sector to the non-state sector. It will also have to accept faster expansion of the private sector. These moves will create more efficiency gains, especially when efficiency performance varies within and between different economic sectors,[9] pushing China's Production Possibility Curve out to generate sustainable growth (see Chapter 1, 'The need for reform' section).

Success in China's economic restructuring will propel further reform momentum, which will in turn generate more growth for supporting more economic reforms. China is indeed in an enviable situation where a virtuous reform-growth cycle is emerging. Of course, if China were to fail to deliver the results, its long-term growth prospects would be quite different. There remain risks associated with cyclical and policy management mistakes, as the price mechanism – be it the interest rate or the exchange rate – has yet to be fully liberalized. The restricted role of the market in adjusting cyclical economic imbalances will remain a key risk factor for economic mismanagement.

Growth model shifting

The key to China's economic expansion lies in how the government redefines its role in the economy and, hence, reshapes the structure of the growth dynamics. So far, the Chinese economy relies heavily on investment growth, supplemented by exports, for economic growth momentum. This development model has created significant economic imbalances.

On the external front, they have resulted in a large current account surplus and an undervalued currency. On the home front, the imbalances have manifested themselves in excess capacity in some major industries eroding pricing power, but at the same time overheating in various parts of the economy and raising fears of an eventual economic crash.

Too much reliance on investment and export growth is not sustainable. Erratic investment growth in China, directed mostly by the visible hand of the government, is prone to inflict large volatility in economic growth. Meanwhile, relying too much on exports for growth will hold the economy hostage to foreign demand shocks. Structural trends in China are also pointing to the end of its fast export-growth era in the coming years (see Chapter 4, 'Labour-intensive model maturing' section).

To solve the economic imbalance problem, the government has put consumption growth as its top policy priority in its eleventh Five-Year Plan in 2006. This suggests that Beijing has set as its medium-term policy goal an expenditure-switching towards domestic consumption from investment and exports to help resolve the structural imbalances between the external and domestic sectors.

Indeed, structural, political and cyclical trends are converging to boost Chinese consumption to a secular uptrend. Crucially, Beijing's experiments to scrap the *hu-kou* system and further financial liberalization, including pilot schemes to allow private investors to set up lending companies, are bold moves toward restructuring the old system by allowing market forces to work better. They are also initial steps to unleashing consumption power by reducing labour market distortion and relaxing consumers' budget constraint. Economic sectors that have exposure to Chinese retail and financial sectors are poised to benefit the most in the coming years.

The structural support for the spending shift towards consumption includes steady income growth, accelerating urbanization and a growing middle class. The expected annual average 8 per cent GDP growth in the coming decade would easily support an average 10 per cent retail sales growth per year. Despite its volatile growth in the early years, overall

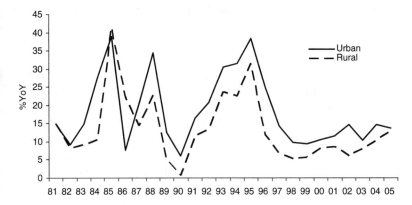

Figure 6.7 Retail sales growth
Source: CEIC

retail sales growth has stabilized at an average growth rate of 11 per cent since the late 1990s (Figure 6.7). This steadier growth trend, which is also reflective of the GDP growth trend, is mainly a result of better economic management, steady income growth and structural reforms that have improved the underlying demand framework and growth stability.

Further, rural consumption growth has been catching up with urban spending, as the income growth gap between the two areas has narrowed in recent years (see Figure 5.10 in Chapter 5). This trend of rural income growth catching up with city income growth is poised to continue (see Chapter 5, 'What about the farmers?' section). This will be strongly positive for boosting future total consumption because, as income rises, the poorer rural population will have a higher propensity to consume than the richer urban population.

This benign growth backdrop is, in turn, a result of structural reforms that have gone deeper than many, including the Chinese, have thought. Using better growth-accounting methodology, Beijing revised the GDP data in early 2006. The service sector, a proxy for market reform progress, now accounts for over 40 per cent of GDP versus less than a third as reported before. Chinese banking bad debts have dropped sharply over the years to less than 10 per cent of total assets (see Chapter 2, 'A reality check on the banks' section). This will act to liquefy the economy's balance sheet for future growth.

Urbanization is speeding up due to economic liberalization, giving rise to increasing retail demand. Beijing is experimenting with ending the half-century old *hu-kou* (or household registration) system[10] (see Chapter 1,

p. 32). By tying individuals to their birthplace via registration that determines their state benefit entitlements, the system has retarded labour mobility, income growth and urbanization and, hence, consumption growth.

As and when the abolition of the *hu kou* system is rolled out to the whole country in the coming years, the effect will be very positive for consumer demand. Meanwhile, a growing middle class is boosting retail demand of all sorts. China's middle class (defined by the World Bank as the share of population with per capita annual income of US$3,000 or more), estimated to be only 4 per cent of total population today, is expected to grow by more than six-fold to about 360 million by the turn of this decade.

The consumption power behind these forces has been unleashed by creative destruction (as inefficient sunset industries are being destroyed to make way for more efficient sunrise industries) and financial liberalization. The latter makes China's greying population a non-binding budget constraint for consumption. This is because financial liberalization allows consumers to borrow for funding current consumption.

China's personal loan market has grown leaps and bounds since it was opened up in 1997, with mortgage lending growing at an annual average rate of 100 per cent and other personal loans at 300 per cent between 1997 and 2005. However, this market is still in an infant stage (Figure 6.8), as mortgage loans still account for about 10 per cent of total bank lending and other personal loans 2 per cent. Further liberalization will have great potential for boosting consumption.

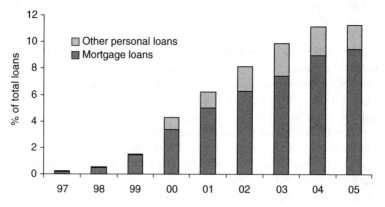

Figure 6.8 China's personal loan market
Source: CEIC

On a cyclical basis, growth momentum from exports and investment are shifting to consumption in the coming years. Slower global demand under the weight of high real interest rates and oil prices will trim China's export growth. Trade friction with the developed markets could also cloud China's export outlook. In the next few years, Chinese exports are expected to grow at half the 33 per cent average rate recorded between 2003 and 2005.

The shifting momentum is reflected in the peaking of domestic corporate profit growth (Figure 6.9), though this is not necessarily a sign of sharp economic decline in the future. Average profit is still growing at over 10 per cent a year, but that is sharply lower than the phenomenal growth rates seen in the early 2000s. Manufacturers' pricing power has been capped due to fierce competition and excess capacity, especially in sectors such as cars, chemicals, steel, cement and electronics. Cheaper prices will benefit the consumer but lower margins will drag on investment, thus switching the growth momentum to consumption.

The bottleneck conditions that boosted investment in 2004 and 2005 are unlikely to re-emerge, as the government has pumped massive investment into the congested sectors, such as coal, power, oil, mining and railways. But these large government spending initiatives have raised concerns that these sectors may even face overinvestment, thus aggravating the excess capacity problem that has eroded pricing power.

Further, contrary to common belief, investment is unlikely to get an extra big boost from the estimated RMB300 billion Olympics-related

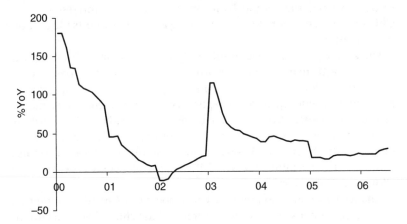

Figure 6.9   Corporate profit growth
Source: CEIC

spending (about 7 per cent of annual national fixed-asset investment). Most of this investment is in urban infrastructure projects, such as roads, telecoms, environmental projects, hotels and commercial buildings that would have been undertaken even without the Olympic Games, which Beijing is hosting in 2008. Sports facilities will account for only about RMB30 billion.

The growth-driving shift may already be starting to emerge, as seen in China's import trends. In 2005, China's imports of industrial commodities such as oil and oil products, chemicals and industrial metals slowed down sharply. On the other hand, imports of consumer items, including high-value ones like beverages, aircraft, biotech products and medical equipment sped up. This could be the start of a mega-trend in changing import composition, from investment-led to consumption-led, in the coming years, driven by gradual expenditure-switching from investment to consumption.

From a micro-perspective, watch the imports of the following sectors, the demand growth of which will confirm the shift to a consumption-led growth model on the back of decelerating investment: cars, aircraft, digital cameras, gold, high-end tech products and services, fast food, nuclear technology, high-value medical equipment, natural gas, telecoms equipment, satellite, water treatment, potassium fertilizer, palm oil, soybeans, processed foods and beverages, and the like.[11]

Meanwhile, government policy is encouraging the shift to consumption-led growth. Monetary policy is going to be less supportive for investment, as the past monetary expansion and a secular rise in energy prices have put the central bank on inflation alert. Interest rates in China have been kept too low for too long and that warrants the authorities' attention.

The government has tried to shift output incentive away from exports to the domestic market. The eleventh Five-Year Plan in 2006 has set policies to boost domestic consumption as top priority. A strong currency policy and the ending of many export tax rebates will encourage manufacturers to switch from exports to domestic markets. To distribute income more evenly so as to boost rural consumption, Beijing is spending more on infrastructure and power networks in the rural areas. It has also eliminated all agricultural taxes and lifted personal income tax exemption allowance to spur consumption.

Financial liberalization holds the key to boosting Chinese consumption in the coming years by making an intertemporal choice between current and future consumption possible (via borrowing and lending). A significant sign has emerged of faster and bolder financial liberalization for the future. Since 2006, Beijing has allowed domestic investors to run lending companies in the Pingyao county of Shanxi province. This acts to increase the consumers' (and small firms') accessibility to capital and thus boost spending.

The experiment could be a harbinger of a national policy that, like the scrapping of the *hu-kou* system, will be very positive for consumer demand. It could also mean that underground finance, or the curb market, will soon be legalized to allow market forces and discipline in the financial system.

China is moving into a tougher reform path, as it goes deeper to shake up the old system. The success of China's economic growth has built up Beijing's confidence to keep the growth momentum. However, it remains to be seen how this confidence will be extended to allow more market forces to function in the coming years. While the growth transformation to a consumption-led economy is still heavily policy-directed, Beijing's bold experiments in ending population control, financial repression and public asset ownership are positive signs that the leadership is willing to tackle the root problems inherited from the central planning system.

Despite the strong policy push, a shift to consumption-led growth has its limits to boost growth potential in the short term. This limitation is due to the government's weak fiscal ability to boost consumer spending and the stubborn Chinese saving habit. Cutting taxes should boost consumption by raising disposable income. In principle, this should work powerfully in China because its larger and poorer rural population has a higher consumption propensity than the smaller and richer urban population, which has a higher propensity to save.[12]

However, tax cuts are not practical, and not powerful enough, for boosting Chinese consumption because of China's small personal and consumption tax bases. Combined government tax revenues from personal income tax and consumption accounted for an average of 13 per cent of total tax revenues, or only 2 per cent of GDP, between 2000 and 2005. By comparison, this is way below the 10 per cent GDP share in the US. Thus, Beijing's plans to raise personal income tax exemption and scrap the agriculture tax will have a limited impact on boosting consumption.

The government can also use fiscal spending to boost domestic spending and trigger a chain effect on pushing private consumption. Given the already high level of public investment, Beijing can only realistically raise non-investment outlays, including education, health care, welfare, social services and pensions, the total of which accounts for less than 4 per cent of GDP currently.

While financially feasible, expansion of these programmes faces technical problems in the short term. On one hand, the rise in spending on these areas is constrained by the lack of technical skills, personnel and knowledge. On the other hand, the current low level of these expenditures means that even a large jump in their outlays would not stimulate growth much, and hence would limit the chain effect on boosting consumption.

An even bigger challenge lies in the Chinese saving habit. If fiscal spending is not efficient enough to boost domestic spending, increase in private consumption will have to come from a reduction in the household savings, which amount to over a quarter of household disposable income since 2000.[13] But reducing Chinese savings is difficult because households are in a high precautionary mode due to a poor social safety net. The reform process over the years has taken away many free social services that were formerly provided by the government and the state-owned firms.

For example, households are now spending an increasing share of their income on medical services and education, as the government is withdrawing from providing free services in these areas. Only about 15 per cent of the population is covered by basic health insurance, while about 16 per cent of the economically active population is covered by the basic pension scheme. In a nutshell, households are more cautious under the new, more market-oriented, system as many of the free goods and services that they used to get from the government, including foods, lodging, education and health care, are gone for good. They have to save for rainy days.

From Beijing's policy perspective, increase in public spending on health, education and other social services should help reduce the precautionary demand for saving, and hence boost consumption, in the long term. This, in turn, implies that the transition to a consumption-led growth model will have to start with more public spending to boost household confidence so that savings can fall to make room for consumption growth.

Consumption is only the expenditure side of the growth model. China should also find new keys to sustaining long-term growth from the production side. Manufacturing is not going to be a sustainable source of new jobs in the long term, as improving technology and productivity are reducing industry's labour needs.

Here, the service sector is a crucial key to stimulating China's economic expansion in the future. And the service sector does not just include low-end, low-skill jobs in the fast food chains, beauty parlours, retail and the like. Such jobs, which are indeed developing very fast in China's service sector in recent years, will account for only a minority of all service jobs when the economy matures. For example, even in the US, widely thought to have too many hamburger-flipping type jobs, they account for about 22 per cent of total service employment.

In fact, services comprise many activities crucial to economic growth, such as financial services, commerce, research and development, health and medical services, power supply, transport and telecommunication. Once an economy reaches the middle-income level of development, service industries become a more important source of job growth than manufacturing; and the skill and pay levels of the service jobs rise along with economic maturity.

In most developed and developing economies, employment has fallen in the manufacturing sector since 1997, leaving the service industries as the net job creation machine.[14] Even the world's factory, China, has lost over 15 million manufacturing jobs since 1997. The new jobs created by the boom in foreign manufacturing investment in China were not enough to offset these losses, due to a combination of corporate restructuring, technological advancement and rising productivity.

China's local services such as retail, financial services and construction are becoming crucial GDP growth drivers because of their sheer size in the domestic market. Access to high-quality local services will affect growth rates in other economic sectors as every enterprise uses them. Good local services will also make a difference in attracting FDI. So expanding the domestic service sector will uncover new growth sources for China in the coming decades. To unlock local services' potential to boost jobs and income growth, Beijing must remove barriers to competition. This will require levelling the playing field so that services can compete freely for land, labour, capital and technology, removing excessive restrictions on tertiary businesses and tackling red tape.

The government's development policy has so far been too focused on the manufacturing and industrial areas. This will have to change. Beijing needs to remove any development biases against services and give them equal treatment in financial, fiscal and development policies so that services firms can compete for resources on the same terms as manufacturing and industrial firms.

In China today, state-owned manufacturing firms still account for two-thirds of all loans, though they account for less than 40 per cent of all industrial output. Meanwhile, rules for listing on the stock markets are still favouring large, state and manufacturing firms. This argues for deepening economic liberalization to allocate capital to the projects with highest returns regardless of sector.

To speed up the development of the service industries, the government should extend special economic zone-type arrangements to them so that they can serve the other sectors more efficiently. This will be increasingly important as manufacturing firms continue to outsource more functions to third-party service providers. As in banking, withdrawal of public ownership lies at the heart of the ultimate liberalization of the service sector. This will also open the door to more FDI inflows, which will bring in more management technology, better business practices and increased competition to boost productivity.

The maths for sustainable growth

Let us re-group our thoughts on China's growth dynamics. Development economics states that China grew rapidly as economic reforms purged structural inefficiencies. Agricultural and industrial reforms altered economic incentives and unleashed 'animal spirits' to boost private spending growth. Increasing private ownership in the industrial and commercial enterprises raised competition and led to cost cutting and innovation. The opening up of the economy to foreign investment and trade intensified competition, resulted in technology transfer, sharpened the commercial sense of Chinese firms and improved their management techniques and knowledge in finance and foreign markets. The Chinese economy could not but grow robustly.

As the economy develops further, efficiency gains are key to sustain growth. The shift of labour from agriculture to industries and services has been crucial in raising productivity growth in China since economic liberalization began in 1978. This shift is far from over, if experience in other East Asian economies is any guide. Their process of labour shift from the farms to the industries and services lasted for an average of 40 years (Figure 6.10), during which time both productivity and GDP growth soared.

In South Korea, farm jobs fell from 65 per cent of the total in 1963 to 10 per cent in 2003, while Taiwan's farm employment fell from almost 50 per cent in 1965 to only 7 per cent in 2003.[15] China's labour shift is likely to be at the middle stage of this typical reallocation process. Its agriculture jobs which accounted for 70 per cent of the total in 1978, only fell to 44 per cent in 2003. Research has shown that moving Chinese labour out of the agricultural sector to the secondary sector had added one percentage point each year to overall GDP growth.[16]

This shift matters a lot because Chinese labour productivity in the service sector is estimated to be four times higher than in agriculture,

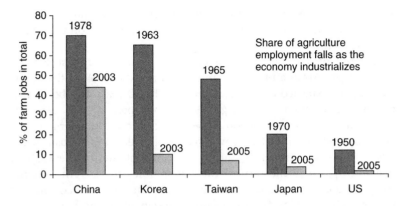

Figure 6.10 Coming off the land
Source: CEIC

and in industry seven times higher. This means that every time a farmer moves into services or industry, the value-added of that labourer jumps four to seven times. If 1 per cent of the labour force were to move out of farming into industries and services each year, this shift *per se* could add 4 per cent to 5 per cent to GDP growth each year. Structural changes will remain a major source of economic growth for the next three to four decades.

The incentive to shift labour out of agriculture to the secondary and tertiary industries is strong, and the government is encouraging that shift. To start with, China's agriculture is overcrowded with labour. The number of labourers per acre in Chinese farmland is about 100 times higher than in the US, which only has 1.6 per cent of jobs in agriculture. But the *hu kou* system and illiquidity of farmland have restricted the movement of Chinese labour out of agriculture.

The problem with the *hu kou* system hindering labour mobility is obvious, and Beijing has embarked on a process of gradual relaxation. Urbanization, especially migration from the rural areas to satellite cities, has become an official policy. Different parts of the country have been asked to experiment with different degrees of reform of the 50-year old *hu kou* system, with the aim of eventually scrapping it altogether.

The inability of farmers to sell their land is a severe financial constraint to labour shifting out of the agriculture sector and moving to the cities to start a new life. That is why it is so important for the government to implement genuine land reform, including fully transferable land rights and establishing an open market for them (see Chapter 1, 'The next steps' section). Despite its current insufficiency, liberalization of rural land transfer has come a long way and is currently back on the reform agenda again.

The shift of rural labour to the cities will be met by robust demand from the industries and services in the years to come. With the young labour pool expected to shrink in the next 15–20 years, this bodes well for long-term labour income growth (see Chapter 4, 'The real story about labour shortage' section). The changing economic structure to boost private-sector spending will keep labour demand robust. In the 1990s, it was government spending on infrastructure that kept labour demand up. Since the turn of the millennium, the government has stepped back and the state sector has shrunk. The job growth engine has been switched to exports, manufacturing and increasingly consumption.

Despite rising wages, especially in the coastal manufacturing hubs, average Chinese wages, at the official exchange rate, are still about 2–3 per cent of those in the US. Meanwhile, the price of labour relative to the price of capital in China is only 6 per cent of that in the US. Before the true labour shortage hits, which is not expected until another 15 to 20 years later, Chinese labour is still cheap compared to the industrial world both in absolute terms and relative to the price of capital.

Meanwhile, China's external trade liberalization and its ascent to the world trade league have allowed it to make the best use of its comparative advantage in labour abundance. The dominance of cheap labour means that average output per Chinese labourer will continue to rise for many years. Hence, foreigners' demand for Chinese labour and incentive to invest in China should remain strong until China's labour and capital prices become equal to those in the industrial world.

Chances are that China's labour quality is going to improve sharply in the coming decades. This will, in turn, sustain steady economic growth rates in the neighbourhood of 7–8 per cent for quite some time. On the surface, China's labour force is poorly educated. China sceptics would like to cite statistics such as the most recent census in 2000, which shows that only 16.5 per cent of China's population had senior high school education, compared with over 80 per cent in the US; and only 1.4 per cent of China's population had a bachelor degree, compared with almost 25 per cent in the US. And for postgraduate degrees, the gap is 0.1 per cent in China versus 8.9 per cent in the US.

However, this evidence is deceptive and outdated. The picture is different if we compare them in absolute terms. Doing the comparison in percentage terms ignores the fact that China's population is over four times larger than that of the US. This means that in absolute number terms, almost as many Chinese had senior high school education in year 2000 as in the US, although at the first degree and postgraduate levels, the US still outnumbered China many times.

More crucially, using the 2000 census figures ignores the education dynamics in the future because the education data in year 2000 say nothing about the education of today's and future young generations. Recent official education data show that although new first-degree and associate-degree enrolment in the US was four times larger than in China in the early 1990s, by 2001 China overtook the US for the first time in new enrolment, and by 2005 it had twice the US enrolment.

This means that the number of first- and associate-degree graduates in China has exceeded the number in the US since 2004. By 2008, Chinese first and associate-degree holders will outnumber those in the US twice over. For postgraduate degrees, the growth trend is similar and China has now reached about two-thirds of the new enrolment numbers of the US. The government is aiming to bring enrolment ratios at senior high school and tertiary education up to OECD countries' levels in fifteen years time (that is by 2020, according to the current plan).

The point is that Chinese labour quality is going to improve sharply in the coming years. This will definitely have a positive impact on future growth. Some basic growth accounting helps illustrate this. Empirical evidence across countries shows that the share of total labour income (i.e. the number of workers times wages) in GDP is relatively constant over time. China should behave the same way in the long term, despite the short- and medium-term structural changes. This means that GDP growth can be divided into labour and wage growth. If the future growth of labour and wages in China is known, the future GDP growth can be deduced.

Let us put this into context by adding up labour and wage growth in the years after the 2000 census, i.e. between 2000 and 2005. The simple calculation from this basic growth accounting predicted GDP growth would have averaged about 6 per cent a year. But actual growth turned out to be averaging 9.35 per cent. Of course, other factors such as productivity growth and short-term fluctuation of labour income would have accounted for this growth-rate difference in the period. But the point remains that with improving labour quality, Chinese productivity and labour income share in GDP is going to rise, boosting overall growth in the long term.

There is no doubt that on the labour issue China's ageing population (and hence its shrinking labour force) is the biggest constraint for future growth. But as we argued earlier (see Chapter 4), the demographic constraint will not come into play for another twenty years or so. Much can happen to the population dynamics in two decades that may change the economy's growth path.

Given its huge population, there are other factors to be considered in assessing China's demographic impact on future economic growth. One is the pool of quality labour. Given China's educational trend and the government's policy to improve it, it is quite possible that the number of geniuses in China would outnumber that in the US in the coming decade. If growth depends on invention and innovation, which in turn depend on accumulation of talent, then China is poised to continue to grow for a long time to come.

China's large population also means a huge domestic market size for growth to hinge upon. But here distribution of the population is more crucial. About 80 per cent of China's population (which is about three times the population of the US) lives in the eastern part of the country. This population concentration opens up huge opportunities for economies of scale and scope, which could boost competition, innovation and rationalization. Further, China is still in a catch-up phase in research and development (R&D) spending. While the Americans spend about 3 per cent of GDP in R&D each year, the Chinese only spend 1 per cent.

However, China's R&D spending is rising rapidly and the future trend is going to speed up for good reasons. Since economic reform, China has been focusing on labour-intensive manufacturing because that is where its comparative advantage lies. Thus, many companies have so far been able to thrive without much spending on R&D. But this labour-intensive model is maturing (see Chapter 4), and profit margins are starting to fall for poor innovators. The intensifying labour cost problem in the coastal manufacturing centres suggests that labour-intensive industries will have to give way to labour-saving and capital-intensive technologies.

A quick and full-scale shift towards high-tech industries would still not be in China's best economic interests until the pool of excess farm labourers has shrunk enough. But the seeds have been sown for more R&D spending to help the transition of the growth model to a more sustainable one in the future (see Chapter 7, 'Strategic drive and vision' section for further discussion).

Challenges ahead

Of course, this does not mean smooth sailing for sustainable growth. China's reform programme lies at the heart of assessing its challenges in the future. It is important to recognize that China's leaders are operating in a tough environment with many institutional deficiencies, like a weak legal framework, poor governance and poor quality of economic data. There is also this problem of the central reform directives not being trickled down to, or implemented by, local governments who have a significant degree of autonomy in local matters. Beijing is walking on a tight rope in balancing between economic reforms, growth and political and social stability.

China has taken a gradualist approach to the reform programme. This typically means taking small steps and/or conducting reform experiments in some provinces before rolling them out as national policies. This cautious reform approach has worked well so far for China. This is because in the world where multiple distortions will make the impact of reforms unpredictable and ignite social and political tensions, China's learning-by-doing approach has helped minimize the costs of policy errors and uncertainty in reform outcomes. It also allows the leaders to gauge political and social sensitivity towards reforms so that any resistance could be tackled effectively when reforms are implemented at a broader level.

However, China's reform programme has come to a cross-roads as its economy becomes more market-oriented and complex. This means that Beijing's incremental and experimental (arguably piecemeal) reform approaches may become increasingly untenable. In some cases, they could even create risks of their own. The increasingly complex economy means that those critical reforms relating to broad macro-economic issues, such as exchange rate flexibility or equivalently capital account liberalization, cannot be isolated to specific geographical areas.

As the economy becomes more sophisticated, some of its factors of production become more mobile, and more able to take advantage of economic distortions in the system. This means that a slow approach to change carries the risk of being overwhelmed by the rent-seeking activities of these mobile factors.

Exchange rate reform is a case in point. Repeated small moves towards exchange rate flexibility will only raise speculative fund inflows to China in anticipation of eventual large RMB revaluations. While this does not mean that China should move towards full RMB convertibility overnight, the case underscores the fact that conducting domestic monetary policy in a more open and increasingly complex economy is much more complicated than in previous times (see Chapter 7 for more discussion).

The complexity extends to the reform programme itself. China's development has come to a point where many key reforms are interconnected. For example, progress of restructuring the banking sector hinges upon SOE reform to end the implicit pressure on state banks to sustain the bad

SOEs with cheap loans. But SOE reform will mean more bankruptcies, adding to banks' bad debts and raising unemployment in the short to medium term. Slow progress in building a better social safety net will, in turn, create social tensions and disrupt reform progress.[17]

Under these circumstances, it will be increasingly difficult for China to undertake individual reforms in isolation. The traditional incremental reform approach may not work well in the future due to the combined forces of an increasingly vibrant private sector and an increasingly open economy. Reform experiments will also become more difficult, as they will have to be coordinated with strong incentive compatibility between the national and local authorities for implementation, which is already a problem. The ability for reform incentives to trickle down from the central to the local levels is also crucial to prevent arbitrage forces from taking advantage of the distortions and negating the reform impact.

But coordination and consistent implementation of reform measures are precisely the biggest challenge in the future. The challenge is already manifested in the 'shang you zheng ce, xia you dui ce' phenomenon.[18] The root problem is the conservative mindset of control imbedded in the system. Economic reform threatens loss of control, which in turn would not only threaten the security of the communist power base but also threaten to destroy the rent-seeking opportunities in the distorted system. Such fears have thus created stubborn resistance to change.

To unleash growth potential and to advance research, invention and innovation, however, the government must loosen control. The Communist Party's absolute control over the system, especially on access to and dissemination of information, will remain a big obstacle to moving the Chinese economy forward from merely catching up to undertaking extensive research and development. While information is more freely available to those who are part of internal circles, public scientific dialogue is almost non-existent. A significant Chinese-language research community with Chinese-language research publications has yet to emerge. The political constraints will not only be a drag on China's long-term economic growth, but will also cause a brain drain, with some of the best local talents leaving the country for freer systems in other parts of the world.

Managing the timing and priorities of the changes is becoming increasingly crucial for the Chinese leadership for the future. The evolution of the Chinese economy towards a more market-oriented system cuts both ways. On one hand, the changes have brought prosperity and a brighter growth outlook. On the other hand, they have set in motion forces that will be increasingly difficult to control. It is the latter that clashes with the control ideology of the Communist Party.

Politics aside, the traditional incremental approach can worsen the risks that are inherent in the transition to a market-oriented system. Take financial reform, which is a core policy priority if China wants to change its financial system to one with efficient financial intermediaries driven by commercial incentives. In the absence of fundamental changes in the financial sector, freeing up the banking system when there is still the implicit 100 per cent government guarantee of bank deposits could create more moral hazard problems,[19] and eventually more bad debts, in the system.

Meanwhile, a gradualist approach can encourage more inefficiency and result in legacy problems that could take a long time and a huge amount of resources to correct. Arguably, the financial sector is where it is most difficult to strike a balance between speeding up reform and keeping systemic stability. If reform gets too far ahead of the institutional constraints, systemic instability will follow. For example, continued interest rate liberalization is crucial for making the banking system function efficiently. But a rush for full liberalization without adequate regulatory and supervisory mechanisms in place could create perverse incentives and systemic instability. Indeed, this was one of the root ingredients in the making of the 1997–98 Asian crisis.[20]

As economic liberalization continues, it will be more difficult to keep a tight lid on certain parts of the economy. Thus, any policy or policy experiment that relies on such control will become increasingly ineffective. Capital controls are a good case in point, as they are becoming less effective with domestic and international investors finding ways to get

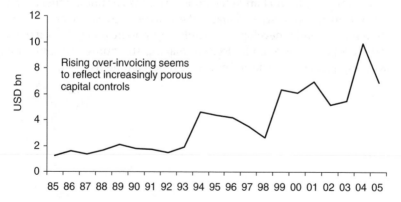

Figure 6.11   Estimated over-invoicing of Chinese imports
Source: CEIC

around them. Over-invoicing in foreign trade is a prime example of capital controls evasion (see Chapter 1, p. 23) and the recent rise in the over-invoicing amount (Figure 6.11) seems to underscore increasing porous capital controls. Keeping a fixed exchange rate while the capital account becomes more open can be a dangerous combination.[21] But full currency convertibility without a well-defined nominal anchor also poses risks of systemic instability.

Evidence and theory suggest that anchoring monetary policy with an explicit long-run low inflation objective would be instrumental in keeping long-term economic stability by tying down inflation expectations and thereby minimizing output and employment volatility. This should apply to China too. A flexible exchange rate (which is already a long-term goal of the Chinese leadership) and an independent central bank are essential for making an efficient monetary framework for delivering macro-economic and financial stability and sustainable economic growth.

Much work remains to be done to sustain long-term growth and to translate the growth into improvements in economic welfare in various parts of the country. China should be mindful that high growth can sometimes mask deep underlying problems. On the other hand, favourable domestic and external circumstances which China has been enjoying in recent years may provide good opportunities for restructuring the economy without causing many economic disruptions.

Beijing has managed its balancing act well so far. But more daunting challenges lie ahead because it will be more difficult for the leadership to continue using controlled policy experiments to feel their way around. The authorities may have to take bigger reform strides, though they will mean moving into uncharted territories. The risks of not moving ahead fast enough are even bigger. A practical way to proceed will be broadening the reform agenda, developing flexible and potent policy instruments and streamlining economic decision-making structures that allow for swift responses to unexpected events and developments.

7
Policy Vision and Inspirations

China's real GDP growth has averaged more than 9 per cent a year[1] since economic reforms unleashed its growth potential. Real per capita GDP has risen more than six-fold, lifting millions of people out of poverty. This spectacular growth performance has been a result of China's move from a centrally planned agrarian economy to an increasingly market-oriented industrial system.

Now China's growth has come to a turning point where its comparative advantage in labour-intensive production is eroding. Government policies are changing to adapt to the increasingly complex economy and facilitate its next transformation towards higher value-added and more capital-intensive production. Since economic policies are moving into 'uncharted waters', sceptics inevitably question Beijing's ability to manage this change and its policy vision, inspiration, direction and their national and global impact.

The government does have a long-term growth vision, but some of its policy aspirations, such as the building of the industrial conglomerates, need to be reassessed carefully. Other policies, such as the exchange rate policy, are puzzling to many observers. Does Beijing want to play by international rules and allow more exchange flexibility? Or does it want to keep exploiting an undervalued currency to gain at the expense of the rest of the global system? China's exchange rate policy indeed has important relevance to its future growth, as Japan's economic doldrums in the 1990s and early 2000s have shown that a wrong currency policy could have disastrous long-term impact on growth.

Policy evolution

China's hybrid economic system, where policy and price signals are often distorted and abused, has raised some concerns about whether its leadership knows what it is doing. However, evidence has shown that

Beijing's policy and reform initiatives have already delivered a benign outcome in the system. For example, take a look at the structural changes in the banking and corporate sectors.

The banking system started off in the 1980s with state control of resources and credit allocation. Banks were *de facto* fiscal lending arms when the government began directing state budgetary allocations to enterprises through the banks. Loans to the state-owned enterprises (SOEs) accounted for all bank lending at the time. Even as quasi-private collectives and non-state enterprises sprang up in the late 1980s and 1990s, banks continued to focus on funding the state sector under the government's planning policies. Not surprisingly, this resulted in poor asset quality and mounting bad debts in the banking system.

Things have changed dramatically since the mid 1990s. The SOEs now account for a much lower share (less than 50 per cent) of total bank borrowing than in the 1980s (Figure 7.1). Even for the state sector as a whole, which includes SOEs, government agencies and departments, its loan share has fallen to about 60 per cent recently. This declining trend of lending to the state sector is set to continue.

More crucially, SOE borrowing has fallen steadily on a flow basis. Some bankers estimated that SOE borrowing would probably account for 35–40 per cent of China's total borrowing today. The steady decline in the SOE loans was obviously a result of the shrinkage of the state sector due to structural reform. Then there was the emergence of the personal and mortgage loan business in the late 1990s. The phenomenal growth of this market underscores the rising, albeit still small,

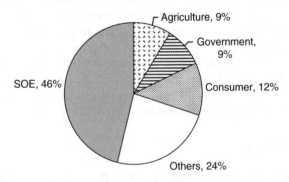

Figure 7.1 Banking system loans (2004)
Source: CEIC

market share of the smaller, more aggressive commercial banks which are less susceptible to policy lending pressure.

The point is that the state sector has lost its monopoly power to dictate capital allocation. The trend for market forces to emerge will continue, even though there is still some way to go for full commercialization of the Chinese banks. Beijing has shown a strong resolve in purging economic inefficiencies. Its creative destruction of the state sector, by allowing the growth of private firms to replace them since the mid 1990s, has resulted in the closure of tens of thousands of inefficient and loss-making SOEs and millions of state job losses. The resultant shrinkage of the state sector[2] and sharp improvement in the profitability of the remaining state firms (Figures 7.2 and 7.3) have led to an equally sharp improvement in the quality of the state borrowers.

All this does not mean that state banks are free from local government pressures on lending (directly or indirectly) to fund social welfare, pensions, housing, education programmes and politically driven investment projects. But the structural improvements in the banks' underlying asset quality mean that Chinese local banks are increasingly spared the task of throwing good money after bad to subsidize large, loss-making state companies. What is crucial to note is the improvement that is happening at the margin of the credit system rather than the absolute amount of lending.

The government's macro-policy management has also improved over the years, suggesting a lower risk of demand mismanagement. Contrast the policy moves in the 1991–95 economic bubble era with the 2002–04 economic imbalance environment. Beijing basically lost control

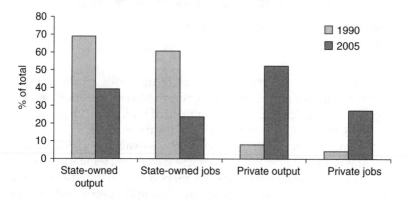

Figure 7.2 State sector declines while private sector thrives
Source: CEIC

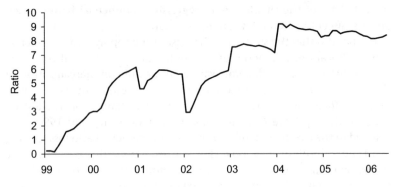

Figure 7.3   State-controlled firms' profit-to-cost ratio
Source: CEIC

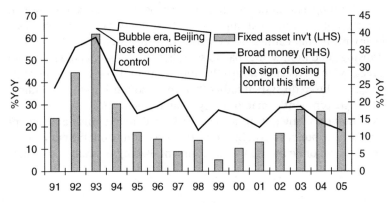

Figure 7.4   Macro-policy management improved
Source: CEIC

in the bubble years during the first half of the 1990s, which saw run-away board money growth fuelling soaring fixed-asset investment growth (Figure 7.4). Inflation soared to an annualized peak rate of 28 per cent in October 1994, leading to plummeting industrial margins.

Between 2002 and 2004, the perception was that soaring bank lending growth was boosting runaway investment growth and leading to an over-heated economy. But evidence did not support that view. Though Beijing did roll out a series of austerity measures to cool the overheated spots in the economy, both broad money supply and fixed-asset investment growth did not show runaway growth (Figure 7.4). In fact, both economic indicators peaked at much lower rates than the pace in the first half of the 1990s. Inflation also peaked at about 5 per cent in the 2002–04 period, almost six times lower than the inflation peak in the 1991–95 period.

All this shows that Beijing was not only in better economic control, it also reacted earlier by implementing cooling measures to prevent the overheated pockets from spreading to the rest of the economy. Better and more responsive economic management has resulted in more effective policies. While it took four years for the government's tightening policies to deliver the desired results in the economy in the early 1990s, the impact of the cooling measures in the early 2000s was felt about a year after their implementation.

Many critics argue that China's demand management depends on administrative controls rather than market-based measures, and government directives will not work in an increasingly market-oriented economy. This is true in the long run, and in fact Beijing has been using more market-based economic tools recently. But in the medium term, the biggest swing factor in driving economic growth, which is investment, is still driven by the state sector either directly or indirectly (Figure 7.5).

As recently as 2005, private-sector investment in fixed assets accounted for 30 per cent of the total. The rest was by companies that still have direct or indirect control by the government. The fact is that investments by these government-controlled or connected firms are not interest-rate sensitive. They are only responsive to government directives. Hence, administrative measures will remain a crucial policy tool for demand management until the market segment gathers a critical mass.

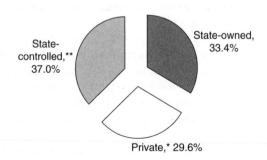

Figure 7.5 Investment still dominated by state sector (2005)
* Incl. foreign funded firms

** Incl. collectives, share holding firms, etc., which still have direct or indirect state control
Source: CEIC

Strategic drive and vision

The Chinese leadership has demonstrated strategic vision in correcting some of the root problems in the system. The most notable problems include an uneven playing field between domestic and foreign firms, round-tripping investments (see below), widening of regional disparity, the low value-added trap of the Chinese industries and the lack of policy flexibility due to the exchange rate constraint. Only time will tell if the policies have worked. But the initiatives and measures in the works show that the leadership knows where the growth stress points are. It is not sitting on its hands, though some of its policy strategies need reassessing and fine-tuning.

Tax reform is the single most important drive and the biggest change for more than a decade to correct some of the fundamental flaws in the system. After ten years of policy debate, the State Council has finally moved on with unifying corporate income tax rates and wage expenses for local firms and foreign-invested enterprises (FIEs). Implementation of the tax reform package is expected in 2008.

This tax reform serves to provide a level playing field for competition between domestic firms and FIEs in two ways. One is through unifying the tax rate. Currently, local companies pay a statutory 33 per cent tax on profit, but over 90 per cent of FIEs pay between 15 per cent and 24 per cent due to the preferential treatment granted to them in the special economic zones (SEZs) and various other development zones.

The other one is through unifying the wage expense. As part of the income tax reform, local firms will also benefit from full deductibility of wage expenses. Currently, most local firms are only allowed to deduct wage expenses of RMB1,600 per person per month from income tax. But the FIEs are allowed full deduction.

The tax reform will also help reduce regional income disparity over the long term. The current tax system has contributed to rising income inequality between the coastal and inland regions. This is because the tax incentives for foreign direct investment (FDI) to locate in the SEZs have boosted income growth in the coastal regions (in which the SEZs reside) to rates far exceeding those in the inland regions for over three decades.

Unifying the tax rates paid by the local and foreign firms should help break this FDI concentration in the eastern coastal regions. Coupled with other sector-based tax breaks, which aim at fostering certain industries to spread across the country (see below), tax reform is expected to encourage a more even growth pattern between the regions.

In the medium term, unifying the corporate tax rates is expected to reduce the incentive for round-tripping investments,[3] whereby capital that originates from China goes through another country, often an offshore tax haven, before re-entering China as 'foreign' investment to take advantage of its preferential tax treatment for FIEs. Such money could be from state- or private-owned mainland firms, Chinese individuals or China-based Hong Kong, Taiwan and foreign firms recycling earnings from their mainland operations. Their overseas vehicles are typically holding companies that hold no operating assets, except their mainland-registered ventures. Such 'fake FDI' might have accounted for a quarter or more of total FDI inflows to China over the years.

Within a few years, the government wants to complete unification of the three tax rates of 15 per cent, 24 per cent and 33 per cent for different types of business ownership to one standard rate of 25 per cent across all firms, disregarding their ownership. However, some sector-specific preferential tax treatments will remain, including environmental protection, high-tech, software, new materials, alternative energy and major equipment, to foster more even development and a green economy.

The tax reform should be expansionary in the short-term, as Beijing's corporate tax intake is estimated to fall by RMB100 billion (US$12.7 billion) in the year when the unification of tax rates takes effect. Obviously, the benefit of a lower tax rate for local firms (from 33 per cent to 25 per cent) will be felt directly and at once. This should lead to increase in investment and hiring, triggering an expansionary effect on the economy.

Meanwhile, the FIEs should see their effective tax rates rise only gradually over five years, due to the phase in process and grandfather provisions. But overall, the FIEs will continue to enjoy slightly lower effective tax rates than local firms, due to their higher exposure to sectors that enjoy sector-based preferential tax treatment, such as environment, high-tech and software.

Big is not beautiful

However, some of the policy visions need to be reassessed, especially in face of the more competitive economic environment after the 1997–98 Asia crisis. Notable is China's 'big is beautiful' mindset. On one hand, Beijing's top leadership has been trying to reduce economic inefficiency by offloading hundreds of SOEs through mergers and sales. On the other hand, it still wants to grow China's own Fortune-500 companies, even though they do not necessarily mean direct state ownership.

Many of China's leading thinkers still believe that by achieving economies of scale, corporate expansion is the way to cut economic inefficiency. This means building corporate giants, such as Korea's chaebol which are non-government-owned business conglomerates but with extensive government connection and financing and fiscal assistance.[4] Such thinking in fact reflects the communist 'grow your way out' mentality, which was also manifested in former premier Zhu Rong-ji's banking reform policy.

The background and structure of the Korean chaebol are quite similar to the Chinese environment. That is why the Chinese leaders are attracted to the model. But the chaebol's collapse during the 1997–98 Asian crisis should serve China as lessons for reassessing its plan for following the chaebol model. First and foremost, the chaebol model showed that distorted incentives were not limited to state-owned companies. Heavy government intervention in privately owned businesses could lead to dire problems too.

The Korean government, which copied the Japanese keiretsu[5] model initially, played an active role in the creation and expansion of the chaebol into a web of interlocking bureaucracies and big businesses. Although the chaebol were family-owned private firms, they had close ties with the government which gave them access to preferential treatments, such as tax subsidies, special grants and cheap credit.

This cosy business–government relationship created serious incentive distortion and moral hazard problems in the Korean system. Excessive risk-taking became an inherent part of the chaebol model. This was because the costs of corporate imprudent decisions and bad behaviour were shared with the general public via government credit and/or tax subsidies. These close business ties with the government effectively allowed the chaebol to socialize the risk of business failure.

China also has a habit of heavy economic intervention, which ultimately creates all the inefficiency in the state sector. Although the government has noticeably reduced its 'visible hand' to direct economic activity in recent years, the effort to purge inefficiency is still hampered by the old mindset towards preserving the state's role in China's mixed economy to influence business decisions.

Thus, Beijing is attracted to South Korea's experience, as it seems to suggest that China could possibly tread a middle road, combining a strong and activist government with a private, albeit not completely free, market system. However, the collapse of the chaebol during the Asian crisis showed that government could fail in a market economy just as miserably as it had in a traditional centrally planned economy.

The goal of China's corporate sector reform should be two-fold: to shrink the state sector sharply and to withdraw government influence in business decisions completely. Beijing has achieved much in the former, but it still has difficulty in letting go of its control mindset. The bottom line for the government is to establish the rule of law and to improve the provision of public goods, but not to micro-manage the economy through business tie-up with private companies, such as building chaebol-like conglomerates.

The chaebol's failure also shows that the industrial policy behind them could be very counterproductive and China should steer clear of it. Arguably, the industrial policies Korea pursued in the earlier decades of its development might have caused huge distortions in resources allocation. For example, Korea built a car industry in the 1980s and early 1990s under government guidance primarily aimed at exporting, despite overcapacity in the world car industry. The chaebol also expanded aggressively beyond their core business of manufacturing into semi-conductors under strong government backing, just in time to see the plunge in global chip prices in the second half of the 1990s.

China has also started building a modern car industry under state guidance and support in recent years. The aspiration to build a national pillar industry is understandable, given China's pool of engineering talent and huge domestic market. However, rapid technological advancement and fast changes in the marketplace on the back of rising competition will quickly outdate any grandiose industrial policies, no matter how cleverly designed.

The overcapacity problem associated with the push for building big is starting to show in some areas. For example, massive investment in new plants in China's steel industry has lifted its steel-making capacity by almost 30 per cent in 2005 to 470 million tonnes; all in the name of Beijing's industrialization policy based on the 'build it and people will buy it' assumption. Feeding all those new mills with iron ore pushed up contract prices for the raw material by a total of 100 per cent in 2005 and 2006. But the demand behind the building binge was never as robust as the policymakers assumed. Hence, steel product prices plunged by over a third in 2006. Similar problems are emerging in other sectors, such as cars and cement.

The point is that bureaucrats cannot outwit the market in picking winners. While the chaebol model was built on the 'big is beautiful' basis, the size of a corporation does not matter much in determining success in today's information age. The Korean chaebol were no doubt masters of quickly creating gigantic, diversified and over-extended organizations that emphasized scope and scale. But these also created inherent problems of controls and coordination and a bias towards growth at the expense of earnings and profitability. As they turned out, the chaebol expanded aggressively, but they lack clear business focus and core competence.

Despite China's recent policy's emphasis on freeing the small SOEs, the old mentality still wants to keep and grow the large enterprises. The conservatives reckon that if China could make its biggest firms successful, then the country would be on its way to becoming an industrial powerhouse like Korea. Such a mindset remains stubbornly embedded despite the creation of the State-owned Assets Supervision and Administration Commission (SASAC), which is empowered with privatizing the state companies.

While the government is planning to cut sharply the 167 central government-owned enterprises, it still aims at keeping about 80 large ones that are of strategic importance. There are more SOEs at the provincial levels that the local governments will want to keep for the same reason.

The temptation is for the government to turn these companies into conglomerates through mergers and consolidations with the smaller companies. This strategy will inevitably come with implicit government guarantee of capital, bank credit, market power and political favours. The danger is that these conglomerates could in time become inefficient and unruly oligopolies.

However, China has improved on one key area where Korea had not, and that is banking. The Korean crisis had its roots in a bad banking system. The Korean government played a big role in directing banks to lend to the politically connected chaebol. Easy credit had led to a dangerously leveraged corporate sector, with a debt-to-equity ratio of over 500 per cent in most big Korean firms just before the financial crisis broke in 1998. The huge risk of concentration, aggravated by borrowers' reckless expansion, had threatened the viability of the Korean banking system in the years running up to the 1998 financial crisis.

Local Chinese banks have also been used as a tool for quasi-fiscal operations. Most of the loans used to be employed to sustain loss-making SOEs so as to avoid soaring unemployment. However, the situation has changed drastically since the mid 1990s, when Beijing started earnestly to restructure the corporate and banking sectors (see Chapters 2 and 3). Today, the state sector accounts for just about 60 per cent of total banking credit, down from 100 per cent in the early 1980s and 75 per cent in the mid-1990s.

The resolve of the Chinese leaders to allow creative destruction to unfold suggests that they were concerned about the systemic risks that the bad

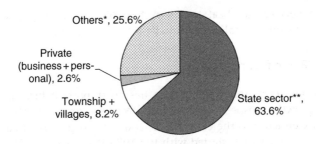

Figure 7.6 Share of loans (September 2006)

* Incl. loans to companies with indirect government control or with minority government stake

** Incl. SOEs, government agencies and departments

Source: CEIC

banking system could bring. The easy parts of the bank restructuring have been done, namely reducing government-directed lending to the SOEs, cutting bad loans and recapitalizing the banks. However, much has yet to be done on the most crucial step of withdrawing government intervention in the banking system and establishing an arm's-length relation between the banks and borrowers.

Only when there is no official intervention would banks be able to operate on a commercial basis. Rather than focusing on serving the SOEs, banks must channel credit to the private sector and individuals. This market has just started and will have to a long way to go. Excluding mortgage loans, private sector and individual loans account for less than 3 per cent of total bank credit (Figure 7.6). Mortgage lending only adds another 8 per cent share to the private sector/individual loans in the system.

In fact, China does not have to follow the Korean chaebol model to build world-class manufacturing. In comparison, Taiwan's development model stands up better. The island's petrochemical and high-tech firms are as successful as the Korean chaebol. But unlike the Korean giants, Taiwan's many small and mid-sized firms are more flexible, focused and disciplined, with the bottom line on profitability rather than size. They have also proven to be more resilient to adverse shocks, including the Asian crisis, and highly adaptable to changes.

The point is that cosy government–business relations will not help improve China's economic structure. Building conglomerates with the backing of industrial policy may not lead to the desired results no matter how good the policy intentions are. Experience has shown that policymakers cannot beat the market in picking industrial winners. China's chaebol mentality needs to be reassessed carefully.

The RMB and future growth

Meanwhile, its currency policy also has an important bearing on its future growth prospect. Japan's lost decade throughout the 1990s, which extended into the early 2000s, could be attributable to a wrong currency policy which started with the 1985 Plaza Accord.[6] The lesson from the Japanese experience is that currency policy could make or break a country's future growth. But the debate on China's currency policy since late 2002 has masked the fundamental trends, and a large part of that debate has been distorted by political incentives.[7]

There are strong arguments for China to pursue a floating exchange rate regime as a permanent policy option. The most common logic is that China is a big and closed economy. The latter is contrary to perception but it is seen clearly in the small size of its trade sector relative to GDP (Figure 7.7). Being big and closed means that the impact of the external influences on the domestic sector should be limited so that China should have enough autonomy to conduct domestic economic policy.[8]

To see this, consider the arguments for why fixed exchange rate is better suited to a small open economy like Hong Kong than a big closed economy like China. Since the trade sector of a small open economy is a large share (often over 100 per cent) of GDP, the cost of currency fluctuation

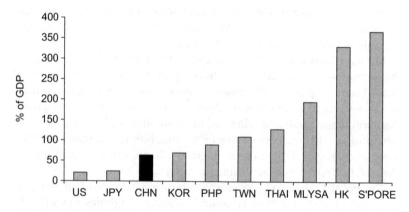

Figure 7.7 Size of the trade sector
Source: CEIC

under a floating exchange rate can often be very high (although there are also other arguments for small economies to have floating exchange rates).

In other words, for a small open economy, external shocks often overwhelm the impact of domestic monetary policy, rendering it powerless as an economic management tool. So it is better to anchor monetary policy on the fixed exchange rate to minimize the currency risk in the economy. By contrast, China's large closed economy, especially with its capital controls and a small foreign debt, argues for a floating rate regime to maximize policy flexibility for economic management.

However, China has adopted a *de facto* renminbi (RMB, also called yuan) peg against the US dollar since 1994.[9] There is a view that a weak central bank needs a currency peg against a hard currency to build confidence in combating inflation. Until recently, that has been the argument for keeping the RMB peg. The Chinese authorities have been strengthening the People's Bank of China's (PBoC) credibility since 2000.

The PBoC has revamped its structure along the line of the US Federal Reserve Board by forming a monetary committee that meets monthly to formulate monetary policy. It has also moved to reduce political interference by slashing the number of provincial and municipal offices from over 30 to just 9. Beijing is also issuing more treasury bonds and bills and nurturing the growth of the interbank market (Figure 7.8) to facilitate the conduct of monetary policy. The authorities have shown a great determination to fight inflation and keep it low since 1994. Chinese CPI inflation peaked at over 25 per cent in 1994 and has since fallen to less than 2 per cent since 2005.

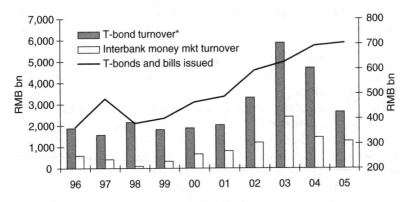

Figure 7.8 Chinese debt market growing

* Incl. trading on Shanghai and Shenzhen stock exchanges
Source: CEIC

So being a big and closed economy with better monetary policy management argues for China to switch over to a floating exchange rate system. But why has Beijing been dragging its feet, despite its repeated promises to change? Meanwhile, international pressure has mounted on China since 2005 to revalue the RMB to correct the international imbalance of payments. The imbalance is reflected in China's persistent current account surplus and the chronic US current account deficit. But even the Americans know that revaluing the RMB *per se* will not solve the problem, which involves a global saving-investment imbalance. Why have they kept pushing for sharp RMB revaluation?

The RMB controversy reflects a battle of economic principles on which a compromise is difficult to come by. For China, the principle is a matter of control of the economic development process by the government and the Communist Party. This is a mindset that the Chinese cannot change quickly despite more than two decades of economic liberalization. The Americans' principle, on the other hand, rests on the reliance on market forces to drive economic development. The two principles clash when they meet over global trade.

Deep down, this controversy is quite different from the usual debate on whether America gains economically from trading with China. It clearly does. But for many Americans, when an exchange rate is determined by the Chinese government and not the market, the Chinese government becomes the implicit decision maker on who wins or loses in Sino–US trade – whether they be creditors or debtors, consumers or manufacturers? The American principle holds that it should be the market that decides the trade outcome and not the policy of some government.

Some China sceptics also refute the mainstream argument that China needs to fix its exchange rate against a hard currency as a check against irresponsible monetary policy so that internal market forces can set relative prices effectively. This argument assumes an immature Chinese central bank. This is still true in a general sense despite recent structural reforms at the PBoC.

Deeper reform of the central bank is needed to purge its structural and institutional inefficiencies. However, before the PBoC reform is completed, a fixed exchange rate can be a tool to help protect the market from damaging policy in setting relative prices. The point is to force the PBoC to run a monetary policy that is anchored on fixing the external value of the currency so that it cannot engage in domestic policy sabotage.

However, the sceptics argue that market forces do not operate freely in China, so they do not set relative prices. A notable distortion is the labour market. As the largest employer, the state plays a key role in setting wages, controlling labour movement and thus blocking the market mechanism from pricing labour properly. The state also determines how many engineers, doctors, accounts, lawyers, factory workers and so on will be educated, who will be in what occupation and where they will be assigned to, at least initially. In the energy and commodity sectors, the government still sets prices for many products.

Under this situation, a fixed exchange rate does not protect the market mechanism from state distortion effected by the central bank. Instead, it protects state policy in setting administered prices from the rigours of the price mechanism set by international markets. This is because the fixed exchange rate takes away the market discipline that a floating exchange rate imposes on the tradable goods market.

Hence, these critics argue, the Chinese authorities are intent on keeping a fixed exchange rate not to discipline the PBoC but to keep state control of the economy. While this line of thinking may be too US-centric, there is some element of truth. Before China can change its old mentality completely, the principle of control will remain difficult to compromise under the current political system and the fight over China's currency policy will go on.

There is no doubt that most Americans benefit from Sino-US trade under China's fixed exchange rate. China's resistance to letting the RMB rise has been partly responsible for capping the global pricing power of tradable goods. This has enabled American consumers to buy goods at low prices, making them the winners in the Sino-US trade. Meanwhile, to keep the RMB from appreciating on the back of a rising trade surplus, the PBoC has been buying excess dollars and accumulating massive foreign reserves (over US$1 trillion as of 2006).

Since the domestic return of capital is low, the PBoC has turned around and lent the dollars back to America by buying US Treasury, corporate and home-loan securities. This, in turn, has kept both the Treasury borrowing costs and mortgage interest rates in US lower than they would otherwise be, thus boosting US economic and asset price growth. American house owners, asset holders and taxpayers are also winners in this arrangement.

On the other hand, the competitive stress created by the Chinese manufacturers has made American manufacturers losers in the Sino-US trade, as their goods are now being made in China. However, the losses to these producers are outweighed by a combination of two benefits. First is the income earned, and eventually repatriated, by American international companies which have moved their production bases to China. Second is the benefit from the Chinese subsidies on US imports of consumer goods (in the form of lower prices) and the reduction in US borrowing costs that have resulted from China's recycling of its trade surplus back to the US by buying US fixed-income securities.

While the economic logic and benefits are clear, the politics behind this arrangement is much more complicated and often distorted by vested interests for political purposes.[10] From the American perspective, it is the Chinese government, and not the market or the US political process that determines the winners and losers and distribution of the Sino-US trade impact.

Radical thinkers even argue that Americans are buying more Chinese-made toys, tee-shirts, lingerie, appliances and are living in bigger homes than they would otherwise be able to afford because of the Chinese government's decision to pursue an undervalued currency. Americans are making fewer appliances and manufactured goods and producing less agricultural output, also thanks to this 'cheap' currency policy of China's.

This thinking creates big political tensions because of the belief that the Chinese subsidies, in the form of lower import prices and interest rates, are changing American behaviour in a way determined by the Chinese but not by the American themselves. This is to say, in the US it is the market that determines relative prices that drive economic decisions. But in China, it is not. And through trade, China's resistance to the RMB rising on the back of a rising external surplus is imposing on the Americans the Chinese decision about resources allocation. The Americans feel that they have lost control of their economic well-being. Hence they want to fight back.

On the other hand, the Chinese want to keep control of the economic decision-making process, at least until they can shake off the communist legacy. Hence, the currency policy becomes a domestic issue for the Chinese, but not the Americans, to decide. International trade, by bringing together the self-interest of the two sides, just provides a catalyst for these different principles to clash. And the fight has manifested itself in the currency policy controversy.

A flexible RMB has to be part of the solution to the global economic imbalances and the Chinese authorities have begun to move towards that, albeit slowly. However, China should not move towards a floating exchange rate regime too quickly. This is because a higher RMB alone is not going to solve global economic imbalance, as some Americans have erroneously argued (see below).

It is also wrong to point the finger at only China. The US is running a large, and growing, current account deficit with other parts of the world too, notably Japan and the Middle East oil exporters. In particular, the

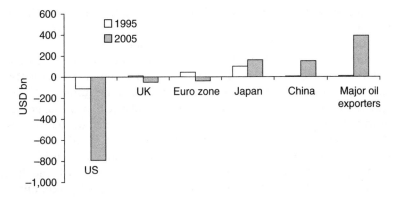

Figure 7.9 Current account balances
Sources: CEIC, IMF, OECD

latter's collective current account surplus was twice as large as China's in 2005 (Figure 7.9). Meanwhile, China has absorbed most of Asia's processing industry and become the last stop in the Asian supply chain before the exports leave for the final markets. Thus, it is natural that China has also accounted for the bulk of the region's foreign exchange reserves building up. In fact, China accounted for over 85 per cent of all of Asia's new foreign reserves in both 2005 and 2006.

The erroneous belief of many Americans that a higher RMB would solve the US current account deficit problem reflects the fundamental flaws in the American Public law.[11] This law requires the US Treasury Secretary to assess whether countries like China that have large bilateral trade surpluses with the US are rigging their exchange rates to prevent effective balance of payments adjustments or to gain an unfair competitive advantage in international trade.

This law is fundamentally flawed because it assumes all current account surpluses are evidence of currency manipulation by the foreign trading partners in question. This assumption has impaired the judgement of many US lawmakers, observers and analysts. They fail to see that China's aim for pegging the RMB is to secure internal economic stability but not to achieve a mercantile advantage in the world export markets.

China did have the world's largest bilateral trade surplus with the US between 2000 and 2004, but not any more. Since 2005, the collective trade surplus of the major oil-exporting countries has become larger than China's surplus. However, what makes the Americans target China with complaints, despite the fact that China's trade surplus with the US is now smaller than that of the oil-exporting countries, is that China is a major competitor of many US manufacturers. But US imports of oil products are seen as vital inputs for the US economy.

Some American politicians have exploited the flaw in the Public Law to distort the debate on China's external surplus and its currency policy.[12] The Law fails to recognize that the persistent current account surplus in China and deficit in the US are results of a savings imbalance that exchange rate movement alone cannot resolve. China's saving is much higher than its domestic investment, which amounts to 40 per cent of GDP, and thus has to export its excess savings. But America's savings are much lower than its domestic investment, which is about 16 per cent of GDP, and thus it has to import the savings shortfall. Note that most Asian economies also run persistent current account surpluses due to excess saving.

This has resulted in a stable disequilibrium where China (and Asia) runs a current account surplus while the US runs a current account deficit. America's large current account deficit reflects its need to borrow from the rest of the world to cover its savings shortfall. This process represents a transfer of savings from the surplus economies, such as China and Asia, to the US so that it can spend more on goods and services than it produces.

This is a disequilibrium situation because, without this savings transfer, the US would suffer a credit crunch; interest rates would soar so that investment would collapse. But the disequilibrium is stable as long as the Chinese (and other Asian) surplus continues to flow to the US to cover its deficit.

However, if there is no correction in the US savings deficiency and if China suddenly stops recycling its savings to the US, the US current account deficit will fall abruptly. This, in turn, will force the US economy into sharp contraction, causing serious economic dislocation. In other words, it will do the US no good if its current account deficit falls sharply and quickly. This brings back the question about the sharp RMB revaluation that some Americans have pushed for so strongly. If they succeed, and the RMB revaluation sinks the Chinese economy so that its surplus recycling ability disappears, they will likely bring an economic disaster upon America rather than save it from one.

Those who push for a big RMB revaluation are naïve to believe that a change in the exchange rate could correct America's savings-investment imbalance. For America's part, if it could raise its savings rate gradually, its current account deficit would fall over time, even without the need for any major exchange rate realignment with its trading partners. For China, it will have to do the opposite to help solve this global disequilibrium by consuming more and saving less. And Beijing is moving in this direction.

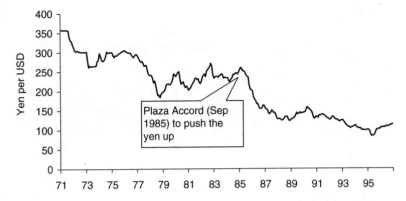

Figure 7.10 Yen/USD exchange rate
Source: CEIC

The consequences of misdiagnosing the US current account deficit as an exchange rate problem could be very bad for China's future growth. Japan provides a lesson. When Japan had the largest bilateral trade surplus with the US in the 1980s, the US government exerted persistent pressure on Japan to appreciate the yen in the same belief that it has today that a higher exchange rate for its trading partner would correct the US trade deficit without structural adjustment by the US. The yen indeed rose sharply by 70 per cent between 1980 and 1995 (Figure 7.10).

Japan's loose economic policy in the 1980s created an asset bubble in both its stock and property markets, which burst in 1991. The high yen aggravated the resultant deflationary slump. Despite a zero interest rate policy (ZIRP) and quantitative easing by the Bank of Japan (BoJ), which flooded the domestic system with a huge amount of cash, a liquidity trap followed. This resulted in Japan's lost decade of the 1990s, which extended into the early 2000s. However, the higher yen led to no obvious decline in Japan's trade surplus (Figure 7.11), as the fall in domestic imports from the sluggish economy offset the fall in exports from the high yen.

Japan's experience is relevant to China's currency policy and its future economic growth. China fixed its exchange rate at RMB8.28 per US dollar between 1994 and July 2005. The purpose was to use the dollar exchange rate to anchor China's price level at a time when financial liberalization and economic transformation made domestic monetary indicators unstable. This policy has been successful in stamping out inflation and reducing economic volatility. China's high inflation of the mid 1990s came down sharply and converged with that in the US

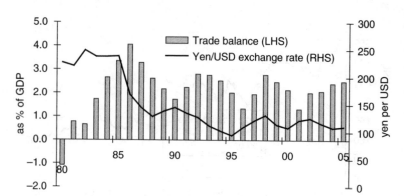

Figure 7.11   Japan trade balance and exchange rate
Source: CEIC

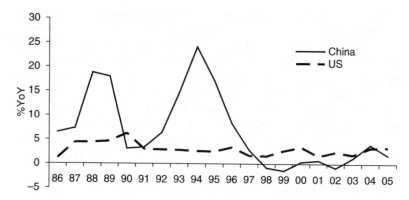

Figure 7.12   Consumer price index
Source: CEIC

(Figure 7.12), just as the principle of relative purchasing power parity under a fixed exchange rate regime would suggest.

Here is why external pressure should not force China to revalue the RMB sharply. China's inflation (a little over 1 per cent since 2006) has fallen way below the US (3 per cent in 2006). Any sharp rise in the RMB exchange rate will easily push China back into deflation. Despite its robust real economic fundamentals, if China is forced to push up the RMB because bad usage of economic theory suggests that a higher RMB would eventually cut its trade surplus with the US, the possibility of a Japanese-style economic quagmire could be the result in China. For the sake of its own growth future and US economic well-being, China should keep its exchange rate stable in the medium term.

Over the longer term, China needs to increase private consumption and reduce its savings glut. Beijing has launched a major policy initiative towards achieving this goal (see Chapter 6, 'Growth model shifting' section and the last section in this chapter). But the US also needs to do its part and drastically rein in its fiscal deficit to boost national saving. If China does its part to address the global imbalance but the US does not, then China's reduced trade surplus would mean less lending to the US. This, in turn, would lead to higher US and global interest rates, with negative implications for US and global growth.

In any event, forcing China to revalue sharply will not help; and China should not move hastily to free the RMB. More RMB flexibility is part of the adjustment package for global disequilibrium. The Chinese authorities have already begun to loosen capital account controls slowly. But all these policies will take time. China's high savings rate will only fall gradually over the next two decades. Meanwhile, its manufacturing and processing clout will likely rise further for a few more years, putting further upward pressure on the current account. As for the world, it will have to put up with this imbalance for a while longer.

Dilemma with foreign reserves

Thus, for its own and the world's benefits, China should move towards a floating exchange rate regime over time. But it should not do it in a hurry. A fixed exchange rate takes away the flexibility of demand management policy. Consider the calls, including those from Premier Wen Jai-bao and Vice President Zheng Qing-hong in 2006, for China to spend its trillion dollar-strong foreign reserves on domestic development, fixing economic ailments and boosting long-term GDP growth. But no matter how admirable those policy goals are, spending the foreign reserves would be a blunt demand management policy tool under the current inflexible exchange rate system.

The RMB has been fixed against the US dollar since 1995. Even after it was re-pegged to a basket of currencies in July 2005, it retained its inflexible nature. Under this currency regime, the foreign reserves represent no more than the asset side of a balance sheet against which the central bank holds liabilities; they are not a *trouvaille* that the government can use for macro-economic policy objectives.

Whether the foreign reserves are used to fund rural education, buy high-tech equipment for Chinese companies or fund environmental protection or medical care, the result is the same: the PBoC's asset is depleted as it does not get an equivalent asset in exchange, while its liabilities remain the same. This is unlike using the reserves to buy US Treasury bonds, which is not an instance of spending but of asset exchange.

In the absence of an asset exchange, all the dollars that the PBoC spent out of the foreign reserves must go back to its vault to balance the books. The current exchange rate regime acts as the conduit for doing this, but at the same time it eliminates any intended macro-policy impact on the economy of using the reserves.

To see this, assume that Beijing wants to use $1 million of foreign reserves to hire more teachers in rural Shanxi, one of China's poorest provinces, to boost the local economy. After receiving the money, the Shanxi school authorities would have to sell those dollars to a local bank for RMB to pay for the teachers' salaries. To raise the funds, the local bank would then have to sell the $1 million to one of China's authorized foreign-currency dealing banks.

This process would create downward pressure on the US dollar. The central bank would buy up the $1 million, thus supplying more RMB, to keep the exchange rate constant. This means that the PBoC would get back its $1 million and the size of China's foreign reserves would remain the same. However, the process would also create an extra $1 million worth of RMB in the economy. The PBoC would have to sell bonds to mop up the extra RMB, or it would risk igniting inflationary pressures in the economy. This manoeuvre, to offset the impact of exchange rate intervention (by increasing domestic money supply) on the local economy, is called 'sterilization' under the fixed exchange regime.

In a nutshell, to keep the RMB exchange rate constant when the currency is under upward pressure, the central bank sells RMB for US dollars. But that would increase money supply in the local economy and risk igniting inflation. Consequently, the central bank sterilizes this impact by issuing bonds to mop up the excess RMB, thus offsetting the inflationary impact of foreign exchange intervention. The process is reversed if the RMB is under downward pressure.

Things would be different if China shifted to a floating exchange rate system and liberalized its capital accounts. The PBoC would no longer have to buy all the US dollars. It could let the exchange rate move by market forces until it found a buyer. Without the need for foreign exchange intervention and subsequent sterilization, China would regain monetary policy flexibility for macro-economic management. As long as Beijing keeps its *de facto* fixed rate regime, it has no policy flexibility in using foreign reserves for macro-economic management.

However, when considering the policy impact of spending China's foreign reserves, one should also distinguish between macro-economic and micro-economic aspects. While the macro-impact may be muted, spending the reserves could still have some distributional effect on the economy.

In our case of Shanxi here, more teachers would still be hired by the new programme funded by the reserves. Its education standard would also be raised. However, the increased spending by Shanxi's teachers would be offset by the fall in demand in other parts of the province, or even of the country, due to the PBoC's sterilization effort. This is equivalent to reshuffling wealth distribution among various areas or sectors, while keeping the size of the cake constant.

Overall national demand would remain unchanged. What changes would be the composition of the economy's balance sheet. For the banks and households who have bought the sterilization bonds, they have replaced lending (consumption in the case of households) with an increased holding of government bonds. Meanwhile, the government's net indebtedness goes up.

The micro-economic impact might even have an indirect effect on China's structural behaviour. Spending the reserves on education could raise China's future productivity, and hence growth potential. If the reserves were spent on social services, the resultant improvement in the welfare system could boost consumer confidence, and thus help reduce China's excess saving. This would, in turn, help reduce China's saving and investment gap, and eventually the current account's structural imbalance.

There is no *a priori* reason to push for a complete RMB regime shift in the near term. Chinese authorities do have a goal of moving to a floating RMB regime in the longer term. They are implementing the needed changes gradually. Given the trends that are unfolding, it is unlikely that China would make the same currency policy mistake as Japan did in the 1980s and 1990s in derailing its long-term growth.

The innovation drive

When China's policymakers want to shift growth momentum towards the domestic sector, they clearly understand that becoming the world factory is not a sustainable strategy. The rapid growth of low-end manufacturing has led to a surge in China's trade surplus. The ensuing political pressure on RMB appreciation and intensifying trade frictions with major trading partners have become one of the most crucial macro-economic challenges

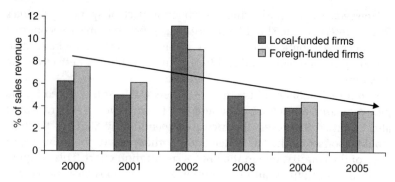

Figure 7.13 Declining profit margin: electronics sector
Source: CEIC

facing China's policymakers. It is also not in China's best interest to remain as the world factory in the long term because dwelling on making low value-added goods could trap China in the low end of the production chain. This, in turn, will hinder its move up the value ladder over the long term (see Chapter 1, p. 20).

The decline in profit margins in low-end exports indicates that the export strategy based on selling cheap labour-intensive goods is not sustainable. For example, the pre-tax margins of one of the most representative export sectors, electronics, have fallen steadily in recent years, disregarding whether it is the foreign- or local-funded firms which made the products (Figure 7.13).

More crucially, the share of value-added gained by China in the global supply chain is also depressed. This suggests that Chinese manufacturers are reaping fewer and fewer profits by selling into the global market. For example, with a retail price of US$200 for a Nikon camera made in China but sold in New York, the design, high-tech components and distribution segments of the supply are estimated to reap over 95 per cent of sale revenues. In other words, Chinese manufacturers get less than the 5 per cent of the pie!

Meanwhile, China's focus on low-end manufacturing and exports has worsened its terms of trade (measured by the ratio of export-to-import prices). This is a result of its need for importing a large amount of raw materials and natural resources at rising commodity prices to make the exports which are selling at falling prices. Since 2000, China's export price index (of electronics, apparels and shoes) has fallen by 3 per cent, while its import price index (of energy, raw materials and technologies) has risen by almost 60 per cent. In other words, Chinese manufacturers have seen their export pricing power being eroded due to rising competition, but at the same time suffered from rapid rising input costs.

This deteriorating terms-of-trade could develop into a secular trend as globalization, rising productivity and excess capacity from Asia will continue to squeeze export pricing power while supply–demand imbalance will keep pushing up commodity prices. The terms-of-trade shock is like a negative income shock on the economy, as China has to make and sell an increasing amount of exports to buy a given amount of imports. This is another reason why the low-cost labour-intensive export strategy is unsustainable.

To break out of the low value-added trap, the government has started to make serious efforts to promote home-grown technologies and local innovation capability. In February 2006, the State Council outlined the national Medium- and Long-Term Science and Technology (S&T) Development Plan for the next fifteen years. Beijing recognizes that China's S&T development capability is still lagging behind other developed countries by a wide margin.

This is seen in China's very high dependency on imported technologies, limited number of domestically owned patents and insufficient research and development (R&D) investments. Official data shows that China ranked 28 among the 49 major countries in terms of S&T innovation capacity (as measured by technology contribution to growth, R&D-to-GDP ratio and dependency on external technology).

The government is striving to push China up the innovation league in the next fifteen years by raising R&D spending to 2 per cent of GDP in 2010 and 2.5 per cent in 2020 from the current 1.3 per cent of GDP. That will put China on a par in terms of R&D spending with Germany and the US (Figure 7.14). This also implies that China's R&D spending will rise at an annual rate 21 per cent over the medium term, significantly faster than the expected average nominal GDP growth rate of 11 per cent.

Following from this initiative are other long-term efforts. One is to raise the contribution of productivity (resulted from technological improvement) to 60 per cent of economic growth by 2020 from less than 40 per cent currently and cut the dependency on imported technologies by half from the current 60 per cent of total technologies used. Another is to boost the annual number of patents obtained by Chinese nationals and the number of scientific research papers being published internationally to the top five in world by 2020.

The government is also rolling out tax incentives to boost innovation. It will allow exemption of 150 per cent R&D spending from the corporate income tax, up from the current 100 per cent. This is especially beneficial for start-up technology firms, as the tax leverage to boost profit, and hence incentive, will be especially high.

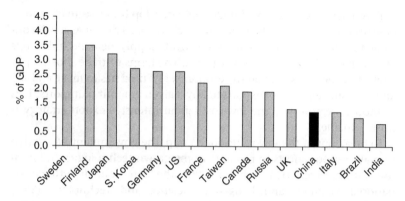

Figure 7.14   R&D spending to GDP
Source: Chinese Ministry of Science & Technology

For a typical high-tech firm with a 10 per cent R&D spending-to-sales ratio, a 10 per cent effective corporate income tax rate and a 10 per cent net profit margin, this policy would boost its post-tax earnings by 5 per cent. For firms at their early stage of development with thinner profit margins (for example 3 per cent), assuming the same R&D intensity and effective corporate tax rate as the typical firm above, the impact on its bottom lines of the tax exemption could be as big as 17 per cent.

High-tech firms will also be allowed to depreciate their investment in R&D facilities faster, which means bigger tax-deductibles boosting bottom-line earnings. Meanwhile, new high-tech set-ups in designated high-tech development zones will be entitled to a two-year income tax exemption from the first profit-making year, and a favourable income tax rate of 15 per cent afterwards (compared with the usual 33 per cent corporate tax rate).

To encourage local innovation, the government is reducing support for importing complete sets of machinery and equipment. It is switching the focus of preferential policy to importing raw materials and key components for domestic firms by exempting them from tariffs and import VAT. The aim is to encourage local capability to manufacture advanced equipment with home-grown technologies.

Fiscal spending on R&D is a key initiative to mobilize/induce more private investment. Indeed, Beijing has been taking the lead to boost R&D spending in recent years (Figure 7.15). The S&T plan aims at boosting the growth rate of fiscal spending on R&D sharply higher than that of overall government spending. Further, any excess fiscal revenue over budget each year will be allocated to R&D activities.

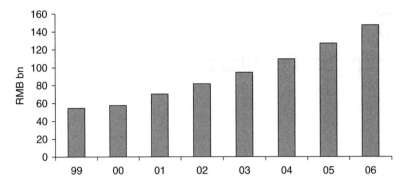

Figure 7.15 Fiscal spending on R&D activities
Source: Chinese Ministry of Science & Technology

Home-grown technologies will be promoted through public procurement policies, in particular by giving buying priorities to domestic suppliers that own intellectual property rights. For example, the S&T plan requires the procurement of local-made equipment to be at least 60 per cent of total purchases in major projects invested in by central and local governments. This practice was in fact common in the early days of car production in the developed markets, when their governments also imposed limitations on import contents and requirements on minimum usage of domestic components.

In a nutshell, the government is making its strongest effort ever to promote home-grown technologies and the innovation capability of domestic firms. Its policy direction and initiatives are not far from the practice of the developed markets during the early days of their technological development – through procurement policies and restrictions on the usage of import contents. Some key sectors are expected to benefit more than others under Beijing's innovation drive. They include IT, telecoms equipment, high-value electronics and manufacturing, alternative energies, new materials, pharmaceuticals, medical equipment and environmental treatments. These will also be the sunrise sectors leading China's future growth.

8
Steps to the Future

Despite China's spectacular economic ascent, it is not a growth miracle.[1] The world has seen similar economic performance before, including Japan, South Korea, Hong Kong, Singapore and Taiwan. To sustain growth, it is encouraging to see that Beijing is taking steps, albeit slowly, to break the classical communist policy icons and free the system.

China's economic ascent is evidence of the success of the numerous reform steps that the authorities have taken. While recent trends and policy initiatives point to a sustainable growth path for the Middle Kingdom in the long term, it is by no means plain sailing. There are still significant hurdles the Chinese leadership has to overcome before the economic transformation is complete.

The most difficult challenge is for China's leadership to break free from its old communist mentality so that deep-rooted changes can be made. This fundamental change is not easy; especially when China is not really as centrally controlled by Beijing as many have thought. The leadership's ability to implement reform thoroughly is linked to its willingness to take structural reforms further, in bigger strides and bolder and more integrated moves.

Financial (including currency) reform will remain at the heart of future changes. China's macro-economic backdrop is robust, its policy initiatives to change are strong and the overall policy directions are right. The odds are high that China will become the next America rather than another Latin American in the not too distant future.

The promising land

Picture this. The average lifespan of the population here is 80 years old. Everyone has access to social and medical services. Economic growth averages 9 per cent a year, with per capita income at US\$16,000 a year. Half of the population own a car and are able to afford overseas travel. Over half a billion of the rural population have moved to the cities, boosting the urbanization rate to 80 per cent; 600 million city dwellers are living in hi-tech suburban homes. The nation is a major power in science and technology. It is one of the most advanced countries in the world in developing biotechnology, exploring space and making major breakthroughs in energy exploration, food and energy-saving technology and clean-energy technology.

Yes, this is China in 2050, or so it is envisioned. These are the forecasts from the Modernization Report 2006 produced by the Chinese Academy of Sciences.[2] The forecast is based on the successful transition of China from an agricultural society to a knowledge-based economy. While cynics (mostly armed with anecdotes and a partial view of China's role in the global system) write off this outlook as purely a fantasy,[3] and even the Chinese Academy of Sciences admits that these achievements would be hard to reach, hard evidence on China's rapid and prolonged economic ascent and its government's policy initiatives to push ahead have raised eyebrows. Arguably, US President George W. Bush's announcement in 2006 that the US would raise its spending on science and education was thought to have been partly influenced by the fear of being overtaken by China.

Nevertheless, the road to the promised land is bumpy. From the social perspective, the biggest challenge comes from the population (see Chapter 4). First, there is the imminent task of creating jobs fast enough to absorb the labour force (aged 15 to 64), which is expected to reach 1 billion by 2020 before it falls off. Then there is concern about food supply in the medium term, when the United Nations predicts that China's population will peak at 1.45 billion by 2030. Last but not least, 320 million Chinese will be 60 years old or over by 2040, straining resources and adding a burden for the shrinking labour force.

Rapid development will also come with a high cost to the environment, which may become a critical stress point affecting future growth prospects. China has one fifth of the world's population, but only 7 per cent of its arable land. Of that, only one third is productive. More crucially, the amount of arable land is declining fast (see Chapter 5, 'What about the farmers?' section) due to soil erosion, pollution, and growing demand for industrialization and residential development. China's rising water consumption already rivals that of the US. Its total energy consumption is second only to the US and China is also the second largest emitter of industrial carbon dioxide pollution.

However, the future development of these issues may change, depending on future technological advances, government population and environmental policies and the population's attitude towards family size, living style, habits, and so on. So it is unfair to conclude, as some cynics have done, that the cumulative bad effects of China's continuing down the present path would become so large that they would crush the economy before it reached the promised land.

From a macro-economic perspective, the slow decline in the economic role of the state remains a pitfall along the way to China's future growth. Although many remaining state-owned enterprises (SOEs) in the core industries such as steel, energy and telecoms now appear to be quite profitable, their profits often coming from monopoly rents and government protection. These profits are costs for the downstream industries, and obstacles for further improvement in economic productivity.

The government's big economic role will also constrain future economic development by encouraging crony capitalism and thus breeding corruption. Many private-sector firms still have very close ties with government officials, and cultivating favours from the government often offers tempting ways for making quick and easy profits. Further, many former officials or family members of incumbent officials have extensive involvement in business, often in government-protected monopoly industries. Some even hold prominent business posts.

This cosy government–business relationship not only creates conflict of interest and moral hazard problems, but it also builds resistance from vested interests against deregulation and the opening up of core industries to competition. This will only make it hard to have an equitable environment for businesses, income distribution and living. The resultant social discontent will make political transformation more difficult to pursue.

State intervention in the economy, especially in the financial system, has made China's GDP growth volatile. This volatility in 1996–98 nearly derailed China's long-term growth prospects, when the government embarked on closing or downsizing tens of thousands of insolvent SOEs and laid off more than 30 million state workers. The bad news is this could happen again. But the good news is it is unlikely to replay.

The economic bubble in the early 1990s was a result of some specific economic development. In particular, there was a burst of economic liberalization at a time when the government had no proper economic management tools. But there has been sharp improvement in recent years, both in terms of policy tools and response.

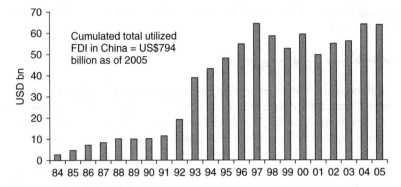

Figure 8.1 Utilized foreign direct investment in China
Source: CEIC

Take the 2002–4 period of economic imbalances. The authorities were still hampered by fixed interest rates and an inflexible renminbi (RMB) exchange rate. But they were quick to act, using aggressive liquidity management and direct administrative controls to reduce the economic imbalances. Most crucially, state-ownership and control in the banking system has been dismantled gradually in recent years; and the trend of financial liberalization is going to intensify (see Chapter 1, 'Reform momentum' and 'The next steps' sections and Chapter 2, 'The fate of the banking system' section).

As for other potential pitfalls that could shock China's long-term growth aspect, such as a banking crisis (see Chapter 2, 'A system that won't collapse' section), fiscal instability (see Chapter 5, 'Fiscal handicap aggravating social tension?' section) and social tensions (see throughout Chapter 5), there are sufficient positive forces balancing them out; often these positive progressive forces have outweighed the negative impact of the economic problems. The overall macro-risks are thus contained and net positive results are being delivered.

For example, China's much-vaunted financial discrimination against private capital has ebbed recently, though there is still discrimination against small-scale capital (which is a problem that still has to be fixed). This can be seen in the rising number of private entrepreneurs in the ranks of the wealthiest in China. This newly rich group has ample access to bank loans. China also boasts some $800 billion accumulated foreign direct investment (Figure 8.1). These are profitable investments growing at an annual rate of 10 per cent a year. These indicators suggest that China is hardly an economy where transparency and governance issues are preventing healthy capital investment.

Wanted: new policy approach

Arguably, the Chinese leadership has skilfully fine-tuned China's growth model with an incremental and experimental approach to economic reforms, while leaving the political system untouched. China's achievement contrasts sharply with the disintegration of the former USSR, which liberalized politics even before its people had enough to eat.

At the general level, China's leadership has guided the reform process by some broad principles, avoiding a detailed blueprint that would create complications and risk making too many mistakes in China's hybrid (planning plus market) economic system. It has wisely implemented reforms by keeping directional planning for the broad issues while allowing the development of market segments in various parts of the economy. The latter has enabled efficient gains at the margin without creating an overwhelming number of losers.[4] This combination of control, flexibility, adaptability and pragmatism has allowed China to grow around the various reform constraints and delivered an extended high growth period without much of a hiccup.

To keep systemic stability, the Chinese leadership has left the political system unchanged since reform started in 1978. It has instead focused on moving towards a 'socialist market economy'. Beijing has adopted an open door policy to augment industrialization, facilitate import of foreign technology and invoke market discipline in the local system (though the impact of this last one remains rather limited so far). As a result, China's trade sector has grown sharply (Figure 8.2), though it remains overall a closed economy relative to other Asian neighbours (Figure 8.3).

China's currency and capital control policies have been instrumental in shaping its economic growth, and they will continue to be crucial in the future (see Chapter 7, 'Currency puzzles for future growth' section). The RMB has been fixed against the US dollar since 1995. Even during the Asian crisis in 1997–8 when there was enormous pressure on devaluing the RMB, the Chinese authorities stood firm, suggesting the importance that Beijing attached to this nominal anchor.

The RMB was revalued by 2.05 per cent against the US dollar and re-pegged to a basket of currencies on 21 July 2006. But in practice, the RMB still remains pegged against the US dollar with limited flexibility. Over the long term, the authorities should move towards a floating exchange rate regime (see Chapter 7, 'The RMB and future growth' section).

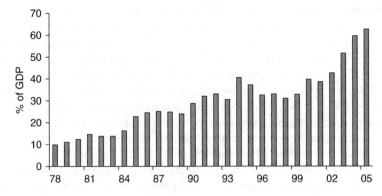

Figure 8.2 Growth of China's trade sector
Source: CEIC

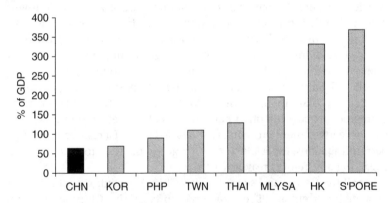

Figure 8.3 Size of the trade sector – Asia
* as of 2005
Source: CEIC

Management of capital flows has been a crucial policy tactic in China's growth model. This has two elements: direct capital controls, and tax and investment incentives. The direct controls act to reduce the impact of hot money flows on the local system, while the incentives work to attract massive foreign direct investment (FDI) inflows. Other forms of volatile inflows, especially portfolio debt, have been discouraged.

The sluggish development of a domestic capital market is indeed part of China's capital management policy. Without other funding and investment alternatives, the banking system is effectively the only financial intermediary for both borrowers and savers. This makes the growth process more manageable amid gradual economic liberalization.

China's strict control on the capital account and exchange rate and its reluctance to allow fast development of a local capital market are indicative of its desire to keep stability on both the external and domestic fronts (see Chapter 1, '... now you don't' section), while opening up to global trade and investment systems. The large stock of foreign reserves amassed from the capital control policies may serve as a cushion to the potential risks arising from a weak banking system.

However, the Middle Kingdom has likely come to a point where bolder changes are needed and things will have to be done differently from before. This is because the distortions resulting from the current policy approach are likely to worsen, raising welfare costs and generating systemic instability down the road. For example, investment growth has become excessive (over 40 per cent of GDP) in recent years because the policies designed to keep macro-economic control have made investment rather than private consumption the key driver of demand growth.

While factor accumulation is a normal path to higher growth for many developing economies, China's high savings mediated almost solely through an inefficient banking system is producing welfare loss, which will only get worse down the road. Depositors bear part of the inefficiency costs in the form of low returns on their savings, while entrepreneurs bear the other part in terms of low return on investment. Excessive investment growth has also raised fears of a resurgence of non-performing loans, especially if a few large sectors were to falter, possibly triggering a systemic breakdown.[5]

For all the virtues and success so far, China's growth model is in need of a major overhaul. The structural shifts of the Chinese economy towards a market-oriented system and its increasing integration with the world economy have changed the growth paradigm. The more open and liberalized economy will soon expose the stress points of the current policy approach of gradualism, control and experiment. Hence, despite all the constraints that still exist due to policy and institutional deficiencies, Beijing will have to move on with bolder and more integrated reforms to sustain long-term growth. To push reform more effectively, the central directives must be able to filter down to the local levels.

But 'shang you zheng ce, xia you dui ce'[6] has been a problem for the central reformers (see Chapter 1, p. 26). This lack of trickle-down problem stems from the fact that Beijing is not really in firm centralized control of the country, as perception has it. This is all because of the incentive problem that exists at the local levels. A good career in the

Party still depends on following, or at least appearing to follow, orders from central government. However, local leaders calculate that as long as they achieve rapid economic growth in their jurisdictions with minimal unrest, they have considerable manipulation leeway.

The discipline to obey has been loosened as the party no longer frets about the ideological purity of its leaders due to continued economic liberalization. In fact, since the days of Mao Ze-dong, each new generation of leaders in Beijing has been less and less able to command absolute obedience across the country. This is not to say that China is heading towards a USSR style of break-up or warlord-ism of the pre-Communist era. The armed forces and the police remain firmly under the Party's control. The central authority is also secure at the provincial leadership level.

Rather, the lack of control is a profusion of township, county and prefecture leadership whose efforts to boost growth in their areas produce impressive statistics, but at hefty social, environmental or macro-economic cost. The lack of centralized control can readily be seen in excessive investment growth, especially the property sector, which has become a policy headache in recent years. Between 2003 and 2005, the government was worrying that the economy might overheat and was trying to curb excessive investment growth by imposing cooling measures, such as tightening capital requirements on start-up investment projects, curbing lending to overheated sectors and curbing investment growth outright.

In many cases, the orders issued in Zhongnonhai, the Party headquarters in Beijing, never left the compound as many local officials ignored the central orders. The problem in the property sector was especially serious, as land development and investment projects were granted illegally through bribery. In March 2005, for instance, amid growing public complaints about soaring housing prices, the central government issued directives aimed at cooling the market. Shanghai, the main target of those measures, dutifully tightened controls and the local market cooled down. But housing prices in other big cities continued to climb rapidly (almost 20 per cent year-on-year in Beijing, for example).

As long as the local leaders remain defiant against central directives, Beijing will have problems in pushing through deep-rooted reforms. Incentive incompatibility between the central and local governments is to blame. What is good for the national economy in the long term, such as more structural reforms, may not be good for local rent seekers. Until recently, local leaders have rarely incurred heavy political penalties for failing to carry out central directives. The problem of 'shang you zheng ce, xia you dui ce' is going to be a tough challenge for China in the medium term. It must be resolved if bigger strides are to be made to sustain China's long-term growth.

Priorities and signposts for future growth

Financial sector reform and development are crucial priorities for China's future growth and stability. However, changes in the country's financial structure must come in conjunction with other broad macro-economic objectives, the most crucial one being the RMB exchange rate policy.

Views on the overvaluation/undervaluation of the RMB exchange rate are irrelevant to analysing China's exchange rate regime. This is because cyclical shocks in the global and local systems affect the valuation of a currency so that any focus on valuation is a moving target and thus irrelevant for long-term policy formulation. For example, the current intense pressure on the RMB to revalue (which Beijing has been resisting) came about only in 2003, while five years before that there was enormous pressure on the RMB to devalue (which Beijing also resisted).

The ultimate goal of an exchange rate regime shift in China is to allow Beijing to have a more independent monetary policy under a floating exchange rate, and also allow the exchange rate to play a role in correcting the economic balance. A floating exchange rate would also remove one of the obstacles to banking reform. This is because the current fixed rate prevents the central bank from using market-based instruments, such as interest rates, to guide credit growth. Instead, it forces the government to rely on moral suasion and administrative measures. This, in turn, stifles efforts to commercialize the banking system.

Beijing's long-term goal of eventual full capital account convertibility and a floating exchange rate should reduce the moral hazard problem that a fixed exchange rate brings. Generally, when the fundamentals are bad, currency speculators always see government effort to keep a fixed exchange rate as a one-way bet. They would continue to short-sell the currency and stand to reap huge profit if the exchange rate were really to collapse. If their bet were wrong, they would lose nothing except a small transaction cost, as they could cover their short position at the same exchange rate.

For the host country, the collapse of the fixed exchange rate will inflict serious damages on the economy. They will come in the form of soaring interest rates, surging inflation and economic chaos. However, a floating rate will take away that government guarantee of the exchange rate value, and hence remove the moral hazard associated with it.

Exchange rate fluctuation will create incentives to develop financial products to hedge foreign exchange risk. This, in turn, will help stimulate broader financial market development.

Beijing is starting to speed up capital development already. The banking system has also been opened up, with increasing foreign and retail investor participation. The changes so far have not yet affected the predominantly state-owned nature of China's banking system. But given Beijing's policy direction and its resolve to change, banking reform will speed up in future. Once recapitalization of the system is completed, Beijing should focus on reforming the institutional and legal underpinnings for bank restructuring.

More Chinese banks will also be listed overseas, as this could serve as a one-stop shop for SOE reform. The benefit is that global management, human resources and investment banking firms will take up the reins of the restructuring process, identifying and shedding unproductive assets, clarifying pensions liabilities, carrying out full audits and redefining governance responsibilities. There is no need to change the civil servants and/or make them do the restructuring, which is always difficult and troublesome.

China is serious about bank privatization and the process is under way, though changes will not happen all at once. It will take years to achieve significant diversification of bank ownership. It will also take years for new investors and owners to bring about big behavioural changes in state bank. In a nutshell, just recapitalizing financial institutions is not enough. Bank reform will not stick until the state withdraws from managing the banking business. Privatization is the final step in forcing the banks to kick their old habits and avoid repeating the mistakes of the past.

Proper financial reform and privatization should improve capital allocation and hence future growth. How growth is distributed is another matter. Beijing has various policy initiatives to divert investment and growth momentum to the less developed parts of the country. It is important to watch how income distribution evolves over time to gauge how well China's transition is proceeding.

Economic reforms since 1978 have substantially cut the number of people living in poverty. But it has also sharply widened the income gaps between the rich and the poor, between rural and urban residents, and between the coastal areas and the inland provinces. As measured by the Gini coefficient,[7] China's income inequality rose 1.7 times between 1991 and 2006 (from a Gini coefficient of 28 in 1991 to 47 in 2006).[8]

Development economic theory suggests that as income continues to rise, the trickle-down process tends to narrow the income gap over time.[9] The issue for China is how fast this process will take place, whether the changes are socially acceptable, and whether there are any institutional and political obstacles slowing or blocking the gains of fast growth from being transmitted to the low-income groups.

From a market perspective, China's 1.3 billion people does not mean a market size of 1.3 billion people. It is the purchasing power of the population that counts. Better income distribution implies a larger domestic market with more people enjoying stronger purchasing power. This will, in turn, facilitate China's paradigm shift from export- and investment-led to consumption-oriented (see Chapter 6, 'Growth model shifting' section) for sustaining long-term growth.

Experience shows that redistribution by brute force, through taking from the rich to give to the poor, is bad income distribution policy. These egalitarian doctrines were the wrong formula trapping China in poverty before 1978. Instead, efforts should be made to remove the restrictions on blocking the benefits of growth from being shared more broadly. Accelerating privatization and granting fuller property rights, especially to farmers, would take China a long way in closing the income gap and easing any future potential social discontent.

In a nutshell, income distribution is an important matrix both for evaluating China's domestic market size and for monitoring the risks associated with social discontent. If China fails to reduce the income inequality gap, fast economic growth will not prevent chaos from emerging. Indonesia's experience during the 1997–98 Asian crisis serves as a good reminder that despite decades of fast growth, a regime remains vulnerable if its political and economic institutions are not solid, income distribution is unequal and social discontent is widespread.

Clues and evidence for success

The Chinese authorities are putting in place the 'hardware' for sustaining long-term economic growth, through industrial retrenchment and economic restructuring driven by a strong will to reform. Beijing is even taking the initiatives to break some of the classical communist policy apparatus, such as population control, financial repression and asset ownership. Some of these moves are happening at the margin of the system and thus may not have been factored into mainstream analysis at this time. They include experiments to:

- Scrap the *hu kou* system and privatize lending rights (see Chapter 1, 'Reform momentum' and 'The next steps' sections)
- Institutionalize and integrate the privatization process (see Chapter 3, 'The future of the SOEs' section),

- Reform the pension system (see Chapter 4, 'The pension puzzle' section),
- Relax interest rate and capital controls (see Chapter 1, 'Reform momentum' section),
- Improve the bankruptcy procedure (see Chapter 1, 'Reform momentum' and 'The next steps' sections),
- Shift the growth drivers to consumption from exports and investment (see Chapter 6, 'Growth model shifting' section), and
- Promote home-grown technology to transform Chinese industries into high value-added and high-tech activities (see Chapter 7, 'The innovation drive' section).

Some of these experiments have already delivered encouraging results, while others have shown progress in the otherwise sluggish reform process. For example, China overtook Germany in the global ranking of patent applications to become the fifth largest source of filings in 2004,[10] according to the most recent data from the World Intellectual Property Organization (WIPO), a United Nations agency.

This underscores a good start for Beijing's drive to promote home-grown technology and local innovation capability. However, half of the patent filings in China in 2004 were made by foreign companies, while most in Japan and South Korea were by local inventors. This suggests that China still has some way to go in developing home-grown technology and pushing China up the world scientific and innovation league.

In breaking the barrier to labour mobility and distortion in the labour market and income distribution, Beijing is giving its blessing to more cities scrapping the *hu kou* (or household registration) system.[11] After Jinan in Shangdong province, two more cities, Harbin and Mudan-jiang, in the northeastern Heilong-jiang province scrapped the 50-year household registration system in 2006. Rural residents can freely move to, live and work in the city as long as they have a legal residential property and fulfil certain residency requirements. The scheme has gone province-wide in 2007. As more cities and provinces are expected to scrap the *hu kou* system in the future, labour mobility, income growth and distribution, and overall consumption power should continue to improve in the years to come.

More steps are being taken to speed up corporate, capital market and pensions reforms. The central government is in the process of transferring shares in the SOEs to the national pensions fund. This move acts to kill three birds with one stone: by reforming the pensions fund, corporate sector and the capital market.

Moving the SOE shares to the pensions fund should inject market discipline into the SOEs, as the pensions fund managers would, in principle, be more concerned with share valuation than the SOE managers and other government bodies. The move also injects a large amount of assets into the state pensions fund, which badly needs to build resources in the coming decade to deal with the ageing population. Last but not least, the move also acts to reform the stock market by getting rid of the large overhang of shares in the state companies that could not be traded on the stock exchanges.

The leadership must break free of its old communist legacy to be able to deliver the desired economic growth in the long term. As argued in Chapter 7, China's reform has come to a crossroads where complicated forces have made the old policy approach of gradualism and piecemeal experiments inappropriate. Beijing's top leaders will have to act more bravely to take larger reform strides in a more integrated way in the future.

To take economic reform further and boost long-term growth, the leaders need to think innovatively, to be more creative, or even to take a gamble at times. To illustrate the point, consider the gaming industry. As shown in the US, Hong Kong and Macau, the gaming industry can be a strong engine for creating demand growth, boosting government revenues and employment, and generating funding for the poor. In China, it is politically impossible to allow a fully fledged gaming industry with casinos and the like. But it could relax control on horse racing to get some of the benefits to start with.

The point here is not so much to reap the monetary gains from legalizing horse racing as to change the policy mentality. Beijing must break out of the communist ideology box. Instead of treating it as a vice, horse racing could be treated as an entertainment sport, with the desirable by-products of generating jobs and government revenues for helping the poor. In the long term, Beijing could even consider licensing casinos for its potential positive distributional impact on economic development, especially in the western hinterland where it is difficult to attract investment.

By shaking off the old thinking, Chinese leaders could be more creative in developing many new industries to boost job and consumption, which fits their medium-term policy of promoting domestic demand as the growth driver. China's rising affluence provides a favourable backdrop for policy creativity to create desirable long-term economic benefits. The key is to discard suspicion of private economic incentive and give the private sector a freer hand.

Take civil aviation as an example. Demand for private jets has been rising as the Chinese are getting richer, with a few tycoons in the Zhejiang province already owning planes. But severe flight path restrictions have suppressed overall demand and kept those tycoons' private planes mostly parked in hangers as a mere show of wealth. If Beijing were to allow flying schools to be set up and relax private jets' flying and landing restrictions, it could satisfy demand and at the same time develop new industries and raise government revenue.

Yachting too could be developed into a multi-billion dollar industry and provide a good source of employment, given China's rising affluence and long coastline. Golfing has the same potential, as it has become increasingly popular among China's elite class and the newly rich. But Beijing's indiscriminate ban on golf-course construction has stifled the industry's development. While the policy intention of protecting farmland should be applauded, the authorities should get a better understanding of the various aspects of the golfing issue instead of blindly pursuing a blanket ban policy. Indeed, golf courses could be developed on barren land not suitable for farming.

One can debate the viability of these new industries at this stage of development in China. There may not be a critical mass of wealth yet to allow them to take off. But who knows; there is no accurate account of private wealth at this point. These industries are certainly the new economic ideas down the road. The problem is that the current narrow thinking often causes the policymakers to be out of touch with the real economy and kills policy ideas.

The change in mindset is easier said than done. But it is achievable, as Japan illustrates. Like China, the Japanese system has very deep cultural and political roots, which many had deemed intractable. But much has changed in recent years, especially after Junichiro Koizumi came to power as prime minister in 2001. The key is the leadership's will to break the old entrenched framework and make the quantum leap. As a result, developments that were unthinkable in Japan before have emerged recently to enhance long-term growth prospects for the country. Management buy-outs are a good example.

Japan, long known for legions of low-profile corporate executives, has recently become one of the world's fastest-growing markets for management buy-outs (MBOs). This is a strategy used by executives to retool their companies by making them private. The partners of these Japanese managers are the same large buy-out firms that have engineered a takeover boom in the US and turned some well-known US businesses, such as Toys 'Я' Us and Dunkin' Donuts, from listed companies into private ones.

MBOs in Japan involve foreign buy-out firms, such as the American Carlyle Group, teaming up with local Japanese management to buy a company – take it off the stock exchange. Japanese managers get advice from the buy-out specialists on how to turn the company around in return for a big payoff on successful restructuring. After fixing the business (usually between three to five years), the buy-out funds and the managers sell the companies back to the public, often by reissuing shares.

Although Japan is ripe for MBOs as its companies are trying to refocus and retool after more than a decade of economic stagnation and amid worries about foreign competition and an ageing population, the buy-outs apparently cannot happen unless there is an attitude change. All those worries existed a decade ago, but nothing was changed. The economy was in the doldrums throughout the 1990s and into the early 2000s, and no one thought of MBOs as a micro-economic solution. But after Koizumi came to power in 2001, he shook up the old mindset, broke the fortress of the conservatives and pushed for fundamental changes.

Thus, the MOBs are a good indication of Japan's effort to move away from its old restrictive thinking. These deals jumped eight-fold between 2001 and 2006 (Figure 8.4). There were an estimated 70 MBO deals in 2006, valued over US$4 billion. That was a quantum leap from only half a billion dollars in 2001. Further, the size of the deals has also been rising over the years (Table 8.1), suggesting bolder actions and deeper restructuring involving larger firms. Granted, these numbers pale in comparison to the US, where there were an estimated 150 MBOs valued at US$84 billion in 2006. But it is the momentum resulting from the mindset change in Japan that is relevant to China. If Japan can do it, so can China, which is already showing willingness and momentum to change.

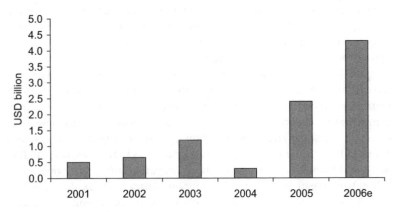

Figure 8.4   MBO deals in Japan
Source: Media reports

Table 8.1   Top ten Japanese MBO deals (to 2006)

Date announced	Target firm	Deal size* (US$ bn)
June 2006	Skylark	2.25
July 2005	World	1.86
October 2006	Qasi	0.53
March 2003	Wanbishi Archives	0.42
November 2003	Toshiba Tungaloy	0.33
August 2005	Pokka	0.21
March 2001	Nissho Iwa Alconix	0.14
June 2006	Skylark	0.13
January 2001	Vantec	0.13
April 2002	Tower Records Japan	0.12

* Excluding debt of target company
Source: Thomson Financial http://www.thomson.com/solutions/financial/

Have the benefit of no doubt

There have been no records of any communist/socialist states being able to make a gradual and successful transformation to a market economy. However, with a consistent tack record of changes and a strong will to move on, China has shown sharp differences from other socialist economies. From a development perspective, China's performance deserves the benefit of the doubt that it could well be the first socialist state able to transform itself into a market-oriented system successfully.

Not only is China the first country among the former centrally planned economies to embark on market-oriented economic reforms, but Beijing has also shown strong commitment and execution capabilities. Despite various domestic political transitions (the biggest step, arguably, being the transition from Deng Xiao-ping's patriarchal regime to Jiang Ze-min's collective leadership system) and testing periods (from the Tiananmen Square incident in 1989 to the Asian crisis in 1997–98 and SARS in 2002–03[12]), the reform programme has been persistently pursued. The policy approach has been practical, gradual and experimental.

The economic reforms since 1978 have brought fundamental changes to the Chinese system. The reforms are irreversible. They have not only lifted millions of people out of poverty, but also created a middle class with rising wealth. All this has created expectations of the Chinese leaders to continue to deliver prosperity to the people in the future. To achieve that, China's future leaders will have to keep liberalizing the domestic economy by freeing markets and allowing the private sector to grow.

Indeed, the private sector has become an increasingly critical force in driving China's growth momentum. Meanwhile, China has been integrating with the world economy swiftly, as seen in the rapid rise of its foreign trade sector and its large share of foreign direct investment to GDP. This integration with the global economy has tied China's self-interest in with the rest of the world, thus instilling market discipline in the Chinese system.

Compared with Eastern Europe, China is a late comer to economic transformation and that gives it the edge of being able to learn from others' mistakes. Granted, there are some policy visions, such as building Chinese *chaebols* and preserving economic controls in the system that need reassessment and refinement, but the lessons and pitfalls of other countries experience will likely help China avoid repeating some costly mistakes in its course of development. On the currency front, in particular, China can learn from Japan's prolonged weak yen policy mistake to avoid some of the potential painful adjustments down the road.

China's move towards a market-oriented system is certainly instrumental for boosting its long-term growth potential. It has at its doorstep an excellent example, Hong Kong, to prove it. Hong Kong followed a *laissez faire* economic policy during its days as a British colony, thanks largely to British civil servant, John Cowperthwaite, who handled Hong Kong's financial affairs between 1945 and 1971 (during which he served as financial secretary between 1961 and 1971). He pushed the free market principle to its extreme by refusing to collect economic statistics for fear this would give government officials an excuse to meddle with the economy.

This 'positive non-intervention' policy, dubbed by Sir Philip Haddon-Cave, Cowperthwaite's successor, delivered remarkable results for Hong Kong. It pushed Hong Kong from a poor backward economy at the end of World War II, with a per capita income about one quarter of that of Britain, to one of the richest in the world, with a per capital income equalling Britain's by 1997 when Hong Kong was reverted back to China. By 2005, Hong Kong's per capita income (US$33,479) surpassed Britain's (US$30,436) on a purchasing power parity basis, according to the International Monetary Fund. This was a striking demonstration of the efficiency gains from having market forces motivate economic growth.

The economic success of Hong Kong's *laissez-faire* approach was, arguably, a major force in encouraging China to move away from a central planning system towards a more market-based framework relying on private-sector incentives. And the results for China are clear – that it too has benefited from rapid economic growth and rising wealth since economic reform started in 1978.

In a nutshell, the final outcome for China's economic future depends on whether, and how far, it continues to move in Hong Kong's direction. Here comes the ultimate challenge for China: half a century of 'positive non-interventionism' has created free-market policy inertia in Hong Kong limiting its temptation to intervene in the economy, despite its reversion to the socialist motherland in 1997.

On the contrary, China has half a century of political meddling, creating policy intervention inertia. Its challenge is thus to break this intervention habit and move to increase market discipline and economic freedom in the system. Given China's track record, reform momentum and attitude, its long-term economic growth outlook remains cautiously optimistic.

Notes

Introduction

1. On a Purchasing Power Parity (PPP) basis, using the 1990 US dollar.
2. See Maddison (2001).
3. Capital deepening is an increase in capital intensity, in a macro-context, where it is approximated by the capital stock available per unit of labour input.
4. For examples, see Maddison (1998), Young (2000) and Rawski (2001).
5. See Lo (2004), pp. 21–4.
6. Hong Kong, Singapore, South Korea and Taiwan.
7. See Lo (2006), p. 167–74.
8. See Krugman (1994) and Young (1995).
9. China does not really have any economic cycles in the normal sense with booms and recessions. Its economic growth rates only fluctuate between high rates and extremely high rates over the years.

1 China's Reform Puzzle

1. This section serves to link the concept of the Production Possibility Curve (PPC) with resources reallocation to illustrate the impact of economic reforms on economic growth. Readers who are familiar with these concepts can skip to the next section without loss of continuity.
2. See Maddison (1998), Young (2000), Iwata and Murao (2002), Wu (2002) and OECD (2005).
3. Total factor productivity (TFP) addresses any effects in total output not caused by input changes. For example, a year with unusually good weather will tend to have higher output, while bad weather hinders agricultural output. A variable, like weather, does not directly relate to unit input changes, so weather is considered a total factor productivity variable. The Cobb-Douglas production function represents total output (Y) as a function of total factor productivity (A), capital input (K), labour input (L), and the two inputs' respective shares of output:

$$Y = AK^{\beta}L^{(1-\beta)}$$

Technology growth and efficiency are two key components of TFP. Studies found that whilst labour and investment are important contributors, TFP accounted for up to as much as 60 per cent of growth within some advanced economies.
4. Bank of China (BoC), China Construction Bank (CCB), Agricultural Bank of China (ABC), Industrial and Commercial bank of China (ICBC).
5. See Lo (2004), pp.106–7.

6. Diminishing marginal returns are also known as diminishing returns in short. The concept refers to a situation where, in a production system with fixed and variable inputs, keeping the fixed inputs constant as more of a variable input is applied, each additional unit of input yields less and less additional output.

7. Economies of scale and diseconomies of scale refer to an economic property of production that affects cost if quantity of all input factors is increased by some amount. If costs increase proportionately to the increase in inputs, there are no economies of scale; if costs increase by a greater amount, there are diseconomies of scale; if costs increase by a lesser amount, there are economies of scale.

8. See Lo (2006), pp. 163–4.

9. In economics, an externality is a side-effect of one activity that has consequences for another activity but is not reflected in market prices. Externalities can be either positive, when an external benefit is generated, or negative, when an external cost is generated, from a market transaction. An externality occurs when a decision causes costs or benefits to stakeholders other than the person making the decision, often from the use of common goods (for example, a decision to do something that results in polluting the atmosphere would involve an externality).

10. See Lo (2004), pp. 99–103.

11. In the financial market context, a 'fixing' refers to an agreement between two or more financial institutions, the central bank and the commercial banks in our context, to fix an interest rate for a borrowing/lending transaction for a period of time ranging from overnight to seven days.

12. For more detailed discussion on this, see Tadesse (2004).

13. A *hu kou* refers to residency permits (household registration) issued by the government. A household registration record officially identifies a person as a resident of an area. It includes identifying information, such as the person's name, date of birth, the names of his/her parents, and name of his/her spouse, if married. Persons without a residency permit in a province are denied access to education and government services and occupy a social and economic status similar to those of illegal immigrants. Before economic reforms, a residency permit was required for any employment and to receive food and other essential consumer products. Since reform started in 1978, it has become possible for some to migrate unofficially and get a job without a valid permit. Economic reforms have also created pressures to encourage migration from the interior to the coast and provided incentives for officials not to enforce migration regulations.

14. Other than in the Pingyao county in the Shanxi province, the authorities will roll out similar pilot schemes for privatizing lending rights in Guizhou, Shaanzi and Sichuan provinces by the end of 2007.

15. See Xiao (2004).

16. See de Soto (2000).

17. See Galiani and Schargrodsky (2006).

2 Financial Fragility Revisited

1. Insolvency is defined as a situation when a bank has a capital-asset ratio of less than 8%, as required by the Bank of International Settlements.

2. The solvency issue may be relevant to regulators in a developed economy for deciding whether to step in and save a bank from collapsing. Typically, they will only save a solvent bank that is suffering from temporary liquidity problems. An insolvent bank will be allowed to fail, with safety measures, such as deposit insurance, to help minimize the shock on the financial system.

3. China's close capital account forbids short-term portfolio flows. Its foreign debt totalled US$281 billion in 2005, compared with US$820 billion in foreign reserves. This means China would have more than enough reserves to repay foreign creditors if they were all to withdraw at the same time.

4. Including township and villages enterprises, joint ventures, private enterprises and personal loans.

5. Short-selling is an investment strategy where an investor borrows a security, such as a bond or stock, and sells it to the market, hoping to buy it back to cover his or her position when the price of the security falls in the near term.

6. Article 5 of the Regulations of the People's Republic of China on the Administration of Foreign Funded Financial Institutions, effective since 1 February 2002.

7. Article 14 of the Detailed Rules for the Implementation of the Regulations of the People's Republic of China on the Administration of Foreign Funded financial Institutions, effective between 1 February 2002 and 10 December 2006.

8. Except in Shanghai, where the authorities disclose the rate at the beginning of the term.

9. See Tsai (2001).

10. Investment pool clubs, or *hui* in Chinese, operate like a credit cooperative. They contain 12–20 members, who receive pooled funds regularly (every month or quarter or six months) on a rotation basis, according to an agreed schedule. Such *hui* existed even before the pre-reform period to finance the family's needs for wedding, house-buying, small investment and so on. For an in-depth analysis of China's informal banking and private entrepreneurs, see Tsai (2002).

11. See Tsai (2001 and 2002).

12. See Tsai (2001).

13. Translated into English, this means 'whenever there are policy directives from above, there are always counter moves to offset these directives from below'.

3   Creative Destruction of the State

1. Lardy (1998 and 2002), Steinfeld (1998), Tenev and Zhang (2002) and Lin, Fang and Zhou (2003) provide detailed analysis on the evolution of China's state sector and economic development.

2. Including private firms, foreign-funded companies, joint-stock companies and cooperatives.

3. See Lardy (2002).

4. Literally, this is translated in English as 'grab the big ones and release the small ones'.

5. See Mako and Zhang (2003).

6. See Lo (2003) pp. 41–3.

7. The rise in labour cost in recent years does not really reflect a labour shortage problem. See Chapter 4, 'The real story about labour shortage' section.
8. As discussed in the first section, the urban collectives, TVEs, farms and private companies all add up to being the non-state sector. In other words, the private sector is a subset of the non-state sector.

4 Ageing Population: What's New?

1. The fertility rate is the average number of children a hypothetical cohort of women would have at the end of their reproductive period if they were not subject to mortality. It is expressed as children per woman.
2. Dependency ratio = non-working population (age below 15 years old and above 60 years old) divided by working population (age 15–60 years old).
3. China's pension debt is the present value of promised future payments to existing pensioners. To estimate that debt, one needs to make assumptions on the pensioners' life expectancy, the long-term growth rate of average wages, inflation and discount rates. A small change in any of these assumptions could make a big difference to the estimates. That is why there is a wide range of estimates for the size of China's pension shortfall.
4. For more detailed analysis and estimation of China's pensions liability, see Holzmann *et al.* (2004) and Wang *et al.* (2000).
5. For more details on China's pension system, see Leckie and Pai (2004).
6. As measured by the total amount of savings in all bank deposit accounts.
7. 'Unemployed' refers to out of work completely. 'Underemployed' means insufficient work – typically defined in developed economies as anyone who is willing to work full-time but can only find work for fewer than 40 hours a week.
8. See also Lo (2006), pp. 167–70.
9. A typical neoclassical production function is the Cobb-Douglas production function, which takes the following form:

$$Y = AK^{\beta}L^{(1 - \beta)}$$

where Y = output, A = technology, K = capital, L = labour, β = the income share of capital and $(1 - \beta)$ = the income share of labour.
10. The law of diminishing returns states that the marginal return of a production factor falls as the quantity of that factor being used increases, and vice versa.
11. This can be seen from the Cobb-Douglas production function, which includes two key parameters – the level technology, A in the production function (see f), and the distribution of income between labour and capital, β and $(1 - \beta)$. The components of the production function are usually assumed to be constant. In the Cobb-Douglas equation, income distribution is expressed by the sensitivity of output to changes in capital and labour. In technical terms, the exponent on capital, β, and the exponent on labour $(1 - \beta)$ give the distribution of income between capital and labour because they must add to 1.
12. Pareto optimality refers to a situation where given a set of alternative allocations and a set of individuals, a movement from one allocation to another can make at least one individual better off, without making any other individual worse off.

5   Socio-economic Disintegration: Myth and Truth

1. The most notable condemnation of China's future was made by Chang (2001; 2006).
2. As measured by the Gini coefficient. The Gini coefficient is a measure of inequality of distribution and is often used to measure income inequality. It is a number between 0 and 1, where 0 corresponds to perfect equality (i.e. everyone has the same income) and 1 corresponds to perfect inequality (i.e. one person has all the income, while everyone else has zero income). It was developed by the Italian statistician Corrado Gini and published in his 1912 paper 'Variabilità e mutabilità' ('Variability and Mutability'). The Gini index (as used in Table 5.1) is the Gini coefficient expressed as a percentage, and is equal to the Gini coefficient times 100. For more details, see Gini (1921), Gastwirth (1972), Chakravarty (1990) and Xu (2004).
3. For more detailed discussions on this subject, please refer to Chen and Wu (2004).
4. Technically, this relationship between demand for food and income growth is summarized by the Engel curve, named after the nineteenth-century German statistician Ernst Engel. In its original form, the Engel curve shows how the quantity demanded of a good or service changes as the consumer's income level changes. For normal goods, the Engel curve has a positive slope – as income rises, the quantity demanded increases. For inferior goods, such as food, the Engel curve has a negative slope – as consumer income rises, demand for inferior goods drops because consumers are able to buy better alternative goods.
5. For example, see *Straits Times* (2005).
6. In economics, a monopsony is a market form with only one buyer, called 'monopsonist', facing many sellers. It is an instance of imperfect competition, symmetrical to the case of a monopoly, in which there is only one seller facing many buyers. The term 'monopsony' was first introduced by Cambridge economist Joan Robinson.
7. Transparency International, Bribe Payers Index (2002).
8. The Heritage Foundation/Wall Street Journal Index of Economic Freedom measures 161 countries against a list of 50 independent variables divided into ten broad factors of economic freedom. Low scores are more desirable. The higher the score on a factor, the greater the level of government interference in the economy and the less economic freedom a country enjoys. An overall score, calculated based on the average of the ten economic factors, is used for ranking economies according to their economic freedom.
9. The Transparency International Corruption Perception Index (TICPI) is a composite index, drawing on 16 surveys from 10 independent institutions, which gathered the opinions of business people and country analysts. Only 159 of the world's 193 countries are included in the survey, due to an absence of reliable data from the remaining countries. The scores range from 10 (squeaky-clean) to 0 (highly corrupt). A score of 5.0 is the number Transparency International considers the borderline figure distinguishing countries that do and do not have a serious corruption problem.

6   Sustainable Growth or Short-term Rebound

1. A *put* option (sometimes simply called a 'put') is a financial contract between two parties, the buyer and the seller of the option. The put allows the buyer the right, but not the obligation, to sell a commodity or financial instrument (the underlying instrument) to the seller of the option at a certain time for a certain price (the strike price). The seller has the obligation to purchase at that strike price, if the buyer chooses to exercise that option. In exchange for having this option, the buyer pays the seller a fee (the premium).
2. Total factor productivity (TPF) is defined as the increase in output growth not accounted for by increases in factor inputs. It is also known as the Solow Residual or Multi-Factor Productivity. TPF is commonly used to measure efficiency of the overall economy. It is a broader concept than merely the efficiency gains from technological advancement. It also reflects better allocation of resources, better management, better political, legal and institutional environment, and so on.
3. For example, see Hu and Khan (1996) and OECD (2005).
4. Hong Kong, Singapore, South Korea and Taiwan. See Young (1995).
5. See OECD (2005).
6. See World Bank (1997), OECD (2005).
7. See Tseng *et al.* (1994) for a discussion on how earlier reforms were being phased in and implemented.
8. The term 'animal spirits' was coined by John Maynard Keynes who used it in his 1936 book, *The General Theory of Employment Interest and Money* to capture the idea that aggregate economic activity might be driven in part by waves of optimism or pessimism: 'Most, probably, of our decisions to do something positive, the full consequences of which will be drawn out over many days to come, can only be taken as the result of animal spirits – a spontaneous urge to action rather than inaction, and not as the outcome of a weighted average of quantitative benefits multiplied by quantitative probabilities' (*The General Theory of Employment Interest and Money*, pp. 161–2).
9. For detailed discussion, see Xiao and Tu (2005).
10. See Chapter 1, f12.
11. For detailed discussions on these sectors, please see Ma and Elledge (2006).
12. The difference in the propensity to consume (save) between the poor and the rich is a typical economic behaviour. When one is poor, and when there is a rise in disposable income, he or she tends to spend a larger proportion of the extra income. But when rich, he or she tends to save a larger proportion of the extra income.
13. See Kujis (2005).
14. According to the World Bank, World Development Indicators, services generated an average of 62 per cent of all jobs in recent years among the middle- and high-income economies. The higher an economy's per capita GDP, the higher the share of service employment.
15. Further development will push agriculture's employment share down further. In the US, for example, agriculture accounts for 1.6 per cent of total employment, compared with over 12 per cent in the 1950s (see Figure 6.10).
16. See World Bank (1997) and OECD (2005).

17. For more details, see Lin, Fang and Li (1998).
18. Whenever there are policy directives from above, there are always counter moves to offset these directives from below; see also Chapter 1, p. 26.
19. The term 'moral hazard' originates from insurance theory. It refers to the increased risk of problematic (immoral) behaviour, and thus a negative outcome (hazard), because the person who caused the problem does not suffer the full (or any) consequences, or may actually benefit. The term is commonly applied to banking where a 100 per cent implicit government guarantee of bank deposits creates incentives in both the depositors and banks to act imprudently without suffering from any of the bad consequences because of their behaviour.
20. See Lo (2003), ch. 1.
21. See Eichengreen (2004); Prasad, Rumbaugh and Wang (2005).

7 Policy Vision and Inspirations

1. Only Taiwan and Singapore performed as well as China in terms of their growth rates during the transition periods. Taiwan grew by an annual average of 9.1 per cent between 1962 and 1989, while Singapore grew by an annual average of 9 per cent between 1966 and 1993. Other Asian emerging economies grew by an average of 7 per cent–8 per cent a year during their golden growth period.
2. State-owned output and private output do not sum to 100 per cent in Figure 7.2. The residue is accounted for by the output of other enterprises which have some government control. These firms are in the grey area between state and private firms. They include shareholding companies, collective-owned enterprises and limited liability companies. The private jobs in Figure 7.2 are expressed as a share of total urban employment.
3. For more discussion on this subject, see Wei (2003).
4. Chaebol are South Korea's business conglomerates. The term refers to the several dozen large, family-controlled Korean corporate groups assisted by government financing. Before the 1997–98 Asian crisis, they played a major role in the South Korean economy in the 1960s through to the 1990s. Some have become well-known international brand names, such as Samsung, LG, and Hyundai.
5. A keiretsu was a set of companies with interlocking business relationships and shareholdings. The prototypical keiretsu were those which appeared in Japan during the economic boom years following World War II. Before Japan's surrender, its industry was controlled by large conglomerates called *zaibatsu*. The Allies broke up the zaibatsu in the late 1940s. But the companies formed from the dismantled *zaibatsu* re-linked themselves through share purchases to form horizontally integrated alliances across many industries. Keiretsu companies would also supply one another, making the alliances vertically integrated.
   Each major keiretsu centred around one bank, which lent money to the keiretsu's member companies and held equity positions in them. Each bank had great control over the keiretsu companies and acted as a monitoring entity and an emergency bailout entity. This structure acted to minimize the presence of hostile takeovers in Japan, because no entities could challenge the power of the banks.

6. The Plaza Accord was an agreement signed on 22 September 1985, by the then G5 nations (France, West Germany, Japan, the United States and the United Kingdom). The G5 agreed to devalue the US dollar *vis-à-vis* the Japanese yen and German deutschemark by intervening in currency markets. The reason for doing that was to reduce the US current account deficit, which had reached 3.5 per cent of the GDP, and to help the US economy emerge from a serious recession that began in the early 1980s.
7. The debate between 1998 and 2001 was focused on preventing renminbi (RMB) devaluation after the Asian crisis. But as the economic tide changes along with a rising Chinese current account surplus since 2002, the debate has changed to pushing for RMB revaluation. See also Lo (2004), pp. 55–9.
8. Both Japan and the US have a smaller trade sector than China (see Figure 7.7), and indeed both of them have a floating exchange rate system.
9. The *de facto* currency peg with the US dollar was officially ended on 21 July 2005, when the authorities revalued the RMB/USD exchange rate by 2.05 per cent and then changed to a crawling peg system against a basket of currencies.
10. See Lo (2006), Ch. 3.
11. Public Law 100–418, Section 3004.
12. See also Lo (2006), Ch. 3.

8 Steps to the Future

1. See Anderson (2006).
2. Published on 9 February 2006.
3. For example, see Dyer (2006).
4. See Lau *et al.* (2001).
5. See Goldstein and Lardy (2004).
6. Whenever there are policy directives from above, there are always counter moves from below to offset these directives.
7. See Chapter 5, f2.
8. Though China's income inequality is not too serious as compared with other developing economies (see Chapter 5, Table 5.1, p. 131).
9. Kuznets (1955).
10. Japan topped the patent league, followed by the US, the European Patent Office and South Korea.
11. See Chapter 1, f12.
12. Severe acute respiratory syndrome (SARS) is a viral respiratory illness that was recognized as a global threat in March 2003, after first appearing in Southern China in November 2002.

References

Anderson, J. (2006) 'China's True Growth: No Myth or Miracle', *Far Eastern Economic Review*, September

Chakravarty, S.R. (1990) *Ethical Social Index Numbers*, New York: Springer-Verlag

Chang, G.G. (2001) *The Coming Collapse of China*, Random House

Chang, G.G. (2006) 'Halfway into China's Collapse', *Far Eastern Economic Review*, pp. 25–28, June 2006, vol. 169, no. 5

Chen, G. and C. Wu (2004) *Zhongguo Nongmin Diaocha (China's Peasants: An investigation)*, People's Literature Publishing House

De Soto, H. (2000) *The Mystery of Capital: Why Capitalism Triumphs in the West but Fails Elsewhere?*, Basic Books

Dyer, G. (2006) 'China Modernisation Report 2006: a Fantasy', *The New Vision*, 20 February (available on www.newvision.co.ug/pa/8/20/482911)

Economist, The (2006), 30 September, 14, 33–4

Eichengreen, B. (2004) *Chinese Currency Controversies*, Centre for Economic Policy Research (CEPR) Discussion Paper 4375

Far Eastern Economic Review (2006), September, 37–8

Galiani, S. and E. Schargrodsky (2006) *Property Rights for the Poor: Effects of Land Titling*, San Andres University and Torcuato di Tella University, March (www.tinyurl.com/ndw69)

Gastwirth, J. (1972) 'The Estimation of the Lorenz Curve and Gini Index', *Review of Economics and Statistics*, 54, pp. 306–316

Gini, C. (1921) 'Measurement of Inequality and Incomes', *The Economic Journal* 31, pp. 124–126

Goldstein, M. and N. Lardy (2004) *What Kind of Landing for the Chinese Economy?* Policy Brief No. PB04-7, Washington, DC: Institute for International Economics

Heritage Foundation (2006) *2006 Index of Economic Freedom* (www.heritage.org/research/features/index)

Holzmann, R., R. Palacios and A. Zviniene (2004) *Implicit Pension Debt: Issues, Measurement and Scope in International Perspective*, World Bank Social Protection Discussion Paper series, March

Hu, Z. and M. Khan (1996) *Why is China Growing so Fast?*, IMF Working Paper WP/96/75, International Monetary Fund

International Monetary Fund World Economic Outlook Database, April 2006

Iwata, S., M. Khan and H. Murao (2002) *Sources of Economic Growth in East Asia: A Nonparametric Assessment*, IMF Working Paper WP/02/13, International Monetary Fund

Keynes, J. M. (1936) *The General Theory of Employment, Interest and Money*, London: Macmillan

Krugman, P. (1994) 'The Myth of Asia's Miracle', *Foreign Affairs*, November/December 1994

Kuijis, L. (2005) *Investment and Saving in China*, World Bank Research paper no.1, May

Kuznets, S. (1955) 'Economic Growth and Income Inequality', *American Economic Review*, 445, pp. 1–28

Lardy, N. (1998) *China's Unfinished Economic Revolution*, Brookings Institute Press

Lardy, N. (2002) *Integrating China into the Global Economy*, Brookings Institute Press

Lau, L., Y. Qian and G. Ronald (2001) 'The Dual-Track Approach to Reform', *Journal of Political Economy*, vol. 108, no. 1, pp. 120–143

Leckie, S. and Y. Pai (2004) *Pension Funds in China – A New Look*, ISI Publications

Lin, J., C. Fang and L. Zhou (2003) *The China Miracle: Development Strategy and Economic Reform*, Hong Kong: Chinese University of Hong Kong Press

Lin, J., C. Fang and L. Zhou (1998) 'Competition, Policy Burdens and State-Owned Enterprise Reform', *American Economic Review*, vol.88, no. 2, pp. 422–27

Lo, C. (2003) *When Asia Meets China in the New Millennium – China's Role in Shaping Asia's Post-Crisis Economic Transformation*, Pearson/Prentice-Hall

Lo, C. (2004) *The Misunderstood China – Uncovering the Truth behind the Bamboo Curtain*, Pearson/Prentice-Hall

Lo, C. (2006) *Phantom of the China Economic Threat – Shadow of the Next Asian Crisis*, Palgrave Macmillan

Ma, J. and R. Elledge (2006) *China Macro Strategy: China's Shopping Shift – From Commodities to Consumer Goods*, Deutsche Bank, February

Maddison, A. (1998) *Chinese Economic Performance in the Long Run*, Paris: OECD Department Centre Studies

Maddison, A. (2001) *The World Economy: A Millennium Perspective*, Paris: OECD Development Centre

Mako, W.P. and C. Zhang (2003) *Management of China's State-Owned Enterprises Portfolio: Lessons from International Experience*, World Bank working paper, September

OECD (2005) *OECD Economic Surveys: China*, Paris, OECD, vol. 2005/13

Prasad, E.,T. Rumbaugh and Q. Wang (2005) *Putting the Cart Before the Horse? Capital Account Liberalization and Exchange Rate Flexibility in China*, IMF Policy Discussion Paper 05/1, International Monetary Fund

Rawski, T.G. (2001) 'What's Happening to China's GDP Statistics', *China Economic Review*, vol. 12(4), December, pp. 347–354

South China Morning Post (2006), 26 September, A4–A5

Steinfeld, E. (1998) *Forging Reform in China*, Cambridge University Press

Straits Times (2005) 'People Power Aids Green Drive in China', 15 November

Tadesse, S. (2004) 'The Allocation and Monitoring Role of Capital Markets: Theory and International Evidence', *Journal of Financial and Quantitative Analysis*, vol. 39, no. 4, December

Tenev, S. and Z. Chunlin (2002) *Corporate Governance and Enterprise Reform in China*, World Bank and International Finance Corporation

Wall Street Journal – Asia (2006) 'Viagra Ruling in Beijing Lifts Foreign Firms' Hope', front page, 5 June

Transparency International Bribe Payers Index (BPI) (2002) Transparency International (www.transparency.org/policy_research/surveys_indices/bpi)

Transparency International Corruption Perception Index (CPI) (2005) Transparency International (www.transparency.org/policy_research/surveys_indices/cpi/2005)

Transparency International (2005), http://www.transparency.org/policy_research/surveys_indices/cpi/2005

Transparency International (2006), http://www.transparency.org/policy_research/surveys_indices/bpi/2006

Tsai, K. (2001) *Beyond Banks: Informal Finance and Private Sector Development in Contemporary China*, Johns Hopkins University, paper presented at the Conference on Financial Sector Reform in China, 11–13 September

Tsai, K. (2002) *Back Alley Banking: Private Entrepreneurs in China*, Ithaca, NY: Cornell University Press

Tseng, W., H.E. Khor, K. Kochhar, Mihaljek, D and Burton, D (1994) *Economic Reform in China: New Phase*, IMF Occasional Paper no. 114, International Monetary Fund

Wang, Y., D. Xu, Z. Wang and F. Zai (2000) *Implicit Pension Debt, Transit Cost, Options and Impact of China's Pension Reform*, World Bank Policy Research Working Paper, July

Wei, Y. (2003) *Foreign Direct Investment in China: A Survey*, Lancaster University Management School Working Paper 2003/02

World Bank (1997) *China 2020 – Development Challenges in the New Century*

Wu, H.X. (2002) 'How Fast has Chinese Industry Grown? Measuring the Real Output of Chinese Industry, 1949–1997', *Review of Income and Wealth,* vol. 48, no. 2, June, pp. 179–204

Xiao, G. (2004) *People's Republic of China's Round-Tripping FDI: Scale, Causes and Implications*, Latin America/Caribbean and Asia Pacific Economics and Business Association (LAEBA) Working Papers no. 24, December

Xiao, G. and Z. Tu (2005) 'China's Industrial Productivity Revolution: A Stochastic Frontier Production Function Analysis of China's Large and Medium Industrial Enterprise during 1995–2002', *Economic Research Journal*, March

Xu, K. (2004) *How Has the Literature on Gini's Index Evolved in the Past 80 Years?*, Department of Economics, Dalhousie University, January (http://economics.dal.ca/repec/dal/wparch/howgini.pdf)

Young, A. (1995) 'The Tyranny of Numbers: Confronting the Statistical Realities of the East Asian Growth Experience', *Quarterly Journal of Economics*, 110(3), pp. 641–680

Young, A. (2000) *Gold into Base Metals: Productivity Growth in the People's Republic of China During the Reform Period*, NEBR Working Paper 7856, NEBR, August

Index